PSYCHOTHERAPY IN THE AGE OF ACCOUNTABILITY

PSYCHOTHERAPY IN THE AGE OF ACCOUNTABILITY

Lynn D. Johnson, Ph.D.

DIRECTOR, BRIEF THERAPY CENTER
SALT LAKE CITY, UTAH

W. W. NORTON & COMPANY • NEW YORK • LONDON

Library of Congress Cataloging-in-Publication Data

Johnson, Lynn D.
     Psychotherapy in the age of accountability / Lynn D. Johnson.
          p.   cm.
     "A Norton professional book."
     Includes bibliographical references and index.
     ISBN 0-393-70209-X
     1. Brief psychotherapy.   2. Eclectic psychotherapy.   3. Managed
mental health care.   4. Therapeutic alliance.   I. Title.
     RC480.55.J64   1995
     616.89'14--dc20   95-23006   CIP

W.W. Norton & Company, Inc., 500 Fifth Avenue, New York, NY 10110
W.W. Norton & Company Ltd., 10 Coptic Street, London WC1A 1PU

1 2 3 4 5 6 7 8 9 0

Contents

Introduction

This book arises from two experiences. First, in 1988 Human Affairs International (HAI), perhaps the world's largest Employee Assistance Program (EAP), with headquarters in Salt Lake City, had created a managed care product and several of HAI's clients had signed on. I was invited to be part of a new HAI committee consisting of a psychiatrist, psychologist, psychiatric nurse, and social worker that would review all inpatient mental health care. The social worker would talk to the psychiatrist or utilization review nurse at the site and obtain information about the case. We would review that information and attempt to help manage the case. When we had concerns about the quality of care, we would talk directly to the physician. In some cases where we felt further inpatient care was unwarranted, we could deny further insurance payments. HAI's initial experiences indicated these committee-based reviews could save a worthwhile amount of money for the companies while at the same time actually improving the quality of care through questions and suggestions. HAI was subsequently purchased by Aetna Insurance, and became one of the largest managed care companies in the country. The Aetna philosophy was to insure the least restrictive and highest quality of care, not to save money, and I was never expected to deny for the sake of economics. The question revolved around whether the care was necessary and appropriate.

Since then, for five to seven hours per week I have been involved in reviewing inpatient and outpatient therapy cases from all around the country. This experience has given me perspective on what kinds of treatment are available. I learned a good deal about how patients across the country are being treated. And I became convinced the quality of care is very uneven: Some brilliant work is being done, a good deal of helpful and competent work, but a surprising amount of inappropriate and occasionally even abusive treatment is being done. I recognized that, at least as we practiced it, far from being a destructive element, managed care could be a great force for quality improvement in my profession.

The second experience was when I began presenting my own version of brief psychotherapy in seminars. Since my earliest days in graduate school, I was interested in doing the most good in the least amount of time. When people seek help, I believe, it is our ethical obligation to work as quickly and effectively as possible, and I had focused my professional skills and identity on briefer forms of treatment.

In graduate school I was exposed to a wide range of modalities, from behavioral and family systems to a two-year internship in a psychodynamic setting. I was most impressed with the short-term therapy approaches, so I specialized in brief treatment, using a strategic and cognitive-behavioral orientation. I was quite aware of many therapists with different viewpoints obtaining similar treatment results, and I realized I had identified some common factors in effective brief therapy, regardless of the theoretical orientation.

This book presents my ideas of what therapists can know and do to succeed and flourish in the next few years. As we approach the end of the century, there is some excitement about our future, perhaps enhanced by the symbolic value of entering a new millennium in our counting of time. The time is analogous to the K-T boundary in geology, a rock layer which marks the transition from the Cretaceous to the Tertiary Periods. During this time, dinosaurs were disappearing and furry mammals were increasing in number and variety. Such a time of enormous and rapid change is marked by highly accelerated rates of evolution. It is as if mammals and dinosaurs were meeting all over the world in focus groups and quality improvement circles to try to keep up with one another. Of course, the mammals found the equivalents of market niches, developed and delivered biologically high quality products, and filled the niches with great skill, whereas the dinosaurs seemed to decide that continuing to do what had always been done was the best way to meet the crisis. Mental health is in a period of upheaval and transition, and it is not yet apparent who are dinosaurs and who are the furry mammals. Will private practice survive? Will corporate-based group practices (which may seem dinosaur-like to some) thunder across the landscape and consume all they survey? Will strategic alliances, combining private and public mental health systems, triumph?

Many of these questions are fascinating but beyond the scope of this book. Rather than discuss models of service delivery, my task is to present a model of brief psychotherapy that is integrative and accountable. My hope is this model will move therapists away from divisiveness and toward a common vocabulary. Just as computers flourished because of a common programming language, as we find common, even universal ways to describe our unique therapy activities, so too we will thrive. At the same time, I am very much aware that the delivery of service depends to a great extent on the kind of environment in which it is delivered. Our "family" and networks also constrain or empower our behavior to a great extent. And I hope this book will encourage the alert therapist to wonder what sort of system will support the highest quality of mental health service, and what she or he can do to sponsor that type of system.

So to the readers of this book: May you sprout fur and nurse your young. Counseling and therapy are very helpful and worthy activities, and this book is my attempt at insuring our profession of psychotherapy will survive and grow in the coming years.

I have attempted to vary masculine and feminine pronouns as randomly as possibly and often combine them. This solution to fair language is constrained and awkward and I am not happy with it, but it is how I have done it. Another word about language. Therapist equals counselor equals psychotherapist equals clinician. I have used these words interchangeably to avoid tiring the reader by the too-frequent repetition of the same nouns.

ORGANIZATION OF THE BOOK

In Section I I attempt to build a general approach to psychotherapy which many, if not most, psychotherapists can agree to. I suggest some basic considerations about psychotherapy, giving my own read on them.

Chapter 1 reflects my odyssey in the managed care industry, and why I wrote this book. I discuss the role of managed care in inpatient and outpatient treatment. Since so many therapists are affected by this industry, the chapter will be of some interest to therapists in both public and private practice.

Chapter 2 outlines my ideas about the components of an integrative model of therapy and introduces the next four chapters. An integrative model must contain concepts that define the role of both the patient and the therapist, as well as the therapeutic relationship. Chapter 3 discusses this therapeutic relationship, arguably the most potent aspect of psychotherapy. Verbal, nonverbal, interactional, and developmental aspects of the relationship are explored, with an eye toward sensitizing therapists to this vital area. Chapter 4 sets forth the idea that focus is what may distinguish brief and/or effective psychotherapy from long-term and/or ineffective therapy. The need for precision in focus, especially in this age of managed care, can actually invigorate and empower psychotherapy.

The next two chapters review the role of the therapist and of the patient. Each has an area of behavior which is complementary to the other, and a clear definition of each seems to be in order. Chapter 5 discusses the role of the therapist and what I believe is the central quality in the therapist's behavior that seems to help patients. In doing this, I realize I am doing something rather foolish, to be kind to myself. The work of a therapist is incredibly complex and artful and any effort to simplify it, especially my chapter, is oversimplified. Nevertheless, I have rushed in and you may make your own judgments. Chapter 6 discusses the role of the patient, specifically the role of patient activity in therapy. I argue for homework and behavioral assignments and experiments as central to the role of the patient. However, the responsibility for effective therapy is still with the therapist, who must understand how to assign homework and other patient activity, and how to increase motivation to make it more likely the homework will be done.

Section II presents two useful concepts and related skills for the integrative therapist. These are seen as supportive to the central argument presented earlier, and are chosen because they are generally overlooked by therapists.

Chapter 7, on time management in therapy, attacks the shibboleth of weekly psychotherapy. I argue that the concept of weekly therapy is for the therapist's convenience and has no relation to the real world. The way the therapist uses time can and should be a powerful therapeutic intervention, and weekly sessions should not be the norm. Chapter 8 reviews some concepts of motivation, emphasizing the role of the therapist in increasing the patient's motivation to change and improve. These two skills—time management and motivation—don't receive enough emphasis in therapists' training, and therapists who emphasize them are likely to cope with managed care and captitated mental health (reimbursement plans which put the therapist at some financial risk) much better than those who do not.

In Section III integrative treatment protocols for three specific problem areas are described. These areas are chosen specifically because they are the three hardest areas for therapists to cope with in the managed care environment. My protocols should not be construed as exhaustive or prescriptive plans, but rather as an invitation for therapists to review their own protocols and as encouragement for HMOs, managed care organizations, and mental health provider groups to create protocols solidly based on a combination of research outcomes and sound clinical experience.

The three areas also are the ones where managed care companies have the most interest in terms of outpatient reviews and avoidance of inpatient or residential treatment. To the extent that therapists and agencies create

protocols that significantly reduce inpatient, residential, or day care utilization, the future of those therapists and provider groups is very bright.

Chapter 9 reviews the treatment of the abuse constellation including
PTSD, dissociative identity disorder, and related syndromes. A review of
outcome studies demonstrates that treatment protocols do exist and can be
followed with this difficult population.

Chapter 10 addresses the treatment of chemical dependency, focusing
on inclusive outpatient treatment approaches. I argue that much substance
abuse treatment excludes and alienates many patients, and propose a protocol integrating research and outcome literature.

Chapter 11 addresses the treatment of adolescents. This is one of the
more difficult areas for managed care, since during the 1980s a good deal
of energy went into hospitalization and other placements for our young
people. These intensive treatments are of doubtful utility and very difficult
to justify financially. Some of the evidence reviewed suggests that inpatient
treatment of conduct disorders (even though the diagnosis may be "major
depression") is not a treatment of choice. An integrative family treatment
approach is proposed, bringing together comparative studies of treatment
effectiveness with teens. An approach to individual treatment based on
systems thinking is also reviewed and recommended. Case examples illustrate the integrative approach. Reports of intensive, outpatient home-based
interventions suggest that these viable, competitive approaches may become the treatment of the future for very disturbed adolescents.

Acknowledgments

Thanks are due to Bill O'Hanlon, who nagged me for years to write. He is a valued friend and a truly empowering person. Yvonne Dolan and Charlie Johnson have been encouraging and helpful; I especially appreciate Yvonne's help in the chapter on abuse survivors. Scott Miller was helpful with the chapter on chemical dependency and improved the manuscript in many places. Richard Ebling and Patrick Morrissette helped to shape and improve the chapter on treatment of adolescents. John Cooper, Paul Finch, Barbara McFarland, and Shauna Bradley read drafts and their comments were very helpful. Jacob Shaha helped proofread the manuscript.

Susan Barrows Munro performed the herculean labor of turning my writing into readable prose.

Coworkers and workshop participants who helped me to refine these ideas were indispensable. Jeffrey Zeig of the Milton H. Erickson Foundation encouraged me to find my voice and gave me place to do that.

Steve de Shazer generously allowed me to study his solution-focused approach at the Brief Therapy Center in Milwaukee. He was liberal with his time, understanding, and resources. My work with his wife, Insoo Kim Berg, has been empowering. She has a rare gift of creative intervention with clients.

Dan Santisteban, Sergio Aisenberg, and Angel Perez-Vidal of the Spanish Child Guidance Clinic and the University of Miami School of Medicine were wonderful hosts and teachers and tolerated my rudimentary Spanish.

I would be remiss not to express a special degree of appreciation and admiration to three fine clinicians who provided supervision, consultation, and support. Bob Finley has been an inspiration as he characterizes integrity, transparency, and creativity. Ernst Beier, a valued supervisor and colleague, has been unfailingly supportive and helpful to my efforts to understand the role of uncertainty in therapy. And John Weakland has been an extrordinary influence, pointing out simple and unique ways of seeing situations. He is unpretentious and approachable, and his consultation with me has been one of the highly valued experiences of my life.

Finally, thanks to my wife and family, who are much more important to me than any career or book ever could be. I especially thank my youngest son, Stephen, who is willing to play by himself while dad finishes writing down a thought, and who at age four remembers and reminds me that playing is more important than working.

SECTION I

An Integrative Approach

CHAPTER 1

The Accountable
Profession

Psychotherapists face challenging times. In both private insurance-reimbursed mental health systems and publicly funded centers, more performance for less money is demanded. Insurance companies have intruded to an extraordinary degree into the relationship between patient and therapist, requiring reports and estimates of length of treatment. In the public sector, budget cuts seem to have leveled off, but the demands on mental health centers have increased. We hear the voices of "efficiency" and cost containment.

Those who are funding psychotherapy are asking hard questions about the results of psychotherapy. While it is clear to us in the profession that psychotherapy is a powerful and useful service, there has been no accountability to the sources of funding for individual outcomes. "How do we know," they ask, "that we are getting value for our money/our constituents' money?" Referring to meta-analytic reviews does not satisfy their questions.

Funding sources are also uncomfortable with the lack of precision with which mental health is often defined. In treatment of blood pressure, readings give feedback about the success or failure of a treatment strategy, so it appears more accountable. But psychotherapy seems too vague to auditors and administrators, and often attracts the attention of budget cutters. Since those decision-makers and those who influence final decisions are almost never aware of the powerful, positive effects therapy has, and of its cost-effectiveness, our profession is quickly targeted for cutbacks when dollars are scarce.

While therapists have often responded to these challenges with anger, there is another way to look at them. These forces are exciting and invigorating for the profession of psychotherapy. Changes in the environment are opportunities to adapt to new conditions and learn new skills. Such challenges help us to specify our own behavior more clearly. Therapists learn and grow from stresses. Across the country they are asking what they have to know and how they have to behave in order survive and flourish.

Because of these pressures, workshops and seminars on briefer forms of treatment are well attended. Clinicians are eager to learn what they can do to make sense of this environment and how to work with higher expectations and fewer resources. The days of planning for a year or two of treatment to address a depressive condition appear to be past, and the new expectation is that therapy should have rapid positive impact.

THE RIGHT REASON FOR BRIEFER TREATMENTS

It would be helpful to bear in mind during this discussion that the external forces from funding are actually the wrong reason for the field to develop coherent approaches to brief therapy. Rather, it is now clear that a majority of patients have always wanted brief therapy, though our distorted perceptions kept us from seeing that. Patients tend to remain in therapy an average of 6–12 visits (Howard, Kopta, Krause, & Orlinsky, 1986; Taube, Burns, & Kessler, 1984) regardless of setting, diagnosis, and motivation. As many as 30% (or more) of patients will attend only one time (Talmon, 1990), but those patients can be helped significantly in that single visit if the counselor is prepared to help them.

Budget and financial pressures toward brief treatment, then, have actually helped. They have called our attention to some facts that therapists and counselors should have been paying attention to all along: Most patients want brief treatment, and most get brief treatment. The only question is whether the treatment will be brief by design or brief by default, caused by the patient's refusal to attend any more sessions.

Quality Improvement in Psychotherapy

The traditional form of brief treatment (treatment by default, in which the therapy terminates before the therapist expects it to) must be replaced with planned brief treatment based on specific skills. Treatments that last a long time and produce no better results than brief treatments cannot expect funding from public or insurance sources. Thus, the comparisons of brief and long-term therapy, which suggest that the brief approaches are as good or better than long-term treatment (Budman & Gurman, 1988; Koss & Butcher, 1986; Strupp & Binder, 1984), are used as justification for expecting all therapists to prefer brief to long-term therapy. After all, the argument goes, if there is no difference, isn't it more humane and ethical to work as quickly as possible? If we do not insist on brief treatment, aren't we failing to protect our insured from the voyeuristic therapists who do not help but only probe and tinker?

So while therapists may feel quite intruded upon by the new mental health review processes, those doing the reviewing feel they are performing a quality improvement oriented service. Reviewers usually believe their mission is to improve the quality of care. While therapists think they are doing very well, reviewers find enormous discrepancies between therapists, with some apparently having much more positive impact in much less time than others. The quest for quality improvement demands that we identify those who are doing the best work and discover how we can all work as they do. The fact that we are challenged to do so by managed care is not the point; quality improvement is the point.

However, we, the psychotherapy profession, must not allow insurance companies to move from providing coverage and even managing care into assessing quality of treatment. This is not an area the insurance companies are well equipped to address. Standards of quality in such organizations may be written by former clinicians who haven't been face to face with a client in years. They will create standards that are clinically irrelevant or even intrusive and dangerous to the proper conduct of psychotherapy. Even standards written by clinicians may be based on hobbyhorses rather than generally accepted, empirically supported factors.

As an example, an insurance company allowed a consultant to write a rule about behavior problems and allergies. The standards stated the company would not pay for child psychotherapy unless there was a note in the chart that allergies had been ruled out as a cause of the behavior problem. Charts could be reviewed after payment had been made to assure the question and answer were in the chart. My child psychiatrist friends tell me that the idea that allergies are behind child behavior problems is not a generally accepted principle; in spite of that, the standard continued to create problems for some time. It reminded me of the scene in Woody Allen's movie *Bananas*, when the new dictator of the banana republic goes crazy and issues a proclamation that from now on underwear will be changed five times a day. "Underwear will be worn on the *outside*," he says, "so we can check."

There are other examples of agencies stepping outside their areas of competence. Consider JCAHO (Joint Commission on the Accreditation of Healthcare Organizations) and Medicaid rules. They have attempted to apply inpatient rules to outpatient care, with unpleasant and unproductive results. When a patient enters outpatient treatment, a case must be opened, and when the patient ends treatment, the case must be closed, and reports created. That actual clinicians would obtain very little from those reports that couldn't be obtained by scanning some progress notes is irrelevant. The fact that in no other area of health do outpatient facilities "close" cases is irrelevant. You may argue in vain that your dentist may go years without seeing you, but she doesn't close your case! And your primary care physician may only see you every two or three years, yet doesn't close your case. There is some vague notion that closing the case will prove there is quality care, or perhaps will reduce "liability."

Where did these ideas come from? Did an empirical investigation find that those therapists who "closed" their cases were more effective and efficient than those who didn't? No, someone wrote up a regulation, and it became the Truth. But consider instead the case of intermittent therapy. The reality is that people often return for some help when they need it, and the process of opening and closing a case is artificial and punishing of therapists whose work is appropriately brief. The therapist who encourages patients to go out and try things has to do lots of opening and closing of cases; the therapist who keeps patients attending year after year doesn't. The notion of opening and closing cases derived from a hospital-based treatment model that has little relevance to outpatient work.

Another example came from the director of one of the finest mental health centers in the country, a facility renowned for its aggressive outreach to the chronically mentally ill. His agency has defined the state of the art with regard to teamwork and case management. This mental health center was audited by Medicaid, and instead of being given kudos for doing such an exceptional job, he was chastised because some of the progress notes were not signed by the counselors. It seemed as if the auditors needed to find something wrong in order to justify their role. I recalled Santayana: "He is a fanatic who has redoubled his efforts and forgotten his purpose."

Accreditation is a similar issue. JCAHO and the federal Health Care Financing Administration (HCFA) both review and certify hospitals and mental health facilities. A study by Hadley and McGurrin (1988) found that although the purported purpose of the accreditation activities is to ensure quality, there is no significant relationship between accreditation status and quality. Barter (1988), commenting on Hadley and McGurrin, stated, " . . . there is no proof that surveys improve the quality of care in the surveyed institution or for the individual patient by one iota. . . . The survey process ascertains whether the facility or program can meet the arbitrary standards of the survey instrument." So the only thing the accreditation accomplishes is to make the surveyed institution meet standards that have no bearing on quality. Similarly, the same outcome can be expected if the insurance companies are not helped to develop useful and empirically verified standards of quality of care.

We must resist this bureaucratic rulemaking, or we will find private insurance companies adopting the same sort of absurd rules which now plague the public mental health centers. But mindless resistance to managed care is self-defeating. We must be proactive and begin to discuss and set standards that are empirically related to psychotherapy quality, or the standards we will have to live with will reduce both quality and rationality. In industry it is generally agreed that those closest to the problem, such as the line workers in a factory, are the ones most likely to understand how to improve the quality of the product. In the psychotherapy profession, clinicians are most likely to improve the quality of their work, not accreditation agencies and insurance companies.

HMOS AND MANAGED CARE

"It is impossible to tell who is right, but it is easy to tell who is in charge."

- Anonymous

In the middle 1970s medical costs were spiraling out of control and insurance reimbursement began to shift. A process of examining claims to determine if the procedures were medically necessary replaced the old indemnity policies, which simply paid for procedures according to policy limits. Insurance companies suspected that much of what was being paid for in psychotherapy was not really necessary, but rather was designed to help people grow or improve. (The insurance industry does not view itself as being in the business of helping people grow — try submitting the bill for your health club membership.) They believed some of the outpatient psychotherapy was for what they thought of as "worried well." In other words, while patients were generally anxious and nervous, their conditions didn't really impair their lives to any great extent. They were still able to "love and work" as Freud would suggest, just not as effectively as they might.

At the same time, it was clearly recognized by most insurers that psychotherapy could be a good buy, helping people to avoid unnecessary medical procedures and making them much more productive and capable. Some patients were very impaired, some were not; the dilemma was in how to distinguish one from the other. Counseling traditionally took place in a cloistered environment, characterized by a high degree of secrecy. The notion of confidentiality in therapy had developed out of a particular theory that suggested repression was a significant part of psychopathology, so it was necessary to create an environment which would allow for the return of the repressed. The feeling that someone was looking over the shoulder of the analyst would distort and destroy the necessary openness. Some of the strongest opposition to managed care comes from therapists who adhere to that notion of confidentiality. Since these therapists are also likely to have been required to undergo a training analysis (or at least were required to go through some kind of extended psychotherapy), they naturally tend to believe that everyone needs long-term psychotherapy. My experience suggests these are the therapists who feel the most outraged when the need for long-term care is questioned.

Health maintenance organizations offer one approach to control of health costs. The HMO staff model has some advantages, such as a closer relationship between primary care physicians and the psychotherapists. Psychotherapy is usually covered with a small payment or no payment at all. Because the therapists are required to stay very busy (30+ hours of direct patient care per week is not uncommon) and eliminate the waiting list, the HMO appears to have conquered the economic incentive to keep people in psychotherapy. Instead of the cloistered confidential relationship of the analyst's consulting room, the therapist might be talking to other therapists, physicians, or nurses about how to be helpful to the patient. Teamwork has flourished and confidentiality declined.

While the HMOs went through some rough times, they appear to be finally producing the outcome they promised to deliver, namely lower medical costs. Premiums for HMO contracts have been rising at a much slower rate than premiums for other plans, and as a result the number of people enrolled in HMOs has risen 400% since 1982. The Group Health Association predicted that HMO premiums would rise 5.6% in 1994, keeping the rate of increase below that of competitive plans. Certainly more and more therapists will find employment within the prepaid health plans, and these therapists will need a jargon-free language with which to communicate to colleagues.

HMOs cover only a small portion of the population—in early 1994 they covered less than 10%. Insurance companies created a parallel to HMOs, the preferred provider organization. The theory was that there would be a limited number of providers who would form a *panel*. The providers on the panel would refer to each other. The providers agreed to take a discount on their fees in exchange for the presumed constant flow of referrals. But PPOs did not yield the kinds of savings it was hoped they would, and the insurance industry became dissatisfied.

The next plan was managed care. Under this system, the PPO providers would be required to preauthorize expensive procedures, and the managed care organization would have the right to examine how the care was going. What this meant to behavioral health was that inpatient psychiatric stays would be closely scrutinized, with a psychiatric review specialist (PRS) who would phone the utilization review (UR) person every day. The UR in a hospital is responsible for communicating with managed care reviewers, and gives reports by reading from the chart about the patient's progress.

In behavioral medicine, managed mental health (MMH) plans have demonstrated financial savings and have become quite popular. By late 1993, approximately 49% of Americans with health insurance were participating in some kind of managed behavioral health program. Since the managed plans allow for some freedom of choice (i.e., participants can chose from a panel of providers, which may range from small to quite large), they are often more popular with the insured than the more narrow and possibly rigid HMO model. Again, however, confidentiality is markedly reduced by the necessity of doing concurrent reviews of the health services. While that might not be a serious issue in surgery or management of illnesses, mental health counselors are strongly affected.

How MMH Programs Evaluate Utilization

MMH programs quickly developed some stringent criteria for inpatient coverage. These criteria typically include evaluating the *medical necessity* of the stay. What this means is that a patient can be covered for inpatient care if and only if there is no less restrictive level of care that can be safely offered. Because some therapists I have spoken with seem confused about what the utilization criteria are, I will present a review.

Typical criteria for medical necessity for inpatient (IP) care include:

1. A patient must be acutely suicidal or dangerous to others. This danger to self or others must be life-threatening, in that there is a plan to commit suicide or assault and a strong desire to carry it out. A patient who makes small cuts on herself without an intention to suicide (as is often seen in people with a history of early abuse) is not appropriate for acute-level (inpatient) care. Likewise, a patient who often thinks of suicide but has no active plan and intent is not a candidate for IP.
2. OR, a patient must have a serious mental disorder and show significant deterioration, in spite of competent and comprehensive outpatient care; the level of functioning must be deteriorating to the point that the patient's life is significantly impaired. In other words, there must be a deterioration in ability to function, reflected by decreasing Axis V (GAF) scales. Low GAF scales in themselves do not necessarily support inpatient treatment, since it is possible for a chronically mentally ill person to not function well but this would be characteristic and not an acute exacerbation.
3. OR, a patient must be unable to perform activities of daily living (ADLs), such as feed and care for oneself. A patient who has delusions that interfere with his ability to eat and sleep and do ADLs is appropriate for inpatient treatment. A patient who hallucinates but is not acutely disorganized (i.e., can find his way around, get food and shelter, and so on) is appropriate for a less intensive level of care.

A patient may meet one of these criteria at admission, but after a few days may not. For example, suppose a patient is admitted who is acutely disorganized, but has a history of response to a major tranquilizer. We would hope for and expect a rapid administration of neuroleptics in an energetic, aggressive style, and a rapid release from acute-level care as the patient stabilizes.

Often a patient is admitted and the managed care organization does not continue to certify inpatient care because the patient appears to have improved and stabilized or returned to a baseline. The physician may appeal for more days based on the fear that the patient will relapse. This is often not considered certifiable since the threat is potential, not actual. A physician's predictions of dangerous relapses must be based on actual behavior of the patient, not on impressions or feelings.

Inpatient care may also be denied because of a failure to energetically pursue outpatient treatment. For example, adolescents may be very difficult to care for at home and may engage in frightening behaviors, such as running away. But most managed care programs do not consider runaway behavior to be an indication for inpatient care, since if the child can plan and execute a runaway, find places to stay, or survive on the street, by definition that child is quite capable of performing ADLs. Competent outpatient care, likely emphasizing changing the family structure and behaviors, would be expected (see Chapter 11). So asking for IP care for that teen would be unlikely to receive approval. Only if there were both a deterioration of behavior *and* competent outpatient care had been offered, would IP be considered. Similarly, a patient who abuses drugs or alcohol may be denied IP if there has not been an attempt to treat the problems in outpatient care (see Chapter 10).

Some treatment centers sprang up around the country in the halcyon days of unlimited mental health benefits. These centers usually specialized in treatment of a particular problem, such as eating disorders or chemical dependency, or particular groups, such as adolescents or Christians. But the general consensus of MMH seemed to be that if a patient was capable enough to fly across the country and enroll in a treatment facility at a new place, there was no obvious reason to suppose that person was highly disorganized, acutely suicidal, or incapable of performing ADLs. By denying coverage for patients well enough to cross the country, the managed care programs demonstrated substantial savings.

Managed care also saves money by encouraging least restrictive care from the onset. A patient who needs some help in organizing her life but is not acutely ill might be encouraged to go directly to a day treatment program. However, the converse is not necessarily true. Suppose a patient was suicidal, is hospitalized, and decides that suicide is not an option and is relieved her plan did not work. She is able to dress and feed herself, and completes a pass. She still weeps and thinks her life is quite bad, thinks about suicide, but she does not want to die. Her history of a suicide attempt (but no current lethal plans) does not mean she is appropriate for day treatment. Why not move her directly to an intensive outpatient care and support her efforts to achieve a better level of adjustment?

The traditional 28-day inpatient chemical dependency treatments came in for hard times when insurance companies discovered there is no evidence that they are any better than outpatient treatment (Miller & Hester, 1986). Therefore, treatment for chemical dependency problems became an outpatient issue, once any necessary medical detoxification was accomplished. (Often detoxification can be safely accomplished with outpatient treatment.) Some of these 28-day programs were shocked to hear insurance companies saying that they certified need, not programs. If the patient was acute, he was appropriate for acute-level care. If he was not currently acute, even if he had been just recently, he was expected to make the transition to less restrictive care. Twenty-eight days of inpatient chemical dependency care became an anachronism.

Similarly, even the intensive day treatment programs did not fare so well, since insurance companies suggested an alcohol abuser may be capable of working and attending an evening program, rather than persisting in day treatment. More than one mental health center found its alcohol and drug program philosophy severely out of step with the times. The chemical dependency programs were based on an unsupported theory that intensive treatment was necessary, when the data suggested the opposite was true and that less intensive treatment did as much good for much less money. Because the theory was like a religious conviction, the program directors have had a difficult time shifting paradigms and offering less intense, less restrictive approaches.

Cutting Fat or Muscle?

In the middle to late 1980s, managed care programs began developing inpatient criteria that were much stricter than traditionally practiced. Inpatient care had been used for those patients who might benefit from the intensity of treatment afforded by that setting. There were vehement conflicts between insurance companies and the private psychiatric facilities, which were accustomed to being able to hospitalize a patient who was not acutely disorganized or dangerous because an intense period of therapy might get him moving. The insurance industry position evolved toward the notion that financial considerations were important enough that the incredible expense of inpatient care outweighed the benefits to the patient of such care. In other words, we as a society cannot afford to allow infinite resources to flow toward the improved functioning of each individual.

As a result of the tightening of criteria, managed care identified certain hospitals (usually, for-profit chains) that were egregiously manipulating the insurance industry and hospitalizing people for little or no reason. The joke was that the most important medical test for psychiatric hospitalization was the wallet biopsy; if positive indication of insurance coverage was found in a person's wallet, inpatient care was indicated. In Texas and in Florida, investigators found that several hospitals had developed sophisticated head-hunting protocols to fill their beds with behaviorally disordered adolescents or with recovering drug and alcohol abusers. Teenagers in these facilities soon learned when they would be released: when the insurance benefits ran out. If a patient was "entitled" to 90 days of inpatient care, then, strangely enough, that patient needed precisely that amount of care.

A number of hospitals and individuals were sanctioned for these abuses; at the same time, the MMH plans began to apply the strict "medical necessity" criteria to inpatient care. Average lengths of stay (ALOS) began to drop and dropped steadily, from 40 days in one Texas hospital to 10–15 days, a common range now for preferred providers. This has saved the insurance companies and their clients a great deal of money. It is not uncommon for MMH to save more than 10% per year on mental and nervous benefits, all without harming the patient.

In fact, one can argue that MMH has improved inpatient care. In the mid-1980s, it was not uncommon for someone to be in the hospital for five to seven days for "evaluation." During this time, there would be no attempt to provide psychotropic medication, treatment, or intervention, since this time was considered an assessment phase. Medications, when they were given, were not given aggressively, but were increased just as slowly as if the patient were in outpatient treatment. Family therapy might be offered once a week. All of this resulted in inpatient care being a leisurely process. MMH brought focus to acute-level care. At admission, physicians are expected to begin discharge planning. If medications are used, they should be pursued aggressively. Family contact should begin at once and continue at an intense level. As soon as the patient is ready for a home pass, she should be considered for discharge. The completion of a successful pass is considered strong evidence that inpatient care is no longer appropriate.

Case Example: The Institutionalized Adolescent

A managed care reviewer encountered an adolescent who had been in an inpatient setting for a full year! The teen had virtually unlimited nervous and mental benefits under the old plan, but when the managed care company began to review cases, they could find no current reason for this child to be in the hospital.

The reviewers found that the young man functioned well on the unit, was able to cooperate and perform ADLs, and was not suicidal or dangerous to others, in terms of stated desires and even from psychological testing. They insisted that he be discharged. The problems followed. He was unprepared for living in ordinary society, and got into a scuffle at school and a fierce shouting match with his father. The two began pushing and shoving each other, and the youngster left his home and returned to the safety of the hospital. The unit called confidently for inpatient benefit authorization, assuring the PRS they would be able to help him, since they had been so successful before. The PRS disagreed, suggesting they had not been successful because they had created a child who was institutionalized. He had not been carefully prepared to handle disagreements outside the confines of group therapy. The psychiatrist was shocked at the position the PRS took. He considered it strange that the IP stay was denied. Instead, the PRS, working with an EAP counselor on site, found a halfway house and the teenager spent two months there, with progressive increases in responsibility and authority, and did well. Family therapy at the halfway house and after discharge helped the boy and his father develop more respectful ways of disagreeing. There was no further IP treatment.

Case Example: The Beleaguered Insurance Company

I consulted to an insurance company that had experienced a dramatic increase in their inpatient nervous and mental benefit costs. When we looked in detail at what had happened, a sad story emerged. The state where most of the insured were living had repealed the "certificate of need" law, which had required that no new hospitals could be built unless there was a demonstrated need for the new facilities. Immediately several for-profit independent psychiatric hospitals were built, and the company experienced a 700% increase in mental health benefits in a single year! The increase was primarily due to adolescents being hospitalized who would have been treated in outpatient family and individual therapy if beds had not been available. It almost bankrupted the company, and of course, the insureds covered by that policy had a stiff increase in their premiums.

Clearly, the managed care programs were cutting fat far more than muscle, but the cutting created "blood in the water." If money is the "blood in the water," then the feeding frenzy of private, for-profit hospitals of the early 1980s shifted to a third-party feeding frenzy as the insurance companies clearly understood there was money in strict inpatient reviews. The first feeding frenzy fueled the second.

The Rise of Outpatient Reviews

Unfortunately, the money saved from improving inpatient service provoked the industry toward a "more of the same" fallacy: If two aspirin are good, 10 or 20 will be even better. If reviewing inpatient care helped, then reviewing outpatient care will *really* save money.

But there is no money there to save. Outpatient care is quite inexpensive, and patients do not tend to stay with it long enough to be able to make a difference. Consider the fact that the average length of treatment (or, the number of sessions per episode of a complaint) is around six to ten. Now suppose it costs $100 to review a case. If you cannot demonstrate a savings that significantly exceeds $100 by reviewing after three sessions, the process is irrational. Assume a review after three visits. If the patient needs more visits, a thoughtful therapist can communicate that to the insurance company. Only if the managed care system is unethically stingy, or the therapist is unbearably stupid, will the case not be authorized for at least three to six more visits. Now consider that by the fifteenth to the twentieth session, around 95% of patients spontaneously terminate. The few who persist beyond 20 visits are likely to need some review to see whether therapy is a necessity or a habit. It is obvious that outpatient counseling is largely a self-governing system, and there is really no need, from a financial standpoint, to do outpatient reviews at less than 20 visits. So it is more than likely that the process of reviewing after only a few visits costs much more than it could ever save.

Some managed care programs did save outpatient money, essentially by harassing clients and providers into terminating psychotherapy while there was still significant need. This led to a widespread discussion about the rationale for outpatient reviews. Here there is much less agreement. The review criteria for outpatient treatment are simply not generally established, in contrast to the inpatient criteria. Further, there is very little good research on the cost-benefit curve in psychotherapy, so reviews can be confusing. Each program tends to make up its own rules for outpatient care, and some outpatient criteria are impossible to comply with. What tends to happen with difficult programs is that the costs of nervous and mental disorders are shifted over onto the medical side. People counsel with their medical doctors who charge a good deal more than a nonmedical counselor would. Emotionally troubled patients tend to seek reassurance from somewhere, and they may find it through CAT scans and exploratory surgeries, more expensive and far less effective than outpatient counseling.

Additionally, since the very strict outpatient controls function mainly by denying needed care (there being little fat to trim), they have created a great deal of hostility in the insured, who tend to go to their employers and complain bitterly to the personnel director. When the time for that contract's renewal comes up, the personnel director will oppose the mental health plan, arguing that the program was only concerned with saving money. Marxist rhetoric to the contrary notwithstanding, most large organizations do care for their workers and do not want to simply pay them as little as possible. Employers want cost savings but also high quality. These programs tend to get punished at renewal time.

A Shift in Emphasis

The MMH industry is beginning to recognize that money is not saved by outpatient reviews. The medical director of a large insurance company privately admitted to me that they do not have any evidence they can save money by reviewing outpatient cases. He conceded that they do it because their competitors do it and the companies they insure think it is a good idea. It has become obvious there is little justification for outpatient reviews, especially the intrusive ones that occur after two or three visits.

Instead of abandoning them, MMH claims the review process will assure "quality of care." Since the review process is sold to the customers on the basis of total quality assurance, outpatient therapists will be expected to demonstrate they are following acceptable diagnosis and treatment protocols. It seems likely we will see a diminishing of the abusive type of reviewing, such as reviews after only three visits. In return for that, therapists should expect to have to demonstrate a clear outcome-based treatment philosophy.

A major problem with all of this is that the review criteria are still idiosyncratic and proprietary with the managed care organization. The criteria tend to be written by administrators who are not in direct patient care, so there is a certain looseness in their grasp of mental health realities. Some of the criteria for quality have no relationship to actual quality.

There is also the problem of hobbyhorses. In talking with reviewers for various MMH plans, I have noticed a general antagonism toward psychoanalysis, based on some cases in which the patient has a diagnosis of mild anxiety of some sort and has been in treatment for many years, sometimes several times a week. The reviewers consider this abusive (which it is) and target analytically oriented therapists for intensive review. But in my experience with outpatient reviews, there is no real relationship between type of treatment approach and excessive therapy. I have reviewed cases of behavior therapists (at least that is how they defined themselves) who had seen a patient with relatively mild problems for a long time. Psychoanalytic techniques appear to be helpful when used by competent therapists. While many analysts rigidly believe long-term treatment is the only approach, others are interested and skilled in briefer treatment (Gustafson, 1986).

Trying to Measure Quality

Instead of focusing on the model of psychotherapy being offered, the best quality reviews focus on certain indicators that presumably indicate quality: a competent assessment and diagnosis, a clear and fairly precise treatment focus, evidence the therapist and patient are sticking fairly well to the focus, and a rational relationship between the focus and what happens in therapy. The therapist's activity should bear a clear relationship to the therapeutic goals, the goals should be accomplished in a reasonable amount of time, and therapist should begin to space out sessions as the goals are met. Therapy is not continued to "solidify gains," but to accomplish goals. Patients are encouraged to be independent and active, and patients with chronic, characterological issues are placed in group therapy.

A comprehensive mental status assessment and psychosocial and medical history are not necessarily what all managed care companies are looking for. There should be some assessment of whether the patient is dangerous to self or others, and whether there is a drug or alcohol problem. A reasonable DSM-IV diagnosis, including all five axes, is appreciated by reviewers, but some of that information can come from pre- and post-session questionnaires and inventories. While treatment traditionally has borne only a tenuous relationship to the diagnosis, the development of treatment protocols is changing that. For example, a diagnosis of major depression should include a treatment plan that follows a specific treatment protocol for depression. Since all treatments for depression, if they are focused (see Chapter 4), appear to have equivalent outcomes, the protocol could be behavioral, interpersonal, cognitive, or psychodynamic.

The therapist needs to bear in mind that, having given a client the diagnosis of, say, major depression, there ought to be some indication that the patient is making acceptable progress. Depression ought to respond fairly quickly to psychotherapy. Within 12–16 sessions, the patient should show a clear and positive response to treatment, and termination or less frequent (i.e., monthly) visits should be imminent. If none of that has occurred by that time, and the therapist has not considered and discussed psychotropic medication, the case reviewer will be suspicious of a poor quality of care. In other words, a therapist should be expecting to see some improvement within a few sessions, marked improvement by a dozen or so.

Other issues of quality include how soon the patient can be seen after calling for an appointment, and whether the therapist has some kind of 24-hour coverage in the case of emergencies. I am most skeptical about this last indicator, since I think it is a distortion of the role of the therapist. But the question of the latency between the first phone call and the first available appointment is certainly an indicator of quality. I recently treated a young woman complaining of an abuse problem with her father. This was an acute situation, with the complaint and the incidents recent. Protective services recommended she get some counseling, and she concurred. She had coverage with a HMO but was told she couldn't be seen for six to eight weeks. This is unconscionable, and I believe it is unethical. In the new era of accountable mental health care, such response should be grounds for sanctions. A patient should have a right to be seen within a few days of calling, or a week at most.*

TRENDS AND FUTURE DIRECTIONS

A trend has developed to "carve out" mental health benefits from medical benefits or to separate them and use a different business entity to administer them. This trend has fueled the growth of multidisciplinary capitated practice groups. Under this system, a group that can offer a broad range of mental health services and is both service provider and insurance carrier. Let's create an example. An imaginary company, Psychotherapy Group, Inc. (PGI) approaches large companies and offers to handle the mental health portion of their health care program. The benefits are "carved out" and the employees and dependents of the program now can only see the therapists in the group. Our imaginary company, PGI, becomes *capitated*, meaning they provide all of the coverage necessary for a flat fee. This is no longer fee for service; in essence, PGI has become a mental health HMO. PGI may also approach HMOs and ask to carve out their mental health package, suggesting that as specialists they can offer the services more efficiently. This program eliminates the external managed care aspect. The group itself now manages the benefits. If therapists are efficient and effective, and if they avoid inpatient care whenever possible, there may be a profit left at the end of the year. If things do not go well, there may be a loss. There is a sharing of the risk.

For PGI to prosper, it must be able to communicate to the groups it provides service for. The therapists must be able to document how many people they are seeing, for what types of problems, and for how many visits. Most importantly, they must report what the outcomes of counseling have been: How much improvement is the typical patient seeing from therapy? How satisfied are the clients?

Such multidisciplinary groups are becoming more and more popular. They have the advantage of offering managed care that is close to the patient, and they might turn out to be more efficient than the managed care

---

*A large EAP conducted an in-house study and found that the sooner the client was seen, the fewer sessions were needed for a satisfactory conclusion. Someone seen within 24 hours was much more likely to be satisfied with two or three visits.

programs run through insurance companies, since they have eliminated the middleman. As long as they maintain high standards and can communicate within the organization, they should do well. However, there is a dark side.

Some groups seem to be turning into the modern equivalent of sweat shops. They offer very low-cost mental health benefits and achieve that through reckless limits on inpatient treatment for dangerous patients. They also tend to hire newer, lesser trained therapists and require that they work long hours for low pay. Qualifications are diminished. Doctoral level providers are replaced with master's level; the master's level counselors are replaced with bachelor's level and paraprofessionals. If such a trend continues, the entire profession of psychotherapy will be rapidly debased and devalued, and the best and the smartest will go elsewhere. Patients will not receive the high quality help they need, and the skill base will be eroded. Therapy is a difficult art, which takes years of concentrated attention and effort to master, and more experienced therapists have somewhat better outcomes than new or inexperienced ones (Stein & Lambert, 1995). Patients will become disenchanted with the low quality of service and a negative spiral will bankrupt the whole profession.

The alternative to this is to work as a profession to create and maintain high standards of professional excellence, to document the value of our contributions to the consumers and to those who control the purse strings. Instead of being managed from afar, providers can and should create practice groups that assume some of the risk for providing services. A practice group can bid on the mental health services for a large company and assume responsibility for providing all the services needed, from EAP to marriage counseling to child and adult psychotherapy to substance abuse treatment. These capitated plans would require therapists to report the results of their work to the employers or insurance companies. In order to work together, we need a common language with which to discuss our profession. Within that language, we must make a commitment to continuous quality improvement both individually and as agencies, so that the cost-control emphasis natural to the funding sources of psychotherapy does not end up corrupting and incapacitating our ability to help.

A Common Language

A new watchword in mental health is accountability. Along with the growth of the HMOs and the managed care programs comes an increase in accountable activity. Whereas in the past the funders of mental health, both the government and the private sector, were content to dole out the money and do systemwide audits, now the individual patient's outcomes are being tracked. This is a challenge, since the ways therapists talk about their processes and outcomes vary widely. To be accountable, we need a common way to talk to each other and to those who review our work. A common language for psychotherapy would allow reversal of the Babel of confusion in reporting on outcomes. That common language is now within our reach, based on research and experience that suggest common factors account for the majority of effects from treatment.

With agreement on common aspects of diverse approaches, common measurements of process and outcome can be developed, leading to methods for improving theory and practice. This common language should have significant benefits. Therapists who base their treatment plans on such a *lingua franca* should be able to communicate with case managers and insurance company psychiatric review specialists across a wide variety of environments.

Accountability influences perceptions; how we look at psychotherapy changes when we report to outsiders. Therefore, as a result of demands for accountability from insurance and funding sources, therapists are developing an emphasis on concrete, specific outcomes. Workshops around the country that emphasize communicating with managed care are well attended, as therapists look for skills to cope with insurance company requirements. But this is the tail wagging the dog: Therapists need to develop their own understandings about accountability and competence, and we need to vigorously assert them, else we run a substantial risk that standards for quality and accountability will be (indeed, are being) imposed from without.

In the pages that follow I will review what I believe are common underlying factors in effective psychotherapy. I have been rather strongly influenced by strategic and systemic thinking, but if you look at my work you see a good deal of cognitive and even the occasional psychoanalytic influence. Since all of those are my own roots, such influences are inevitable. And they illustrate my own notion that there is no one theory of human behavior that is capable of the most efficient and effective application across the wide variety of human problems the psychotherapist confronts.

CHAPTER 2

An Integrative Model

In the early seventies, when I was attending graduate school, there were many interesting and exciting theories to choose from. My behavior therapy professors were claiming they brought science and responsibility to psychotherapy. The gestalt therapy class taught me I should encourage patients to exaggerate their symptoms and talk to an empty chair. My analytic supervisors suggested theirs was the only real therapy; the rest was shallow and symptom removal techniques that wouldn't last. I learned to facilitate T-groups and create behavioral contracts in families; I learned to administer psychological tests and to make defense and transference interpretations in individual therapy. It was confusing, refreshing, exciting. Surely one of these systems would be proved to be more true than the others and would triumph.

Twenty-plus years later it is clear that there is no value in any one system that other systems do not likewise offer. I remember the enthusiasm our behavior therapy professor had for phobias. He was unequivocal: Systematic desensitization is the treatment of choice for fears. Years later I was shocked when I came across a study that demonstrated brief psychodynamic psychotherapy was as effective as behavior therapy for the treatment of phobias (Klein, Zitrin, Woerner, & Ross, 1983).

But I was just learning what was being confirmed by serious researchers: Systems of psychotherapy did not seem to make a useful difference. Neither behavior therapy nor psychoanalysis was superior, and neither was inferior. This understanding invited psychotherapists into an examination of common factors in therapy. Jerome Frank (1974) suggested that all therapies helped by instilling a feeling of hope in clients. The patients come to us feeling discouraged and disheartened. Life seems to them the same thing over and over and they cannot see a new way to deal with it. The therapist gives hope through the listening process, a relationship of caring and safety, and communicating new ideas. Because of that hope, the patient begins to live life in a new, more assertive way, trying new behaviors and new explanations about life, which change the way life is experienced.

THE INTEGRATIVE APPROACH

The Common Elements Argument

In 1975, Luborsky, Singer, and Luborsky published an analysis of psychotherapy outcome studies. Focusing their attention on studies that tried to compare different models of psychotherapy, they asked, "Is it true that all have won and all must have prizes?" Their analysis, which since has been well supported, was that psychotherapy makes a positive and significant difference in clients' lives; however, no significant difference in effect can be demonstrated by any specific model. It does not seem to matter what particular psychotherapy school one belongs to; rather, the process works for reasons other than those the schools postulate.

For example, Sloane, Staples, Cristol, Yorkston, and Whipple (1975) demonstrated that neurotic outpatients were helped by psychotherapy, and that behavior therapy and brief psychodynamic psychotherapy were equivalent in effect. Various reviews have confirmed that the theories psychotherapists hold do not seem to have any relationship to the therapy outcomes; rather, positive outcomes must be due to other, common factors (see Bergin & Lambert, 1978; Meltzoff & Kornreich, 1970; Shapiro & Shapiro, 1982; Smith & Glass, 1977; Smith, Glass, & Miller, 1980). There has been some discussion about how cognitive and behavioral approaches seemed somewhat superior, but this is probably an artifact of those approaches specifying with greater precision their targeted outcomes, and then attempting to achieve those outcomes. If more general measures of functioning are considered, the approaches seem equivalent (Steenbarger, 1994). For example, Eysenck (1993) continues to assert that traditional approaches, by which he means primarily psychoanalysis, have failed to show significant power, whereas prescriptive (i.e., behavioral or cognitive-behavioral) approaches show larger effect sizes in meta-analysis. But in the same volume, Elliott, Stiles, and Shapiro (1993) point out that when using nonreactive measures of change (meaning measures that are more broad or general and presumably more relevant to the patient's desire to generally function better), all approaches continue to demonstrate roughly the same power.

One convincing way to explain this seemingly counterintuitive argument that technique makes very little difference comes from Lambert (1992). In an analysis of the outcome research, he suggests that technique accounts for only 15% of improvement in psychotherapy, equivalent to the expectancy (or so-called "placebo") effects. Common factors account for 30%, or twice as much as technique, and extratherapeutic factors, such as client characteristics and fortuitous incidents in the patient's life, account for 40%. And of the common factors, the strongest single factor appears to be the therapeutic relationship the patient has with the therapist.

The Death of Systems Thinking

The early years of mental health were characterized by adherence to models of treatment, such as insight-oriented, behavioral, and humanistic. Over the past ten years there has been a pronounced and dramatic shift in research and practice away from systems and towards an integrative model (Omer & London, 1988). While there are other ways to interpret the data on equivalent outcomes (Stiles, Shapiro, & Elliott, 1986), the premise of this book is that an integrative model is the most parsimonious and useful one for accountable mental health.

This doesn't mean that every therapist is the same as every other therapist, nor does it mean that specific techniques are the same as a vague, general approach. It is becoming quite clear that therapist skill in engaging and understanding the patient is a crucial aspect of treatment. There are enormous differences between therapists (for example, see Luborsky, McClellan, Woody, O'Brian, & Auerbach, 1985). Some are quite good, and some things therapists do are "psychonoxious" or harmful to patients. Therapists can help or hurt (5–10% of patients deteriorate in psychotherapy; Lambert, Shapiro, & Bergin 1986; Ogles, Lambert, & Sawyer, 1995), and to the extent we can develop process and outcome measures that addresses these effects, we can improve our profession and help therapists develop themselves toward more and more helpful approaches.

Over the past few years, some specific, targeted interventions have been developed for specific complaints (for example, see Barlow, 1993). It does appear that the intense focus on specific problems is yielding some very good results. Conversely, a nebulous sort of supportive therapy is likely to produce ambiguous or even equivocal results. But the consistent finding is that models of psychotherapy have not produced advantages in designing treatments. Rather, it appears that there are many useful ways to achieve particular outcomes, and that it is the sharp focus on the problem rather than the theory from which the interventions are derived that is the operative agent.

The Limits of Theory

To put it more simply: Psychoanalysis cannot be a true model for human functioning, since it is not a necessary component of effective human change. If the psychoanalytic theory were true, then the results from behavioral interventions could not last, but would be characterized by symptom substitution and other untoward consequences. Since there has been no convincing demonstration of symptom substitution, we must assume psychodynamic formulations are unnecessary elaborations.

At the same time, the notions of behaviorism, cognitive therapy, or humanism are not correct or true understandings. Since they all appear to "work" equally well (with the caveat that the focus is clear and interventions are specific and targeted), none of them can have a unique truth. Rather, they all appear to have accessed some common factors that allow them to help people in various kinds of human dilemmas.

Furthermore, even the constructivism of the strategic therapists cannot be true, since constructivism postulates that one cannot know about the world, and that all theory is merely a construction and not a reflection of any actual world "out there." But if this is true, then it is paradoxical, since the theory is saying, "We can know this about the world, that we cannot know anything about the world apart from our own constructions." Such a paradoxical position is fun to meditate on, and is even useful in inducing an hypnotic trance. But because it is paradoxical, that is, self-referential, it also is merely another way of looking at the world. The value of constructivism would appear to be in the claim that one cannot know the truth, so it helps the therapist have less faith in his or her theories. If we stop believing in our psychotherapeutic theories, we can be more respectful both to our clients and to other therapists with diverse approaches.

This puts the therapist in a difficult dilemma: To know what to do next, one needs a theory, just as a pilot needs a map so as to know how to navigate. However, if one looks at the evidence, none of the theories appears to have any unique validity. How can one know how to see these problems? How is one to know how to act? There are a few, simple common elements that have pragmatically shown good impact; if the therapist can master those common skill areas, the particular theory she or he follows will be irrelevant. In fact, the effect of integration is to discourage the therapist from being a "true believer" in any single system, and thus more open to developments from a variety of sources.

To that end, however, an accountable therapist must be aware of current research and be a sophisticated consumer of that information. Retreating into a "know nothingism" in which research is discounted as any useful source of knowledge would mean abandoning any pretense that psychotherapy can be a profession. And while common wisdom holds that published research is frequently characterized by trivial results produced by academics desperate for tenure, for the alert reader there is a good deal of very useful information to be harvested. Especially in this day of computerized databases, which can rapidly review any topic and point out articles that are likely to be useful, it is time for the accountable therapist to become aware of the literature.

This is a difficult challenge. Therapists too often tend to learn about new developments in the field simply by attending continuing education workshops. Since one will perhaps attend only those workshops that appeal to one's own theoretical stance, there is a certain circularity to this process. How does one really learn something new?

Furthermore, in many continuing education workshops, material is presented on the basis of "clinical experience." The presenter speaks *ex cathedra*, saying "This is the way it is." The content often implies the presenter has unique understanding that makes his or her theory more potent than others. This is quite frustrating for one who has read the literature and knows that the general thrust of research has not confirmed those pronouncements. In saying this, there is no intention to point an accusing finger at any single theory. This phenomenon is present in presentations ranging from object relations to strategic, solution-focused, and Ericksonian perspectives. The cognitive therapists are a refreshing exception; their workshops tend to be well-founded in research findings. But unfortunately this is not generally the case. Therapists simply must become more aware of what their own literature says, and not accept pronouncements based on what the presenter's clinical experience may be.

The trouble with "clinical experience" is that it is notoriously unreliable. It is well to remind ourselves at this point that George Washington died of medical treatment that was both state of the art and based on sound clinical experience (Flexner, 1984, p. 404, although, as Flexner points out, he might have died even if he had not been bled four times.). Therapists are very poor evaluators of their own theories and techniques, and often we do not know whether we are actually attending to what makes a difference. Certainly this is a dilemma, since the research base is currently inadequate to actually provide guidance on a moment-to-moment basis. So we must rely on our clinical experience, and certainly a case presentation is more helpful to illustrate a technique than a journal article usually is. However, the literature can give us some general direction and help, and to the extent that it does so, we should attend to it — and to the extent that it does not provide that help, we can encourage good studies.

Many academic departments are full of professors who have never been in a full-time clinical practice since their internships. They are brilliant and thoughtful persons who were unusually productive of research and moved directly into the teaching arena after graduation. So sometimes the research is cleverly and thoughtfully designed, but not relevant to the questions of the practitioner. The practicing clinician often has a notion about research that suggests all articles have titles like, "Visual tracking of identical Bosnian schizophrenic twins." Practitioners and academicians can do a better job of communicating with one another about likely research topics.

For example, solution-focused techniques form a well-defined system that is very popular among clinicians. At workshops, the solution-focused approach seems very well received, and it would appear to be more easily applied than some other, more complex approaches. Unfortunately, there is little actual research on the topic, and our profession has a history of becoming enthusiastic about approaches that show no advantage over a well-designed attention placebo (i.e., a research design in which the control group is not simply ignored but is given an equivalent amount of therapeutic-appearing attention from the researcher). Is this because the techniques have been developed and expounded outside of the academic settings, so that the graduate schools are often unaware of even the existence of the skills, let alone having an idea of how to evaluate them?

My intention, then, is to utilize as far as possible the actual research base and to construct an integrative model of therapy that seems to attend to the major research findings and is appropriate for a wide variety of clinicians. I recognize the value of case examples to provide illustration of how a colleague or I have applied those findings and approaches.

COMPONENTS OF INTEGRATIVE
BRIEF PSYCHOTHERAPY

The Therapy Relationship

The therapeutic relationship or alliance is certainly a common element. The relationship is not difficult to measure, and accounts for a large portion of positive change in psychotherapy (Gaston, 1990). It appears that, according to the review by Luborsky, Crits-Christoph, Mintz, and Auerbach, (1988), outcome correlates with alliance or relationship at approximately the .50 level. Patients need to experience certain kinds of relationship with the therapist so as to benefit from treatment. Chapter 3 will review what seems generally accepted about relationship, as well as offering speculative ideas.

Related to the topic of relationship and working alliance is awareness of patient motivation, how to assess and utilize it. Effective therapists are skillful at increasing patient motivation for change (Meichenbaum & Turk, 1987). In fact, as Patterson and Chamberlain (1992) imply, the therapist is the strongest component of resistance to change in patients. Chapter 8 discusses various approaches to motivation.

Another aspect of the relationship area is focus. In a strong working alliance, the patient is convinced that therapy is doing what she or he wants it to do. There is agreement between the patient and therapist on the goals of therapy. Focus distinguishes brief, effective psychotherapy from counseling that is neither brief nor effective. Therapists must understand how to co-create and manage a useful focus, and how to communicate that to reviewers.

So in discussing the therapy relationship, we must examine the emotional bond between the therapist and patient, the ability of the therapist to motivate the patient, and the skill of the therapist in understanding and addressing the crucial issues in the patient's life. All of these are recursively related, each influencing the others.

The Impact of Therapy: The Role of the Therapist

The second component is that of emotional and/or cognitive impact. Patients may change thinking and feeling primarily because of what the therapist says and does. The therapist must have a set of skills that creates some kind of change in the view of the problem. Because various approaches in psychotherapy yield comparable results, this work will present a modest attempt to integrate them into a simple theory.

This second area, therapist activity, is where most emphasis is placed in treatment manuals and protocols. A treatment protocol suggests various steps in a treatment, gives suggestions about decision points, and models stopping points for treatment. Such manuals are an attractive idea for managed care organizations, since they ensure that treatment decisions are made based on whether some well-recognized treatment strategy is being followed. Therapists will probably be judged by managed care organizations by whether their activity in treatment conforms to a recognized treatment manual for that condition. A good number of protocols already exist and they are increasing.

A challenge to the protocols is that distinct protocols show equivalent results. For example, the NIMH depression studies demonstrated that different approaches to depression had very similar outcomes (Elkin, Shea, Watkins et al., 1989). Here I attempt to formulate an integrative approach based on this observation. Treatment protocols are useful for providing coherence and focus to the therapy relationship, but there are few data suggesting the superiority of one over another. In cases where data do suggest some advantage, that is noted.

The Impact of Therapy: The Role of the Patient

The third element is patient activity. What the patient does and what happens to her outside of therapy accounts for more of the therapeutic impact than technique or relationship alone. But even here the therapist can have some influence. Successful treatments involve the patient in changes of behavior, and those changes are then reported to the therapist, discussed, and form the basis for further change. Homework is not universal in psychotherapy, but among eclectic or integrative approaches it is a common element, so a good deal of emphasis must be placed on that. How does the therapist effectively design and assign homework? What kind of homework appears to be useful? What types of homework are available? The systematic evaluation of homework is a skill the accountable therapist must have.

In addition to homework during therapy, the patient in briefer therapies can benefit from skills at maintaining the gains he has achieved. Therapists may call this goal maintenance or relapse prevention skills. This area, pioneered by substance abuse counselors, can be adapted to problems that do not involve substance abuse. The patient depends on the therapist to understand and educate him about maintaining gains; the therapist depends on the patient to do the actual maintenance.

Since the patient is strongly influenced by factors outside of the therapy hour, it may be important to give attention to the role of family and other significant persons in the patient's network. While the outcomes of family-based interventions are variable, today's therapist should at least be aware of how many treatment protocols utilize significant others. For example, Budman and Gurman (1988) emphasize how they try to get significant others, even roommates or coworkers, to attend occasional sessions of therapy. This involvement of others is a particular example of the general rule that the effective therapist uses a variety of ways to increase patient motivation. A chapter will emphasize approaches to increasing patient motivation.

In other words, examining the role of the patient does not relieve the therapist of the responsibility to make therapy a useful experience for the patient. It only helps the therapist realize what the limits on her or his power are, and implies ways even to influence those parts of the therapy domain that are beyond the traditional verbal give-and-take.

CHAPTER 3

The Therapeutic Relationship: An Integrative View

In a television documentary, *The Heart of Healing*, a woman in Africa suffering from cancer was not being helped by Western medicine. She decided to seek help from a shaman, and she and her daughter journeyed several hours to reach the native healer's hut. They pleaded for help, and the medicine man decided to take the case. He went into his hut, and then emerged wearing the skin of a leopard, symbolizing that the spirit of this consummate hunter had entered him. Presumably he would hunt out the cause of her suffering as the leopard hunts prey. Crouching, he circled her, and then spat on her back! She sat quite still during this, as if it were standard part of a healing process.

After some healing rituals the patient said she felt better and would return for another treatment. I was struck by the way she credited someone who would spit on her with such power! Obviously, in her culture spitting doesn't mean the same as in mine. And I was impressed with the parallel between that healing relationship and the ones we try to create in our consulting rooms. In both situations we hope the client will attribute some kind of legitimacy and power to us, so that our healing efforts will meet with the client's own good will and best efforts.

This chapter will review the therapeutic relationship and how to improve it by using helpful tools such as relationship rating scales and the customer status assessment. While the therapeutic relationship is something that is co-created, at the same time it is primarily the therapist's responsibility. Rather than following rigid rules for creating that relationship, the therapist must be flexible and adaptable.

Originally, the notion of the alliance focused on the therapist's providing key conditions such as empathy and congruence. However, this approach has run into many problems in research. For example, there has to be some way of scoring empathy. The approach has usually been to employ experts to rate the therapeutic interaction and judge whether the therapist offered those conditions. This has not led to useful findings, since it became apparent that the therapist could offer the conditions and they might not be perceived as helpful by the patient. A shift toward researching the way the patient perceives the relationship has given us more useful information.

Gelso and Carter (1985) focus on two factors in the therapy relationship: (1) the attitudes and feelings therapy participants hold toward one another; and (2) the manner in which these are expressed. This suggests that instead of looking at the therapy relationship as the result of the therapist's empathy, a theory that has not yielded helpful results (Lambert, DeJulio, & Stein, 1978), the focus should be on the way the client and the therapist cooperate together. This approach is harder to test, since the way two people cooperate is as variable as the varieties of two personalities involved. But it helps us understand such interactions as the shaman and his patient in the earlier example. The spitting symbolized something about which the two participants agreed. There might even be an expectation that spitting had to take place.

Eric Berne told a story about being consulted about a tribal chief in New Guinea who seemed to have some symptoms of mental illness. The local governor, concerned about the chief, asked the famous doctor to examine and diagnose him. Berne agreed to visit the tribe. When he tried to talk to the chief about how the chief was feeling, the chief would turn his comments around, asking how Berne was feeling. "How are you feeling, chief?" asked Berne. The chief responded, "How are *you?*"

"No," replied the psychiatrist, "I mean, I hear you aren't feeling so good."

"Well," replied the chief, "you don't look so good yourself. Are you all right?" Finally, Berne announced he was a doctor and was there to help the chief. The chief said, "Oh, why didn't you say so?" and disappeared into his hut. He emerged with a pile of yams, saying those were to pay Berne for healing him. Then he said, "Where's your mask?" The psychiatrist admitted he did not have a mask, and the chief was incensed. "Huh!" the chief exclaimed, "How can you be a good doctor if you don't have a mask?"

The governor asked Berne what he thought. He replied, "I think that if I am going to be a doctor around here, I had better get a mask."

And this is the fallacy in using expert ratings of therapist behavior. Some patients may need a good deal of empathy, and others may not. Hill (1989) points out that for many patients empathy comes first; establishing a warm, caring relationship is crucial. Only then does the therapist introduce interpretation and other change-oriented techniques. But this is not true for all clients, she argues, for "(b)efore some clients will trust and disclose to a therapist, they might need to be confronted to have proof that the therapist can see through their defenses" (pp. 20–21). The therapy process is far too complicated to say that all therapists should be empathic with all patients in all sessions. Some patients need empathy; some need to see the therapist's mask.

In other words, there is a good possibility that the patient enters therapy with a notion or plan, albeit unconscious or unaware, as to what sort of relationship is needed to heal his or her wounds (cf. Silberschatz, Curtis, Sampson, & Weiss, 1991). The patient presents the therapist with various tasks and tests to see whether the plan will be understood and responded to. For the patient to recover most rapidly, the plan must be perceived and responded to appropriately. This is the dilemma of the therapist, in that the rules change according to the particular situation, as Hill said.

THERAPEUTIC FLEXIBILITY

New therapists used to be taught the importance of remaining a blank screen onto which the patient projects conflicts and transference. Richard Fisch, the well-known psychiatrist with the Mental Research Institute, told of an incident early in his training when he was on call at a hospital emergency room. A large man was brought in manacles, ranting and threatening. The policemen smiled, and said, "He's all yours, doc!" The young physician reached for a syringe and major tranquilizer, and the angry patient began to make threats about what he would do if that needle came near him.

"You don't understand," said Fisch. "This shot is not for you, it's for me."

"What do you mean?"

"Well," replied the doctor, "you are a very large fellow, and I am quite small. You are scaring the hell out of me, so if I can give you this shot, I will feel a lot better."

"You're scared?" asked the patient. "What about me, being brought to a nut house? Well, if it will help you, then OK, I'll take the shot."

In this case, it is likely the blank screen ("Why do you think you feel so threatened?") or the one-up position ("Take this medicine, it is good for you") would have escalated the conflict. The sensitive response, taking a one-down position, and revealing personal data worked far better. And, admitting one's fear in such a situation is a true example of courage.

Hill (1989) found in her study that therapists who judiciously revealed personal vulnerabilities in therapy were seen as more effective therapists and were more helpful than those who did not. The rigid rule, always remain a blank screen, is counterproductive when we examine individual experiences or research findings. The clinical experience and the research support the idea that flexibility is crucial.

Bond, Goals and Tasks

A good general scheme for understanding therapeutic alliance is offered by Bordin (1979). He suggests there is (1) a *bond* between the therapist and patient, (2) an agreement on *goals* for the relationship, and (3) an agreement on *tasks*. The three areas of bond, goals, and tasks constitute the foundation of a positive therapy relationship.

Clinical experience and research confirm the importance of these factors. There is now evidence that two major factors that predict the patient's response to therapy are the relationship and the level of patient activity. Patients who feel their therapist likes and respects them, is honest and trustworthy, and agrees with them on goals and tasks, will work hard outside of the psychotherapy hour and gain the most from therapy (Burns & Nolen-Hoeksema, 1992). And these factors are recursive; they constantly influence each other. The bond may be strengthened by the therapist's agreeing that the client's wants are reasonable and good; the agreement on goals influences the tasks. At each stage, a negotiation is happening.

Now the therapist's theory is both a help (tells the therapist what to do next) and also a barrier between the patient and the therapist, and may interfere with the therapist's respect for what the patient wants. If I visit David Burns and complain I am depressed, I will find the tasks recommended flow out of the goals. His goals are to modify my cognitions, and the tasks will include a strong component of tracking and modifying my thinking. But if I visit Peter Sifneos for the same depression, I may discover that I competed with my father for my mother's attention and love; I continue to feel competitive but anxious and guilty, and I still expect male figures to compete with me. The problem is the same; the negotiation about goals and tasks depends to a great extent on the skills and interests of the therapist.

If I am convinced that I must examine my past and understand it in order to be free of my depression, then Sifneos is likely to be more appropriate for me; if I prefer to look at the present and the future, perhaps Burns will suit my needs much better. Although this is an oversimplification (e.g., excellent therapists will subtly modify their technique to fit the patient), I believe therapists often let theory get in the way of flexibility and adapting to the patient.

The Customer Status Assessment: A Flexibility Tool

One way of improving the therapy alliance is to focus on what the patient wants, rather than diagnosing what is wrong with the patient and deciding how to fix it. This related to Bordin's concept of the agreement on goals and tasks. Of course, some patients may want to know what is wrong with them, and the diagnosis can be useful and a relief. For example, a patient who cannot understand why her heart pounds and why she thinks she is going crazy may find it a relief to understand the diagnosis of panic disorder, and such understanding may well be a significant step toward recovery. But other patients may have some goals which they feel committed to but unable to achieve. They may be disinterested in, or even insulted by, a diagnosis, and helped by focusing on those goals and ways to achieve them.

I like to call this the "customer status" assessment because that term emphasizes that the client in our office may be interested in, or a customer for, many different things. Effective therapy may be the result of, among many other things, finding a good fit between what the client wants and what the therapist can do. For example, some patients may want to call the therapist at home when they are in crisis, but such calls are probably a very bad idea, so the therapist must frustrate such a need (cf. Yeomans, 1993). By frustrating that need, it may well be that the therapist that will have much better impact. But such frustrating can also be dangerous and should be done carefully and with great respect for the integrity of the patient.

Patient involvement is essential to brief therapy; in fact, the best predictor of patient progress is how involved the patient becomes. The client who says, "Yes, I have a problem, but there is nothing I can do about it. The problem is really my (pick one) husband, wife, son, daughter, parents, school, etc.," is *complaining* about a problem that is seen as outside of him. When you ask, "Are you willing to work very hard to solve this problem?" he is likely to say, "Are you talking to me? Didn't you understand what I said? I am not the problem, my son is! You need to change him." If the therapist demands that this patient take responsibility for his part in the problem, the result is likely to be an unpleasant conflict that leaves both sides unhappy.

Similarly a patient might tell you, "I don't have a problem, it is my probation officer who makes me come. He's the one with the problem, so naturally I am not willing to do anything different from what I am doing, since there really isn't any problem."

Motivation can be conceptualized as a readiness to change, and can be measured by how much actual effort a person puts into changing behavior, thoughts, and feelings. Prochaska, DiClemente, and Norcross (1992) and McConnaughy, DiClemente, Prochaska, and Velicer (1989) have proposed that clients be assessed by a four-stage model of motivation. The four stages are: (1) *precontemplation*, during which there is not a serious intention to change; (2) *contemplation*, during which people are thinking about confronting their problem, and preparation (sometimes seen as a separate step), during which they are ready to take action to solve a problem, (3) *action*, efforts made to solve the problem; and (4) *maintenance*, or efforts to keep the gains. They propose that the therapist can better serve clients by responding congruently to their motivational stage. For example, it is not helpful to attempt to force a client at the contemplation stage to take active steps to deal with an addiction or a problem. We are all familiar with the alcoholic who rejects the idea that he should do something about his drinking; similarly, an adolescent who is giving her parents grief but does not accept the idea that she has a problem is not prepared for action.

A similar idea, independently arrived at, was proposed by Segal and Watzlawick (1985, p. 73) and elaborated by de Shazer (1988, 1991) and Berg and Miller (1992). This is the concept of *customer status*. De Shazer proposes the therapeutic relationship be described as one of three types: *customer, complainant,* or *visitor.* Two questions are asked to determine whether the client is relating to the therapist in the customer, complainant, or visitor/guest role, namely, "Do you have a problem in your life?" and "Are you willing to work hard to solve that problem?" The customer will say "yes" to both questions; the complainant will say there is a problem but he is not willing to work hard, and the visitor will say "no" to both. The customer is appropriate for intervention, behavioral change assignments, and so on. The complainant and visitor are not appropriate for typical psychotherapy interventions. We might correlate these concepts by saying the customer is at the preparation or action stage, while the complainant is at the contemplation stage and the visitor is at the precontemplation stage.

The stage model and the customer status model both suggest that the patient may move from one stage to another. When a therapist responds appropriately to the stage the client functions at, this invites a movement from visitor to complainant, and from complainant to customer. In other words, when we do not ask the client to change, that allows the client to shift from visitor or complainant to customer.

Additionally, it should be noted that the customer status assessment is a way of describing the *relationship between the patient and the counselor, not of describing the patient.* Having said that, I will talk as if, during this discussion, we are describing the client. That is simply a handicap of our language, which tends to classify persons more easily than it classifies processes. Please bear in mind that the description is not of the client, but of the kind of relationship a particular therapist invites from a particular client. When we say a client is a "visitor," it only means the relationship is currently that of a visitor. It may be that another counselor dealing with the same client would be able to create a more cooperative relationship.

In other words, since the relationship is mutable, the actions of the therapist partly determine customer status. (Here I depart from Prochaska's model, which does seem to assess the patient and not the relationship.) In our model, the therapist follows a schema that will often move the patient from a less motivated to a more motivated relationship, so our view is more interactional than Prochaska's appears to be.

For instance, complainants are given compliments for their skills at coping with problems, as well as assignments to collect data. They are not asked to change their views or actions. The "visitor" could be the unintentional result of a counselor pressuring a client (who might have entered treatment at a complainant stage) to be a customer, and the client may well react to the therapist's confrontation by feeling less motivated to change. If the counselor were to restrain the client, warning of the dangers of improvement and congratulating him for the things he does well, the client may very well decide this is a counselor he can trust and share a problem he actually wants to solve.

Table 3.1 summarizes the relationship between customer status and tasks. Following this matrix seems to reduce stress on the counselor and

Table 3.1 The Customer Status-Task Matrix

Status	Do you have a problem?	Are you willing to work hard to solve it?	Appropriate tasks or responses
Customer	Yes	Yes	Reframing, homework, confrontation, interpretation; the patient is asked to change his views of the problem and his behavior.
Complainant	Yes, (but . . .)	No	Give client compliments and ask him to *observe* (but not change) own behavior for coping strategies and what works best, or observe others' behavior for times when the problem is absent or not so much a problem. Ask whether the client can predict those times when problem is absent. Changing of the views is implied, not explicit.
Visitor or Guest	No	No	Emphasize positive relationship; give compliments about strengths and abilities; perhaps warn about the dangers of change and recommend no change "for now" and engage in pleasant conversation; look for the "hidden customer" by asking how the referring person/agency would know when the client no longer needs to come to therapy.

improve the bond between therapist and patient, since there is a better agreement between them about the task and methods of the relationship.

APPLYING THE CUSTOMER STATUS ASSESSMENT

This discussion focuses on using the customer status assessment. With a bit of thought, the same general principles will apply to Prochaska's concepts.

Counseling with the Customer

The customer is the easiest of the three relationships for the therapist to work with. Here we are able to agree on goals (i.e., "something needs to change") and on tasks (i.e., "the patient will work hard to change what needs changing"). We still need to form the kind of bond that will assure that we are seen as helpful persons who can be cooperated with, but that is relatively easy when that the client is a customer.

Some care must be taken in a family where one person is a customer and willing to work hard and others are in complainant or visitor status, since the customer may begin to feel resentful over doing most of the work.

Cooperating with the Complainant

A complainant presents a particular challenge. Berne (1964) wrote of a "game" or a repetitive, predictable interactional pattern with an ulterior motive, which he called "Why don't you – Yes, but." In this game, the first player complains about something; the second player offers suggestions about how the complaint should be solved, and the first player discounts those suggestions by saying "Yes, but . . . "

It may be helpful to think of this pattern as a game, but it is more helpful to think of it as iatrogenic (a disorder caused by the physician). It reflects a basic flaw in the therapist's strategy: She has failed to ask whether the patient is willing to work hard to overcome the problem. The customer will say "yes," but the complainant will say, "You don't understand, there is nothing I can do; it is really not my problem. You need to change this other person." This relationship might be analogous to Prochaska's concept of the "contemplation" stage, in which a person recognizes that there is a problem, but no real plan of action to solve it has been formulated. However, Prochaska's label fails to capture the essential ambivalence about "owning" the problem in the complainant relationship. The patient has taken the stance that he should NOT be responsible for the problem or its solution. There is nothing the therapist can ethically do to change that, since the patient's decision belongs to him, and he has not invited the therapist to help him evaluate that decision.

This answer, "the problem is not my fault," is disappointing to therapists who have been taught the Western value of taking responsibility for one's actions and the importance of self-initiated action. The therapist may then "confront" the patient, meaning she tries to force her values onto the patient.

However, confrontation is rarely helpful, and may result in "hardening of the categories." Miller, Benefield, and Tonigan (1993) compared two approaches to counseling with alcohol abusers. The patients were given two sessions of counseling around their alcohol intake, designed to encourage them to reduce abusive drinking. One group was given a directive-confrontational style of counseling, and the other was given client-centered counseling that did not involve confrontation. Both groups reduced their alcohol use at six weeks and at one year. The only difference seemed to be that the directive-confrontational style produced more resistance and poorer outcomes at one year. An interesting finding that emerged was the more the counselor confronted, the more the client drank.

The therapist and client must find a task in which they can cooperate. The complainant wants someone else to change, which is not within the skills of most therapists.* The therapist wants the client to be responsible, but the client is not interested. The therapist may drift into confronting and challenging the patient, in an effort to "make the patient be responsible." A better approach (Berg & Miller, 1992; de Shazer, 1988) emphasizes cooperating with the client through compliments and coping questions. If the complainant seems to emphasize how difficult the problem is (and we feel pressure to change someone who isn't present), we can become very curious about how the client is able to cope with the situation. What sorts of things has he found to make it worthwhile to continue? What factors give him satisfaction and contentment in his life, even for brief moments? We might ask questions like:

- "It sounds like this is a serious problem. How do you cope with it?"
- "If I hear you correctly, you are alone in being concerned about this problem. How do you keep going in the face of discouragement?"
- "When these things happen to you, what have you found helps you to bounce back from feeling down?"
- "It sounds like this is a very challenging problem. What things give your life hope, in spite of this problem?"

---

*Nevertheless, therapists at the Mental Research Institute in Palo Alto, California (John Weakland, Paul Watzlawick, Richard Fisch, Lynn Segal, etc.) have developed technical specifications for helping a patient who is not actually attending sessions. They focus on the way the family helps maintain the problem through efforts to solve the problem. See Fisch, Weakland, and Segal (1982) and Watzlawick, Weakland, and Fisch, (1974).

If the patient becomes aware of how he copes with the problem (probably something new or surprising to him), he might be willing to give less attention to changing the other person and focus on improving his own coping skills. In this way, the complaining relationship becomes a customer relationship, reminding us that the labels are not categories in which patients fit but are statements of where the relationship is at this time. The situation can change quickly when the therapist and client arrive at a mutually acceptable goal.

Case Example: You're Driving Me Crazy

A young woman complained that she was "going crazy" and was about to have a nervous breakdown. The basis for this was that she was living with a man who liked to go dancing with his friends at nightclubs, but he wouldn't take her. She would stay at home, fantasizing about the women he was dancing with and what other things might be going on. When he would return at two or three in the morning, she would scream at him for some time, crying hysterically. He would accuse her of being crazy and rail at her for not trusting him.

Her initial complaint ("I am out of control and having a nervous breakdown") shifted when she was asked what she wanted. It became clear that her agenda in therapy was to find a method of changing this young man, and she saw her temper and crying as ways of responding to the situation.

I felt very sympathetic toward her. It seemed to me that her crying and raging were reasonable responses to a crazy situation. I asked her how she coped with such a situation besides crying and raging hysterically. She couldn't think of any other coping skills, except occasionally to talk with friends who were sympathetic. I asked whether she could do more to cope. The notion of increasing one's coping with a difficult situation was a new one to her, but with some empathy and realism (I took the position that while her boyfriend certainly might need therapy, he was apparently not willing to get it, so all that could be accomplished would be to help her cope with his behavior), she did agree to look for ways to cope. In agreeing, she had shifted to a clear customer status, and away from a more complainant status.

By the third session, the patient had agreed to new behavior or homework I suggested. She would keep track of the total time in minutes he was away from the apartment in the late evenings. Then the next day she would spend the identical amount of time finding ways to help herself cope with the challenge of living with him. She thought that going out to dinner with friends (and keeping that a secret from him) would help her cope.

By the fourth session (three weeks after the third, to allow time to complete the homework experiment), she had tried the coping two times. On both of those occasions she had had a very good time. In her own words, she wasn't hysterical anymore; in fact, she was fairly calm while thinking of things she would do the next day. On one of the coping times, she had gone out to eat with some friends from work, they had gone to a dance club after supper, and a young man had given her his phone number and asked her to call him. She was amazed to learn she was interesting to men other than her boyfriend.

Oddly enough, the boyfriend stopped going out to his clubs. Her complaints resolved, she stopped therapy, saying she was happy with the outcome and would return if she had further problems.

It also helps to be interested in the *exceptions* to the problem. Since no problem occurs all of the time, there are some times when the problem, whatever it is, is absent or has less impact. We wonder about those. What seems to be different when your wife does NOT criticize you? What does she do INSTEAD? Can these times be predicted? Are they random? Is there a subtle pattern you have overlooked? We might ask:

- "What is different when this problem is not so much of a problem?"
- "What seems to be behind the times when the problem is not so serious or is absent? What is going on then?"
- "When the problem doesn't happen, what seems to be going on instead?"
- "Who in the family is best at predicting when the problem will NOT be there?"

It can also be helpful to ask the complainant questions about degree of motivation, so as to help clarify who feels most strongly about the problem. These questions might include:

- "Who feels the most strongly that this problem needs to be solved? Rate how much each person involved would be willing to work on solving the problem."
- "What would your husband say about your concern over this problem? How would he explain it?"
- "On a scale of 0% to 100%, how successful have you been at getting others to address this problem? What seems to be working best to help them take it seriously?"
- "If you continue to be the one most concerned about this problem, how will the others in the family react? What will they do because of your concern?"

- "If you were not concerned about this problem, who would be the most concerned? How would they handle this problem? Can you live with that?"
- "If you were not concerned about this problem, what would you do with the energy and concern you devote to this problem?"

These questions help clarify for the complainant the advantages and disadvantages of (a) continuing to complain without taking responsibility for solving the problem or (b) letting the problem go.

Our responses form a pattern of first focusing on supporting the patient by pointing how we understand the problem is a difficult and serious one and requires coping strategies, and then shifting responsibility from outside, other-directed (e.g., "My happiness and meaning come from outside of myself") to internal, self-directed. However, this does not take the form of confrontation, pointing out the flaws in such thinking, but rather the form of implicit learning. By consistently modeling patterns that follow the form of "complaint . . . specify own coping . . . experiment with increasing own coping . . . ," we teach the client to redirect his attention away from what others do and toward what he can do to help himself cope.

Anytime we can find a strength or positive aspect of the complainant, we acknowledge that. Here we are following two principles: (1) Emphasize strengths and resources and (2) increase therapeutic impact by offering something surprising and compelling (Beier & Young, 1984), creating "beneficial uncertainty." For example, perhaps the complainant has been involved in the "Why don't you — Yes, but" transactions with persons other than the therapist. At some level, the patient expects that sort of pattern to continue with the counselor (Beier & Young, 1984). When this expectation is not confirmed, a state of *beneficial uncertainty* is created. When the therapist veers into a new scenario, the client cannot continue with the expected script, because the client is now uncertain about what to do next. That uncertainty is within the context of a warm, positive relationship, so there is a chance new behavior can emerge.

Validating the Visitor

Another problematic patient is the visitor or guest. This relationship style is difficult for therapists who feel a strong need to be helpful. Like the proverbial horse who can be led to water, the patient does not want to change. Trying only results in frustration on everyone's part.

When I was young, I would sometimes wait on customers in my father's jewelry shop. I learned that not everyone who entered was looking to buy something (i.e., had a problem and was willing to spend resources solving it). Some came in to just pass the time, or to get in out of the weather. Similarly, we find some people in our office who do not see a need to change. They may have been forced into treatment by "bad weather," pressure from family, work, or the authorities.

The general model of dealing with this type of person is to create a pleasant environment to which the visitor will want to return. In other words, we must be gracious hosts. However, part of being a good host is tactfully to draw out the guest and engage her in a discussion of her interests and goals. And here we sometimes find a *hidden customer*, that is, a person who might be a customer for something other than what she has been referred for.

For example, we might ask:

- "What would the person who sent you here say you should change?"
- "How would the person who encouraged you to come here know you didn't need to come? What would be the first sign to the judge or probation officer that sending you here was unnecessary? What would they see you do, if they could watch you all the time, that would tell them you didn't need this?"
- "How much of a problem is it to you that you are forced/encouraged/constrained to talk to me? Are you willing to do some work so as to get them off your back?"
- "Are you willing to do something so that you won't be required to come here anymore?"

So while a patient may not agree to "work on her drinking problem," she might be willing to work on ways to avoid trouble because she drinks. We can cooperate with her. Often she will spontaneously decide to reduce or stop drinking once she finds she can work with the counselor (that is, the counselor will not try to force changes on her).

However, now let us suppose we offer our guest various questions to elicit a "hidden customer" relationship and we fail to find one. Then our goal is to encourage the guest to return. We can do this by engaging in pleasant conversation that has a purpose, namely to learn what the guest does well. As we learn things the guest feels she does well, we can offer sincere compliments about them.

- "It occurs to me that you have been quite cooperative in coming here and working with me today. I am sure you might have felt tempted to not cooperate, and I do appreciate your work."
- "It seems to me that in many situations your drinking does not cause

problems. That takes some planning and thought, and I think you should be complimented for that."

- "You have been pressured to come here, yet that pressure doesn't upset you. That says a lot about your ability to remain calm when others are upset, and you should be complimented on your stability."

Another way to deal with complainants and visitors is to invite family and other significant persons into the therapy sessions. Having another person in the session seems to motivate a patient, so that often he ends up talking more and more like a customer. With an uncooperative patient, such as a teenager or a court-mandated referral, it is useful to assume that there must be a customer somewhere around, since this visitor has shown up in the office. If I can figure out who that customer is and involve him in the first session, much time and effort can be saved. In addition, I can then use the position of each person in the situation to improve the therapeutic fit.

For example, suppose a teenager has been skipping school, failing classes, and generally being a difficult child. His mother is desperately worried about it; his father is also very upset but feels he has done all he can and the boy just has to straighten himself out. Our customer status analysis suggests that at this time (and it can change at any time, so we need to continually reassess) the boy is a visitor ("I don't have any problems except having to come to this dumb place"), the mother is a customer ("I am willing to do whatever I need to do to solve this problem"), and the father is a complainant ("I'd really like to see him change, but there is nothing I can do about it").

Now, following our paradigm, we offer the following plan: The son should be complimented for anything positive we can catch him doing. His behavior should be reframed into the most positive context we can think of. Then we can explain to him that the problem is that his parents need to develop creative and innovative ways of dealing with teenagers. For this reason he should keep doing just what he has been doing. This will give the parents a chance to practice creative forms of discipline and rewards.

The son might be dismissed to sit in the waiting room. The parents are then complimented on bringing him in. Since therapy is something easily ignored, and since he is not ready to work in therapy yet, we need to do some things to help him see a need for therapy.

Since the mother at this time has the most optimism, she should take the lead in responding in creative ways; the father is supportive and concerned, so he should be collecting data. He should especially collect data about times when the son would be expected to act up, but doesn't. He should carefully watch for what the mother does that seems to have the best effect on the son. If he notices her doing something that doesn't work, he is to forget that as soon as possible, but if he sees her doing something effective, he should make a point of mentioning it to her as soon as they are alone. And the therapist will expect a report from him on that in the next session. These interventions match the position of the three family members, while offering positive compliments to everyone so that no one feels judged as wrong because he is not a customer.

While these suggestions are far from exhaustive in dealing with complainants and visitors, they do give some idea of how this could be done. The most important thing to remember is to adjust therapeutic actions to what the client wants. Don't try to force someone into good mental health on the assumption that the counselor knows best. Respect for the points of view and decisions of others is the foundation of good relationships.

ASSESSING THE RELATIONSHIP

A positive therapy relationship (measured by patient ratings) has been demonstrated to be a significant and powerful factor in creating good therapy outcomes. It may be that the feeling of alliance the patient has with the therapist is the most powerful single factor in solving the patient's problems (cf. Hill, 1989). However, empathy research has tended to look only at what is said, and, worse yet, has often used "expert" judges to rate the empathy! After all, we are interested not in whether the therapist can say the right thing, but in how it is received. Empathy should be measured only on how it is felt by the client. The client should feel that the counselor not only understands, but also somehow sees into her inner world, perceiving things there which the client either had hidden or was not aware of.

Verbal empathy is a topic about which counselors generally have heard a good deal. It does not need to be reviewed here. Rather, therapists should work on the nonverbal aspects of empathy. My supervisor, Ernst Beier, likes to say, "In therapy we give all the nonverbal signs of being in love with the patient." When you watch people who are in love, they tend to do certain things. They listen intently to what the loved one is saying, nodding and demonstrating good attention. They gaze into each other's eyes. They tend to synchronize their movements, so that if one person shifts, the other will shift in a similar way within a few seconds.

Some ways we can convey this nonverbal empathy include posture and postural shifts (not mirroring, but similar posture and movements), repeating back to the client favored phrases and ideas, and matching rate of speech and latency of replies. The last two aspects—latency of replies and rate of speech—were powerfully illustrated with a student who sought supervision.

Case Example*

When he was a graduate student, Scott Miller presented a case of a patient who was complaining of obsessional thoughts and compulsive behaviors, and in his speech demonstrated obsessional slowness. By this I mean he spoke very slowly — when we listened to the tape, I estimated it at less than 70 words per minute. He also would pause for long periods after the therapist would make a comment — 30 to 60 seconds was common.

I was puzzled about where to intervene with this case, but after some reflection I compared the rates of speech and latency of reply the patient demonstrated with those of the therapist. There was a striking difference. The therapist spoke around 170 words per minute, and he had no latency of reply — when the patient was finished with a statement, the therapist began to speak immediately. This, I thought, was not an ideal match.

Scott (who was a customer for a change in his own behavior) was given the assignment of speaking at the same rate as the patient, while continuing to make similar interpretations and interventions. When he finished a statement, he was to silently count the number of seconds it took the patient to reply. When the patient was through with his reply, Scott would count (silently!) the same number of seconds before beginning his reply. The intervention had a powerful effect on the patient: He speeded up his speech and the latency of reply dropped dramatically.

In general, therapists should give more attention to the nonverbal aspects of the client's experience. Nonverbal pacing is probably more important than attending to verbal content in enabling the patient to feel understood and validated. I have systematically experimented with these aspects in my own practice, at times matching carefully the client's nonverbal and paraverbal (i.e., voice tone and inflection) behavior while disagreeing with the client at a verbal level. Oddly enough, some patients feel much more understood in that condition!

Using Rating Scales

A post-session rating device is quite helpful. Some scales have been used in research into therapy process and outcome (Hill, 1989). For example, the *Working Alliance Inventory* (Horvath & Greenberg, 1986) measures the factors I mentioned earlier: therapy bond, agreement on goals, and agree-

*This case was previously reported in Johnson, 1988.

ment on tasks. The three areas—bonds, goals, and tasks—each have 12 items that the client rates on a 1-7 scale. So after each session the client quickly rates these 36 items, which yield three scores.

The *Session Evaluation Questionnaire* (Stiles & Snow, 1984) measures the depth and smoothness of the session, two factors that have been shown to be distinct and orthogonal. The questionnaire is composed of 12 adjectives on a 7-point scale. Depth has six adjectives and smoothness has six, yielding two numerical scores.

Burns (Burns & Nolen-Hoeksema, 1992) uses a 10-item *Empathy Scale*, focusing on five factors. The client rates each item on a 0-3 scale, with 0 = not at all, and 3 = a lot. The five factors are (1) trust in therapist, (2) valuing by therapist, (3) friendliness by therapist, (4) therapist depth of understanding, and (5) therapist concern. Five of the scales are arranged so a high score is desirable, and five are arranged so the high score denotes a poor relationship. Thus, the scale yields two scores; ideally, one will be high and the other low. Burns encourages his patients to complete the Empathy Scale at the end of each session, and the scores are discussed in the next session. He has found that half of the patient improvement in his clinic can be attributed to the relationship between the therapist and the patient (Burns & Nolen-Hoeksema, 1992).

Clinicians have tended to look at such rating scales as research tools; Burns (personal communication, May 1993) advocates their regular and systematic use. Imagine, he argues, that all therapists administer symptom rating scales and therapy relationship rating scales after each session, and further imagine that these ratings—for symptoms and for relationship—are collected and collated, so that we can come to know which therapists are good with which types of problems. This would create a wonderful database. Instead of thinking up theories, creating therapies to go with those theories, and then testing them, we would approach things the other way. Let's find out who the best therapists are, and find out how they are getting results.

This illustrates how the goals of psychotherapy and the bond are recursive. If a therapist is sensitive and respectful of the goals the patient presents, then the patient feels more of a bond. But conversely, when the therapist can bond emotionally with the patient—by empathy, by encouraging the patient to express suppressed thoughts and feelings, and by nonverbal matching—then the patient is more likely to accept the formulation offered by the therapist, carry out homework assignments, and experience improvement.

Regular use of relationship scales seems to be a most promising development, particularly since this enables the patient to be the judge of the empathy in the relationship. The approach is also quite egalitarian and respectful, supporting and empowering the client's perceptions. After each session, the therapist gives the patient a rating form. The patient fills out the form in the waiting room before leaving. The results of such a rating can help guide the therapist's future behavior.

By combining relationship ratings with goal attainment scales, such as depression rating scales, anxiety rating scales, relationship satisfaction scales, and so on, the therapist and patient can track improvement in treatment with reasonable precision. From a pragmatic point of view, the regular use of rating scales after each session involves more than just attending to the therapy relationship. It could have a powerful impact on psychotherapy funding, since bidding on capitated contracts is much easier and more precise with such information. There are many well-recognized scales for specific syndromes, such as anxiety, depression, marital distress, dissociative experiences, and so on. Other scales measure a broad range of complaints and symptoms. Well-conducted therapy ought to show some sort of progress over time. The wider use of rating scales would promote good communication within and outside of the profession. Consider, for example, the difference between saying a patient is improved and reporting a drop in the scores on a well-recognized depression scale to the normal range. As a consultant to managed care, I am constantly disappointed by the lack of objective scores reported to the mental health reviewers, even by psychologists who are presumed to have some special interest and expertise in objective measurement!

Case Example: Things Could Be Worse

I treated a patient who was covered by a managed care program that was not overly generous with benefits. In reporting, I included a Welsh Code for her MMPI, demonstrating (1) she was not exaggerating or malingering, and (2) she did show very high levels of unhappiness and maladjustment, including indications of poor prognosis for traditional psychotherapy. Thus, when I had to work with her 25 hours, instead of my more usual six to ten, the managed care program was quite understanding. It also helped that before coming to me she had seen a psychiatrist who looked at the same MMPI and strongly recommended hospitalization! The plan was quite glad to pay for longer outpatient psychotherapy to avoid the $1,000 per day inpatient charges.

Using tests and objective ratings is one way for therapists communicate economically with managed care programs. Another is to establish in the first or second visit several issues that the patient wants to work on. For example, a theme of assertiveness might emerge. "I hope for and want things from others, but I am afraid to tell people how I feel, because I think they would fall apart if they knew what I want. I would be seen as selfish and demanding. They would hate me and I would be cast off and left alone." A simple set of scales would translate this complaint into some goal-directed activities. For example, the patient can begin by rating on a 1–10 scale how strongly she believes the theory, "people will be devastated by knowing what I want." A rating of "1" means the idea has no relevance or importance to her; a rating of "10" means she would bet her life on the truth of it.

Imagine the patient rates the idea, "If I ask for what I want, it will be a catastrophe" as having a validity of "8." Then various interventions, or experiments can be undertaken to see whether this is a valid idea. One easy experiment is to generate the pros and cons of that idea. All the advantages of believing that should be listed, and the disadvantages are also listed. The therapist should sympathetically encourage the patient to look for hidden or subtle advantages of such a belief. Then the patient can assign numerical weights to each advantage and disadvantage and sum them, seeing whether the pros outweigh the cons.

Now, scale the belief again. Does the pro-con analysis affect the level of belief she has in that idea? Scale the willingness to actually speak up and say what it is she wants. As the confidence in the belief diminishes, does the willingness to speak up increase?

Such individually constructed rating scales are easily understood by managed care reviewers and help communicate the vital issues of seriousness of the problem and progress in solving the problem. Thus, when we use rating scales — either well researched ones or scales constructed for the individual patient — our relationship with the reviewer is improved, since the reviewer's job is aided. And the client feels better about the work, since we are making every effort to understand the client's subjective world. By reporting scores on relationship and goal attainment scales to managed care reviewers, the review process could be considerably shortened and made more objective. Fischer and Corcoran (1994a, b) offer a comprehensive list of useful objective instruments and sources. The more objective the measures used are, the easier it is to be accountable both to our clients and to managed mental health organizations.

In my own practice, I am experimenting with the scale in Table 3.2, which yields useful information about several aspects of psychotherapeutic quality. As it now is, the scale has several psychometric flaws. It is vulnerable to response bias. Demand characteristics are not controlled. The scale is completely transparent and would be easy to fake, but the purpose is only to encourage good communication and problem solving between the therapist and the client, and I find it a useful tool for that. You may use it as long as my copyright notice is attached. I would also ask you forward suggestions and norms to me.

Table 3.2 Session Rating
Copyright ©1994 by Lynn D. Johnson

Name _____ Date _____

Please rate today's session. Be honest and frank, to be the most helpful to your counselor. Read each set of descriptions. Circle the number that best describes your reaction, from 0 to 4. Use the rating system below:

AGREE WITH THIS SIDE		NEUTRAL	AGREE WITH THIS SIDE	
4	3	2	1	0

(*Under* each set of statements, circle the number that best describes your feelings about today's session)

1. ACCEPTANCE
I felt accepted.   I felt criticized or judged.

4	3	2	1	0

2. LIKING, POSITIVE REGARD
My therapist liked me.   The therapist pretended to like me or didn't like me.

4	3	2	1	0

3. UNDERSTANDING
My counselor understood me and my feelings.   My counselor didn't understand me or my feelings.

4	3	2	1	0

4. HONESTY AND SINCERITY
My therapist was honest and sincere.   My therapist was not sincere, was pretending or was not honest.

4	3	2	1	0

5. AGREEMENT ON GOALS
We worked on my goals; my goals were important.   We worked on my counselor's goals; my goals didn't seem important in the session.

4	3	2	1	0

6. AGREEMENT ON TASKS
I approved of the things we did in the session or what I was asked to do for homework.   I didn't like what we did in today's session or what I was asked to do for homework.

4	3	2	1	0

7. SMOOTHNESS OF THE SESSION
The session was smooth; I felt comfortable.   The session was rough; I felt uncomfortable.

4	3	2	1	0

(continued)

Table 3.2 (*continued*)

AGREE WITH THIS SIDE		NEUTRAL	AGREE WITH THIS SIDE	
4	3	2	1	0

8. DEPTH OF THE SESSION

The session was deep. We got to the heart of things.			The session was shallow. We stayed on the surface.	
4	3	2	1	0

9. HELPFULNESS, USEFULNESS

I found the session helpful.			The session was not helpful	
4	3	2	1	0

10. HOPE

I felt hopeful after the session.			I felt hopeless after the session.	
4	3	2	1	0

What could help the next session go better? _____

_____

_____

CHAPTER 4

Focus in Psychotherapy

Conflict is painful but useful. When one set of needs conflicts with another, the result is frequently a better understanding of options and opportunities. Therapists are increasingly in conflict because they have multiple customers for their services. Along with the patient or client, the therapist may "work for" or have a customer relationship with employee assistance programs, managed care companies, health maintenance organizations, and other funding sources requiring some kind of accountability from the therapist.

Reviewers for the managed care programs, for example, want to know what the psychotherapy intends to accomplish. Reviewers like specific goals: They make their jobs easier since specific outcomes can be measured. For example, the goal may be to help the patient return to full employment. This is measurable: The patient is or is not showing up for work. But therapists often want to frame goals is very general or broad ways, such as "the patient will make a realistic assessment of his strengths," or, "assist the patient in thinking through her options in the marriage." Such goals sound like no goal at all to reviewers.

This is a common difficulty between reviewers and outpatient therapists. Some counselors are either unwilling or unable to write coherent, precise definitions of outcome. Commonly the reviewers see such goals as "develop self-esteem," "work through the trauma," "develop better coping skills," and "solidify gains." When a reviewer is charged with assuring quality of service, that charge becomes impossible with such vague goals. The accountable therapist should be able to write quite specific outcome statements after the initial one to three sessions. Therapists accustomed to thinking in such specific terms will flourish in the managed care environment.

Treatment for broad or "deep" issues will likely not be covered as accountability and limitation of benefits come to prevail. Rather, treatment will center on the current motivations that bring a patient into therapy, so the first issue in managed care is the *therapeutic focus* or goals of treatment.

Creating a focus is a powerful intervention for the patient, who benefits from co-defining with the therapist what the problem is. Of course, the problem is not any one thing. Rather, the focus is the combination of what the patient wants plus what the therapist can do.

Once a focus has been established with the client, therapy is organized by efforts to achieve the goals. The organizing of effort creates the *strategies* of the treatment. Even though this war-like word offends some, it conveys an important principle: The therapist is responsible for creating interventions to help the client achieve her goals. The strategy is the plan the counselor creates. For example, the idea of making transference interpretations to give the client insight into the oedipal nature of the problem is simply a strategy, as is a plan to create a hierarchy of fears and systematically expose the client to those fears for longer and longer periods of time. All therapists have strategies if they expect to be compensated for their time and efforts, since without the strategy the patient is no better off than talking to a friend.

To intelligently use therapeutic strategies, it is necessary, Omer (1991) points out, to define goals with precision. He says, "Hazy goals make clear strategies inapplicable. It is preposterous, for instance, to plan in detail for achieving goals such as 'getting in touch with oneself,' or 'increasing self-fulfillment'" (p. 564). His rationale is that application of a strategy must be evaluated to see if the goals are being achieved. The planned action and the outcome should recursively influence each other. Plans cannot be achieved or even evaluated without feedback, and feedback is impossible without some precision in defining outcomes. It is the focus that makes precision possible, and the very creation of the focus is an important intervention. Without clear goals as the reason for psychotherapy, the counseling process becomes a muddle.

Of course, being involved in a muddle has a good many advantages. Muddling along results in confusion, and confusion can be the precursor of comprehension. Before the light, there must be darkness; before the creation there must be chaos. So the scientifically inclined may welcome the muddle. But the scientist will still strive to move from the muddle to the clear definition of the problem and to create a systematic way to test hypotheses about the nature of the problem.

Another advantage of a muddle is that it prevents progress, and there may be some therapists and patients who have some fear of progress, especially rapid progress. The natural human conservative tendency means that when rapid progress is possible we feel an urge to slow down, to even throw a wrench into the guts of the new machine, to stop this monster called change. The desire to sabotage progress is human and understandable. It is often quite wise, since progress often creates more problems than it solves.

A disadvantage of clear focus is the inconvenience. While we are involved in a muddle with our client, there is relatively little danger of making the kind of progress that might tempt this patient to end treatment, so the pain of starting therapy with a new patient is obviated. In private practice, that means we don't have to promote the practice to obtain more referrals; in public practice we don't have to go through the difficult and time-consuming task of opening a new case from the waiting list.

A further advantage of a muddle is avoidance of the competency issue. When we have a clear focus, we can be held accountable; without it we cannot. If I say I will cure a patient of anxiety disorder, and I specify what symptoms will wane and what new behaviors will wax as a result of my treatment, I am on the hook. But if I say I am working to help the patient gain insight into the origin of the disorder, there is no measure that can be economically and practically applied to determine if I am meeting that goal. So I am spared the pain of evaluation. If I really can't change the patient's anxiety symptoms, then I don't have to face that painful fact. My ego remains unbruised.

The reader convinced by these arguments need go no further in this discussion; he can stay comfortably muddled.

CREATING A THERAPEUTICALLY RELEVANT FOCUS

As treatment planning becomes more sophisticated, the role of a DSM-IV diagnosis may be replaced by therapeutic focus statements. The diagnosis often has little relationship to activities in therapy. While there is a fairly good relationship between diagnosis and treatment in biologically oriented psychiatry, psychotherapy is another matter. Someone with a DSM-IV diagnosis of major depression can justifiably be treated in family or individual therapy, with behavioral, cognitive, psychodynamic, or strategic therapy (Johnson & Miller, 1994). It can be argued that a client-centered philosophy can assess the client's preferred focus and center treatment strategies on that. Thus, the choice of all those treatment protocols can be rationally made on the basis of what is most important to the client (cf. Yapko, 1988).

Many therapists do not have a clear understanding of therapeutic focus and its role in effective treatment. Outcome-oriented counseling uses the assessment process to create a specific, limited area of change for the client and therapist to achieve. The changes should have the following characteristics:

1. Goals for feelings, thoughts, or behaviors (or possibly all three) are created. These are the outcome of therapy.* The goal is not necessarily directly related to the diagnosis, since a DSM-IV diagnosis is based on a deficit model (tells what is wrong with the person) and the goal is an attainment model. For example, a patient may complain of feeling anxious and having periods of intense anxiety or panic. The inverse condition, namely the patient will not experience anxiety, is unlikely and even foolish. It may be possible to achieve an anxiety-free life by ablating certain portions of the brain, but in normal persons the experience of anxiety is normal, even desirable. Rather, the result of treatment should be to change the feelings from extreme to uncomfortable but tolerable. After all, anxiety is a helpful emotion, and if the anxiety were not uncomfortable, it would lose its value as a signal device, i.e., a person with no ability to feel anxious might do dangerous or harmful things.

So the goal may be shifted from a change of feelings to *behavior*, what the patient will be able to *do* as a result of therapy. If the patient is limited, so that she cannot perform well at work, cannot shop alone, and is afraid to drive on freeways, then the goals may be to be able to work well at her job (as evidenced by what? The goal must specify particular behaviors), to shop alone (such as going shopping twice a week by herself and staying in a store long enough to make all her planned purchases), and so on.

Another goal may be for the patient to change her *thinking*. She may interpret the symptoms of anxiety (such as rapid heart rate, dizziness, and tingling in the extremities) as being dangerous. The result of treatment may be that she will interpret those not as symptoms but as uncomfortable but interesting and useful physical sensations.

The goals may have aspects that are literal and direct, or they may involve symbolic and relationship-oriented features. Goals with a good deal of relationship focus might be profitably addressed in family or couples therapy.

2. The goals are something the patient feels *committed to* and willing to

---

*I am aware this position is seen as philosophically naive to students of de Shazer (1988, 1991), whose view is that the language in the interaction changes in psychotherapy. We cannot *see* the change in thinking, feeling, or behavior; we only hear the change in the description of thinking, feeling or behavior. So it is more parsimonious to acknowledge that the language is all we do change. My view is much less scientific but more satisfying to me: patients' descriptions do reflect an approximation of reality.

work hard to achieve. The notion of achieving one's goals without hard work will probably not survive managed care. In brief treatment, the patient must work hard to achieve her goals. The goals are achieved through the efforts of the client, more than through the therapist's skills. If the therapist is more committed to the goals than the patient is, there is a problem with that therapist's boundaries.

3. There should be some means of measuring progress toward goals, either through objective measures (such as anxiety rating scales, see Fischer & Corcoran, 1994b) or by subjective means (such as asking the patient to scale her own progress each week on a percentage basis). Some goals may be achieved by behavioral measures (how long the patient was able to remain in the store), and others by introspection ("How comfortable am I with the idea that a rapid heartbeat is not a danger but a useful thing?").

Goals focusing on symbolic aspects can be measured by scaling questions (e.g., "Rate on a 1–10 scale how self-actualized you feel right now. What would tell you that you were one step more self-actualized than you are now?") Relationship-oriented goals ("My family would respect me more") would similarly be assessed with subjective ratings, as well as through objective rating scales (cf. Fischer & Corcoran, 1994a).

The focus is like a contract between the therapist and client, formed early in therapy, that informs both parties of the kinds of operations appropriate in the therapy. Therefore, the way this focus is created depends on both the expectations of the therapist and the hopes of the client. The therapist's area of expertise usually (but not always) becomes a powerful influence on which goals and methods are selected. To illustrate, below I review of some approaches to creating a useful clinical focus.*

The Role of the Expert in Focus

Gustafson (1986) provides a comprehensive review of the sorts of foci dynamic therapists tend to select for their patients. The common element seems to be a message that implicitly or explicitly says, "This is what you are *really* concerned about." There is an unwitting one-upmanship here, since the therapist presumes to know the true workings of the client's mind. The therapist thus seems to encourage dependence. The unintentional result may be a "corrective emotional experience," such as Alexander and French (1946) refer to. For instance, the patient may have been dependent

---

*Thanks to Patrick Morrissette who helped formulate many of the following concepts.

in the past on an important person who was unstable and inconsistent, producing a chronic high level of anxiety; although once again dependent, the patient is now dependent on the therapist who is consistent and fair.

We should be aware of the danger of being an expert. My own expertise may lead me to disqualify the client's interests; I may suggest I know better than the client what is good for her or him. As the Spanish saying goes, *En el reino de los ciegos, el tuerto es rey,* or in the land of the blind, the one-eyed man is king. The client feels some respect for our expert opinion, so we may fail to empower our patients through our allegiance to our theories.

The Role of the Patient

When the emphasis is on pathology, the characteristics of the patient are considered paramount. Malan (1976) argued that focus could be achieved by identifying a current conflict that corresponded with a nuclear conflict from the patient's past. He suggested that a single theme, running through the patient's life, was predictive of successful brief therapy; conversely, a patient with many themes and many complaints without a common affective theme would not respond well to brief treatment. Sifneos (1979) also suggests that certain patient characteristics (such as a history of having close, trusting relationships and psychological mindedness) are prerequisites for brief treatment.

The common element seems to be an emphasis on what the patient brings into the therapy hour, rather than what the therapist brings. Unfortunately, evidence that patient factors are central is not robust. For example, Beckham (1992) found that patient characteristics did not predict dropout; rather, the relationship between therapist and patient did. In other words, the argument that it is the *patient* who is most powerful in determining whether the focus will be adequate and therapy effective is flawed. Rather, the therapist is a much more powerful influence. Paradoxically, the more expert opinions the therapist brings to formulating the focus, the greater the danger that the expert ideas will not fit with the patient.

For instance, the therapist's strong opinions about who is appropriate for brief therapy will contaminate the therapy relationship. Such opinions inevitably leak out (as my old supervisor Ernst Beier used to say, "The unconscious is always showing") and the patient will either consciously or implicitly experience those negative evaluations. Therefore, the rules about who is not appropriate for brief treatment are statements about the therapist's rigidity. Or, if a biologically oriented psychiatrist believes that talk therapy is only for motivating the patient to continue with medication, and that change of viewing and doing has no real power, the patient is likely to adopt a similar attitude, making cognitive, emotional, and behavioral changes unlikely except as a result of the medication.

Approaches to Focus

Although there are a number of suggested ways to establish a focus with the client, there is no empirical evidence demonstrating superiority of any one particular model. I have my opinions, and will try to support them rationally, but empirical work is lacking in this area.

The two basic approaches are to establish (a) a focus that is influenced by the therapist's model (such as a pathology-based or normative-based model) or (b) a focus created by a non-normative (i.e., idiopathic) negotiation of the client's goals. The pathology-influenced or normative-oriented therapist tends to see herself as a diagnostician, discovering what is wrong. Problems should fit into categories. The categories then imply operations that can be applied to the problems. This is the most common view and represents the thinking behind the DSM-IV and its predecessors, and must be understood and used by therapists to communicate with reviewers. However, it is not reasonable to think we are being accountable just because we are skillful in the use of that system, since its very foundation is arbitrary and not based on a systematic comparison with other approaches. Specifically, the non-normative or idiopathic approach tends to be widely ignored, although it appears as good or better at solving the problems of living our patients present.

The non-normative view encourages the therapist to apply some kind of learning-based or interactional view of problems. There is no pathology in this model, only a variety of possible patterns. Therapists do not advocate a particular kind of approach as being healthy; they only apply some set of principles to help patients change. It is quite easy for therapists to be accountable with this approach, since the patient is the expert on what is wanted. It is then relatively simple to encourage the patient to express his views in measurable units or subjective ratings. This is the process exemplified by Joseph Wolpe's Subjective Units of Disturbance (SUDs), in which he asks the patient to rate his own discomfort on a scale of 1–100, with 100 equal to the worst upset imaginable and 1 equal to calm and peace.

Some of the following models contain elements of both views (and many therapists use both), so the effort to distinguish is a bit artificial. Bearing that in mind, let us proceed.

Foci Informed by Models of Pathology

These models suggest there are predictable problems that occur to persons, and the therapist's task is to resolve those problems. The problems are the result of early traumas that create certain kinds of behaviors. The biological variation on this is that a person has some physical predisposition toward a kind of problem, and under environmental stress this problem becomes actualized. The problems are seen as occurring in predictable ways and times in a person's life. Typical problems would include ego loss and separation, oedipal conflicts/neurosis, early trauma or losses, and biologically based disorders (the "medical model"). Some of these will be discussed below.

Life Theme and Termination Anxiety Focus. In brief dynamic psychotherapy, the therapist is influenced by models of psychic conflict and applies that understanding early in the therapeutic process. Mann (1973) and Mann and Goldman (1982) formulate the goal into simple themes of striving for conflicting goals. They present those goals to the patient in a formulation, e.g., "You have always wanted to gain love by achieving success through your work, which you tried to make as flawless as possible. But you found that you have not achieved love and appreciation from those you wanted it from, perhaps because you were gone so much. So now you feel angry and fearful about the loss of that love and appreciation." Thus, attention is paid to striving and the conflict caused by putting that striving ahead of all others. Things like security, love, and achievement are formulated as basic strivings that can apply to a wide range of problems.

Mann and Goldman also suggest that, independent of the client's stated problem, the focus needs to be on the time-limited nature of the therapy. These authors suggest that a common underlying problem is "termination anxiety" associated with the completion of therapy and the concomitant loss of the relationship with the therapist. They contend that when patients successfully resolve the anxiety associated with the termination of therapy, other emotional problems are also resolved. So the theme presented to the client is combined with a focus on the limited nature of therapy.

This led Mann to set a firm 12-session time limit in therapy. The therapist alludes to the time limit in each session. If the patient expresses anxiety that the problem may not be completely resolved in the 12 sessions, the therapist offers interpretations about termination anxiety, linking that anxiety to unresolved dependency issues. His view is this is a common theme in human beings, namely wanting to be at one with others, to merge, and simultaneously wanting to be independent.

While Mann's focus is popular among dynamic therapists, it has short-comings. Budman and Gurman (1988) assert that the notion of termination anxiety may be a projection of the therapist. Clients often assume the treatment will be brief and feel relief and pride when completing therapy. Pekarik (1985) suggests that a major factor underlying early termination may be the different expectations that clients and therapists have about treatment. Williams (1985) points out that clients generally expect treatment to be brief and problem-oriented, whereas therapists expect treatment to be extended and character-oriented. Rather than being too short, the 12-session treatment offered by Mann is twice as long as the average number of visits to a mental health counselor! From this we would suggest that nonspecific factors, rather than the specific focus, are responsible for Mann's positive therapeutic outcomes (cf. Frank, 1974). Further, it seems likely that Mann's approach, like other dynamic focus models, is too narrow to be useful in the general outpatient practice of community mental health centers and private practice.

Separation and Ego Loss Focus. Strupp and Binder (1984) suggest that a major purpose of psychotherapy may be to help the patient deal with previous separations and ego losses, so that the issue of separation is crucial in the conduct of therapy. Consequently, addressing the issues of separation and loss is the foundation of treatment. According to this model, the task of the therapist is to identify issues of loss that the client needs to address without excessive or pathological reactivity. Within this framework, the therapist designs experiments to help the client deal with an outside loss, not with the loss of the therapeutic relationship.

While Strupp and Binder are exquisitely sensitive to the therapeutic relationship, they tend to see therapy as occurring in the present and future, and as focusing on current and future relationships outside the therapy relationship, as contrasted with Mann, who tends to see the resolution of the transference in the session as the crucial issue. This distinction influences their thinking in several ways. While they focus on transference interpretation as the central technique for achieving the goal of therapy, their orientation toward the external context leads them away from a rigid time limit. Their brief therapy may last from a few to over 20 sessions. Yet, the therapy as construed cannot have the general application it should, since the emphasis is on multiple sessions, while a single or few sessions are the norm in the pragmatic world of the mental health clinic.

Core Conflictual Relationship Focus. Luborsky (1984) has proposed a similar formulation, the "core conflictual relationship theme." While this work is independent of Strupp's, it shares the emphasis on formulating a fairly simple and elegant focus. Luborsky tends to formulate the conflict into an easily understood core statement, such as, "You want X from person A, but you can't have that because of Y (fears and conflicts)." The core theme is summed up in the X part of the equation, such as "I want affection from my wife," and the Y portion is summarized by "But if I ask for that, she will think I am weak and unmanly, so I must not show my vulnerabilities." Luborsky believes that these themes recur across various core relationships and that the therapist can help by focusing not on the goal but on the adaptation part of the conflict, shifting the way the client tries to resolve the conflict. This focus is quite similar to the MRI view of problem resolution as best focusing on the patient's attempted solutions, which are presumed to maintain the very problem they are intended to resolve (Watzlawick, Weakland, & Fisch, 1974).

The Oedipal Focus. Sifneos (1979), arguing for an emphasis on oedipal issues, maintains a focus on eroticized attachment to a parent. Issues the patient sees as central are addressed within the context of examining the childhood relationship with parents, especially the opposite-sex parent. Sifneos advocates energetic interpretation of oedipal and transference material, linking it to the patient's concerns. Similar comments to those made about Mann's focus apply here: The notion of oedipal issues may simply be a projection of the therapist; the theory forces the therapist to construe all problems through the lens of oedipal issues. And again, since Sifneos cannot demonstrate that his approach is more powerful than, say, behavioral or humanistic approaches that eschew oedipal issues, Occam's razor* requires that we reject his theory as being responsible for the improvement he documents. Again, we suspect patients improve not because of his focus, but in spite of it.

Another problem with the oedipal focus is its lack of generalizability. I once asked Sifneos how many people could meet his criteria for brief therapy, and he acknowledged that the number was very small. A general model of therapy, to have any value, must be able to treat the vast majority of patients effectively, regardless of gender, race, education, or social status. Many of the psychodynamic models fail in this regard, requiring degrees of psychological mindedness and openness to insight that is not present in many patients.

Biological Focus. Medical approaches to psychopathology also tend to impose a focus on the client. A DSM-IV diagnosis shapes therapy toward medical interventions, primarily psychotropic medication, and more rarely, phototherapy, electroconvulsive therapy, or even surgery. Thus, in biopsychiatry, the focus is on the biological aspects of the presenting problem. The medically oriented assessment is primarily based on symptoms

---

*William of Occam, or Ockham, 1284?–1347?, a philosopher who taught that entities should not be multiplied unnecessarily, or in modern English, the simplest explanation is always to be preferred over complex ones, in which entities of explanation are multiplied.

that are likely to be perceived by the patient as outside of her or his control, such as psychomotor retardation, sleep difficulties, panic attacks, hallucinations, and delusions.

These interventions can be extremely helpful and open a patient to learning new skills. Certainly, the mental health field has benefited from biopsychiatry. However, there are some drawbacks to a strictly medical focus. Attention only to biological aspects could promote a feeling of disempowerment and passivity in patients. This sense of powerlessness might account for the fact that clients who experience depression report more lasting improvement if treated with psychotherapy than with medication (Beck, Rush, Shaw, & Emery, 1979; Evans, Hollon, & DeRubeis et al., 1992; Frank, 1991). In moderate and severe major depression, it appears that focused psychotherapies, such as cognitive therapy or interpersonal therapy, have outcomes equal to antidepressants, although psychotherapy takes longer (but, see Johnson & Miller, 1994, for a discussion of how to create more rapid response to psychotherapy). Similarly, Barlow (1988) has shown that focused cognitive therapy is superior to medication (alprazolam) for anxiety disorders. Because with drug treatment there is little emphasis on changing the patient's understanding or actions in regard to the anxiety, when the medication is withdrawn the relapse rate is very high. Almost all patients return to panic after discontinuing the medicine, so the unpleasant alternative is to continue the patient on medication indefinitely.

Even schizophrenia, which seems to have been conceded to a medical focus by most mental health professionals, is clearly better treated by psychological means combined with judicious use of medication than primarily by medication (Karon & VandenBos, 1975, 1976, 1981, comparing psychoanalytic with psychiatric/medical treatment; Paul & Lentz, 1977, comparing token economies with medication for chronic schizophrenics; Muerer & Glynn, 1993, reviewing family therapy and token economies with schizophrenia). While medication does help patients with depression, anxiety, and thought disorder, that help may not be what the patient is mostly interested in.

This point brings us to a criticism of the medical model — that the focus is generally on symptoms that respond positively to medication and not necessarily on those symptoms that are most important to the client. With depression, for example, should a client's somatic symptoms improve with medicine, his or her concerns with interactional, cognitive, or symbolic aspects of his or her distress may go unaddressed (Yapko, 1988). Consequently, the client is dissatisfied after what the therapist considers successful treatment — a conflict between the client's goals and the therapist's interests. In their meta-analysis of depression treatment studies, Greenberg,

Bornstein, Greenberg, and Fisher (1992) found that if only patient ratings in antidepressant drug trials are used (excluding the clinician ratings), effect size for medication was very small, and probably not significant. Since the clinicians who prescribe the medication are likely to overvalue the biological changes the medication can produce, this parceling out of patient ratings is very significant.

It is now clear that medication does not change the underlying pessimism about oneself and the future; it mostly changes the amount of energy and pleasure available (no small feat but not curative, see Seligman, 1990, p. 81). And in treating schizophrenia, as mentioned earlier, Karon and VandenBos (1975, 1976, 1981) reported psychologists were superior to psychiatrists in outcome, largely because the psychologists tended to use less medication and hospitalization to control the symptoms of schizophrenia, relying instead on therapy.* The medical focus can blind therapists to the factors that are most salient to the client. And certainly the wisest biopsychiatrist combines psychotherapy with medication.

Another very serious problem with the medical model is noncompliance with medication. Meichenbaum and Turk (1987) present evidence that 30% to 75% of patients do not comply with follow-up or take medication as prescribed. If our focus is on the aspects of the problem that are only addressed by medication, only a minority of our patients will be helped.

Normative-Based Foci

Norms or criteria of expected behavior are quite helpful for establishing a focus, since they help shape the treatment in ways that enable the therapist to be powerful and competent. These foci convey greater respect to the patient than pathology-oriented approaches. The underlying feeling shifts toward the idiopathic approach; the implication is not, "you are a sick person," but rather, "You have gotten off track; let's get you back on track again." There is an implicit positive reframing of the problem away from a disease model and toward the idea that struggling with norms is a norm-al process. But the norms are still present, albeit with less emphasis on an illness model.

Using norms has a great advantage in making therapy accountable, since there are many measurement tools for tracking progress in working with specific syndromes. An anxious or depressed patient can be given

---

*Although one variable investigated by Karon and VandenBos was profession, namely psychology versus psychiatry, clearly the important variable was the greater or lesser reliance on psychological versus biological intervention. So anyone, Ph.D., M.D., et al., can learn from these old but valuable studies.

rating scales, such as the Beck Depression Inventory; more broadly focused therapy can be tracked through the use of something like the Symptom Check List or other multidimensional rating scales.

Normalizing Cognitions. Beck et al. (1979) and other cognitive therapists attend to the cognitions or self-talk of the patient as being sufficient for change. They teach the patient to attend to her own thinking processes, document them, and challenge those that are outside the norms of rational thought, such as all-none thinking, mind reading, labeling, and so on. As the patients restructure their styles of thinking, the complaints tend to lift.

Developmental Focus. A developmental focus emphasizes disorientation and reorientation during one's life. Haley (1973), for example, posits these developmental stages:

(a) Young adulthood, in which the norm is to leave home and establish an independent life
(b) Courtship and marriage, in which one locates an intimate partner and makes a long-term commitment
(c) Adjustment to children and child-raising, in which one faces the inclusion of a new person into the marital relationship
(d) Retirement and adapting to relationship shifts between spouses and with life roles
(e) Death and adapting to losses, pain, suffering and grief

These steps often trigger conflicts and difficulties. Each phase can also suggest useful interventions, reframing, homework, and so on. For example, complaints of youth (such as rebellious or depressive symptoms in adolescence) can often be reframed as an unconscious but wise desire to become more independent and leave home. If the clients, the family members, "buy" this focus, the meaning of the bad behavior changes and useful behavior can be prescribed in its place. The advantage of a developmental focus is that it provides useful guidelines and suggests interventions that have worked with other patients at similar stages of life. The disadvantage lies in the danger that loyal adherence to a singular model of treatment will influence the therapist to limit perceptions and respond rigidly.

Symptom Categories Focus. Yapko (1988) conceptualizes eight systems of client complaints and utilizes these to create a clinical focus. The eight systems, along with examples from depression, are:

1. *physiological*, e.g., sleeplessness, racing heart, knot in the stomach
2. *cognitive*, thoughts of one's own worthlessness or how others are unfair
3. *behavioral*, fleeing a phobic situation, staying in bed when depressed
4. *affective*, feeling of doom, sadness, nervousness, jealousy
5. *relational*, the reactions of others to the patient
6. *symbolic*, such as the "organ language" of somatic symptoms, e.g., something is a "pain in the neck" or the depression feels like "a deep, black pit"
7. *contextual*, specifying in which situations the symptoms do or don't occur
8. *historical*, the meaning of the symptoms in relation to the patient's history

According to Yapko, the patient is mainly aware of one or two systems. Direct therapeutic work should be done in those systems, and indirect work should be done in the systems outside of the client's awareness. Yapko's focus is useful since it leads directly to task assignments (homework). The advantage of this focus is that it encourages of the therapist to consider a range of systems, some of which might be otherwise ignored. The difficulty is that his foci are too subjective and are difficult to measure. Since some of them are presumed to be out of conscious awareness, the rating is entirely with the therapist.

Thematic Focus. Budman and Gurman (1988) emphasize a set of common concerns around which the therapist can organize psychotherapy. By asking the question, "Why therapy now?" they organize problems into the following categories:

- *Loss and unresolved grief, anniversary reactions.* They assert this is a very common and easily overlooked focus, and suggest a careful attention to "why therapy now?" as a way of discovering overlooked grief.
- *Developmental dyssychrony*, such as not working ("I should have had a job by now") or not being married ("I should have been, by now"). The patient's internal sense of where he should have been at this point in life conflicts with where he actually is.
- *Interpersonal conflicts with intimates, coworkers, or family members.* They behave in ways that conflict with the patient's expectations, or she behaves in ways they criticize.
- *Symptomatic complaints*, such as insomnia, tension headaches, or phobias. The patient does not want insight or understanding into the origin of the problem, only symptomatic relief.
- *Severe personality disorders or chemical dependency*. Budman and Gurman contend that these issues take precedence over the others, since progress in these areas is necessary before other issues can be resolved.

Thematic foci can be quite useful, since they are general enough that patients are likely to be able to agree with them, and each theme results in helpful interventions and homework. Since there are only five major factors, this system is easy to remember.

Idiopathic Focus: An Alternative to Diagnosis and Norms

The behaviorists (Wells, 1982) and some strategic therapists (de Shazer, 1988; Fisch, Weakland, & Segal, 1982; O'Hanlon & Wilk, 1987), although maintaining different therapeutic styles, respect client goals as adequate and reasonable points of focus. These schools tend to negotiate goals that are restatements of the client wants and desires, and do not impose a clinical framework within which the client needs to operate. Generally, focus is placed on changes requested by the client and not on the changes prioritized by the therapist. Due to the human element within psychotherapy, however, clinical focus is necessarily influenced by the personal bias of the therapist.

The focus is achieved by carefully questioning the client, asking, "What will tell you that coming in to see us has been a good idea?" These theorists attempt to conceptualize the focus in a completely idiopathic manner, rather than the nomothetic style of fitting the client's complaints against a diagnostic scheme. Members of the MRI group (Watzlawick, Weakland, Fisch, and their colleagues, of Palo Alto) are the foremost exponents of this view.

There are advantages and disadvantages to this. One advantage is that the patient tends to be quite happy with the goals of therapy and more accepting of the means of achieving those goals, since there is no attempt to change what he presents. Conner-Greene (1993) illustrated the difficulty a therapist has when the patient does *not* agree with the formulation of the therapist. She attempted to treat a patient who did not accept her diagnosis of choking phobia and the subsequent attempted treatment of systematic desensitization. The patient did not respond, since she thought the problem was a physical one and not psychological. Not until the therapist discovered a way of framing the problem that allowed the patient to accept psychological treatment did the patient improve.

Those who hold to a strict view of patient-selected goals are less likely to try to "get the patient to accept" the view of the therapist. Rather, the emphasis is strongly on reframing the complaints and symptoms so as to make psychological intervention a natural and useful process (Fisch, Weakland, & Segal, 1982). A therapist strongly committed to an idiopathic view of symptoms would sidestep the kind of power struggle that Conner-Greene illustrated. The goals and methods for achieving goals should theoretically be better matched or agreed upon in this school.

However, there is a significant political disadvantage: It is difficult for funding and certifying organizations to accept this view. They expect an intake formulation that meets the medical model and fits (forces?) a DSM-IV diagnosis. While a therapist may believe in idiopathic diagnosis/ formulation, there is an undeniable necessity to pretend to believe in the medical diagnosis model. Purists may rage that the lesser of two evils is still evil, but within the present system there is no alternative.

Another serious problem is that the strategic system is a very difficult one, since one must invent a new theory and treatment for each patient. This may be unreasonable in the day-to-day life of a frontline therapist. Therapists need models and diagnoses not because they are true but because they inform the therapist of what to do next. It may be that the therapist's acting confidently and assuredly conveys the hope and confidence the patient needs. In other words, perhaps the shaman, with her rattles and drums, who acts confidently (because she has a world view that informs her of what to do from moment to moment) is as helpful as the cognitive therapist with his drawerfull of charts and forms and checklists, who conveys the same sense of certainty. In classic strategic therapy, a therapist has the much more difficult challenge of creating a unique intervention for each person, even when there are six or eight more people to be seen that day and there is little time to sit and ponder this particular case. To some extent, the solution-focused approach has reduced that problem.

The focus can be constructed by asking the following sorts of solution-focused questions (Berg & Miller, 1992; de Shazer, 1988, 1991) and guiding the patient toward very clear descriptions of changes in thinking, feeling, and acting.

- "How can I help?"
- "What do you want to change?"
- "If we had a videotape of what your life will be like after therapy, what would we see than we don't see in your life these days?"
- "How will you know when you have gotten what you want from therapy?"
- "Who will notice that you are getting what you want from therapy? How will they notice? Who will be the first to notice those changes?"
- "If a miracle happened tonight, and that problem were solved (but because it happened while you were asleep, you didn't know), how would you figure out the problem was solved?"
- "Who else would know the problem was solved? How would they figure that out?"
- "Are there signs that the miracle is already starting to happen? Have you noticed any times lately when you were seeing even some of those signs of progress?"

- "How do the first signs the miracle is starting to occur help you in your life?"
- "At the very least, what kind of changes would make you feel that therapy had been somewhat worthwhile? What is the very least you would be satisfied with from therapy?"
- "What is the very first change you would notice that lets you know you are starting to get better?"
- "Why did you decide to come to therapy at this time? What made you decide you needed to talk to someone at this time? Is there anything about this time of year that bothers you? Can you remember any traumatic events at this time of year?"
- (*When several problem areas are mentioned*) "If we only have time to work on one of those areas, which would be the one you would like to solve?"
- "Sometimes solving one problem is like starting a snowball rolling down the hill, and it may be if we solve only one of these problems, the others will just follow along. Which would be the easier to solve?"
- "Have you ever had a problem like this one before? How did you solve it?"
- Some patients frame their goals in a negative sense, that is, they say, "I won't feel/think/do X anymore." Ask, "What will you do INSTEAD?"
- "How committed are you to solving this problem? If you have to do really hard things to solve it, will you do them?"

USING THE FOCUS IN THERAPY

As we have seen, there is a wide variety of ways of achieving a focus. While I prefer normative and idiopathic foci, and am especially impressed with the parsimony of the solution-focused group, I concede that many styles of focus can work well in brief forms of treatment. Once a focus has been agreed upon, and some outcome criteria have been created, then well-conducted therapy tends to stick with that focus. While there is a good chance that things will come up in the course of treatment to shift the focus, the counselor should be very cautious about such a shift. It may be better for the counselor to suggest that the client stick with the original focus until something is achieved in that area, and then shift to the new focus. Another, perhaps preferable option, is to take breaks from therapy after achieving a good deal of progress in one area, to see whether there is some generalization, a ripple effect, so to speak.

Assessment Skills in Accountable Therapy

The accountable therapist needs to be skilled at rapid assessment and intervention. This therapist is not likely to be a devoted follower of a school of therapy, but will probably subscribe to a generic or integrative system.

The era of systems thinking, in which one therapist was a behaviorist and another was a psychoanalyst, is rapidly drawing to a close. In its place there is likely to be awareness that there are several common elements in psychotherapy and that good therapists will address all of those elements.

The models given thus far all have advantages and disadvantages. However, while in the long run all models produce similar outcomes, that is not true with briefer forms of intervention. It is clear that behavioral or cognitive approaches, when contrasted with dynamic approaches, are superior in terms of immediate outcome (Steenbarger, 1994). In Steenbarger's review, for therapy of less than eight sessions, the behavioral approaches were clearly more helpful and effective. However, with therapy lasting more than 12 or 20 sessions, the dynamic approaches were just as good. It is not clear what is going on here. It may be that, since the dynamic approach focuses on goals that are strongly influenced by the model, it takes more time to socialize the patient into the therapy system; the behavioral systems tend to be more idiopathic and accept the patient goals, so there is less socialization needed.

Another (perhaps equally likely) explanation is that patients who need more than 12 visits are working less on symptom relief than on character issues and need more time for that. It may be that the dynamic approach is less effective with patients seeking symptom relief, but equal to cognitive and behavioral approaches in working with character problems.

The Future of Assessment

Some better ways to assess patients must be found, since the first session is a critical moment for creating change. To use that first session to pursue extensive social and family history, unless the patient feels it is crucial, is a grave error. As much as 30 to 55% of patients will only attend a single session (Talmon, 1990). Since this is the case, to spend that session in anything but an intense focus on solving as much of the problem as possible, *today*, is unethical.

The use of questionnaires and self-assessment tools is preferred to establish focus quickly (see Fischer & Corcoran, 1994a & b). The experience of those who have tried such assessments on computer is that many patients resist the computer-based evaluations (e.g., they are afraid of sitting at the computer) and they feel more comfortable with a paper-and-pencil activity. However, in the near future, there is little doubt the computer will administer the questionnaire and receive input verbally, so that problem may soon be solved. The computer's voice recognition technology can give questions and record answers and print out a report about history and areas of concern. Once material collected by pen-and-paper or computer is scored and condensed into the areas of concern for the client, the counselor and patient can quickly scan the results and proceed directly to what the patient wants to gain from the visit today. The Symptom Check List (SCL-90-R, Derogatis, 1977) or the Brief Symptom Inventory (Derogatis & Melisaratos, 1983) and similar checklists are relatively brief instruments that can be easily administered and have obvious implications for therapy.

Another approach to assessment is some kind of goal attainment rating scale. The patient can be asked at the beginning of therapy (in the first session) to co-create, with the therapist, three goals most relevant to her life. The therapist then asks the patient to rate on some kind of scale how much progress has been made and what a reasonable amount of progress would be.

How does one apply these ideas? Imagine a depressed patient who sets as a goal "being able to enjoy life." This is quite broad and very difficult to measure. The goal to "help the patient overcome depression" or "help the patient enjoy life" is not acceptable, so a method of making therapy accountable must be found. Some ways of doing that would be:

1. Administer a symptom-oriented inventory each time, such as the Beck Depression Inventory, an anxiety inventory, a marital functioning checklist, and so on.
2. Administer a more global functioning scale, such as the SCL-90, at the beginning of therapy and every three or four sessions. An alternative would be a personality inventory, such as the Minnesota Multiphasic Personality Inventory (MMPI) or the Millon Clinical Multiaxial Inventory (MCMI), or other objective assessment done at the beginning and the end of therapy. The problem with that is often the patient feel good and may simply cancel the "last" session, so it is probably better to use shorter inventories administered each time.
3. Specify some very specific indicators of "beginning to enjoy life." Ask the patient to rank them in importance. Select the top three, ask the patient to rate on a percentage scale, how much of those are in her life. For example, the patient says, "Telling people how I really feel." And what rating would you give yourself on that right now? "Oh, I am at 2% now." And, we would ask, what is your goal? "Well, if I can get to 70% of the time, I will be happy."
4. Specify actual behaviors, such as sleeping six or more hours per night, sleeping until 6:30 a.m., without early morning awakening, initiating sex with partner one time per week, and so on. Then simply count those behaviors.

Obviously, the norm-oriented treatments have the edge in ease of accountability, because of the problem-specific measurements available. But that doesn't mean that norm-based foci are better than idiopathic foci. With any of these systems, the patient can report on progress in each session. This helps the therapy stay focused and makes both the therapist and the client accountable. Reviewers will understand these means of tracking response to treatment.

Challenges to the Focus

The reality is that the focus in therapy is likely to change. Milton Erickson liked to define psychotherapy as "two people talking together until they find out what the hell one of them wants." Not uncommonly, a patient will say after several sessions, "What I *really* want to talk about is . . . " We have a beautiful theory (find and maintain a focus) and patients keep messing it up. Some therapists argue to shift and meet the new focus of the patient; others argue to maintain the original focus.

Keeping the original focus can be difficult but rewarding. A therapist influenced by psychodynamic thinking will note that shifts in attention may be a way of avoiding the anxiety of working on a single issue. A shift can serve a defensive function, avoiding confronting the adaptive compromise.

From a cognitive perspective, it is a useful skill is to stick with one focus and achieve that, instead of running after one and then another goal. The shifting of focus can be motivated by a perfectionistic attitude, with the underlying schema being, "I *must* discover what is really bothering me." This pursuit of the very best topic and goal may prevent achievement of a reasonable goal.

The strategic therapist can mention how it is best to keep one's expectations limited in psychotherapy, since attempting too many changes too fast could upset many people in the patient's environment. It is kinder to all to limit, at least for now, the area of focus.

So it may well be in the patient's best interest to encourage the original focus. This may be difficult if the patient enters an area in which the therapist is "engaged" or unable to operate freely (Beier & Young, 1984). Engagement means a person is constrained to behave in a certain way, usually because of social conventions. If we pass in the hall, and you nod and smile, I am constrained to offer a similar behavior. I have been properly socialized, and such behavior is necessary for me to function smoothly in society. If I am socialized to think that sexual abuse as a complaint takes priority over all else, then if the patient mentions it, I am constrained to pay attention to that topic.

A person may also be "engaged" when he or she has a personal investment in being seen in a certain way. If it is important to be seen as caring, intelligent, tough, or any other attribute, the person with that desire is

engaged and unable to operate freely. If I have an investment in being seen
as a therapist for codependency, then I am unable to operate freely; an alert
patient may be able to ward off talking about certain topics by bringing up
my favorite topic, codependency.

If the patient is working on panic disorder, and if I follow Barlow's
(1988) treatment protocol, there are some uncomfortable homework activities that I must encourage the patient to follow. Since avoidance is the heart
of panic disorder, the patient may be unconsciously constrained to avoid
the discomfort of discussing and confronting the panic symptoms. There is
now a substantial motivation to avoid the here-and-now work, and if the
patient engages me in a (perhaps intellectualized) discussion of remote
trauma, I have unwittingly supported the very process that underlies both
the panic and the PTSD: namely, the tendency to avoid uncomfortable
feelings.

Instead, I could suggest, "Early childhood sexual abuse is certainly one
of the most devastating and crippling experiences you could suffer. It is
likely your panic has at least some of its origins in that. On the other hand,
we have agreed to work on the panic condition, and if we are successful at
that, we could work more effectively with the more serious material. And if
I cannot help you with the panic, which bothers you now, I probably
couldn't help you with the more deeply rooted material."

Now I can wait and see what the patient is going to do with that. If she
insists on a shift of focus, then I will follow that, but if we can stay with the
original focus, that may well turn out to be more helpful than shifting.
Gustafson (1986) cites an example where a patient of Wilhelm Reich behaved in lurid and provocative ways. The young man spoke of sexual
feelings toward his mother and implied she felt the same toward him. Reich
was struck by the patient's need to impress and please the doctor, and
thought the material derived from the patient's readings of Reich's own
works. Reich ignored what he felt were provocations and pursued his original focus, which was character analysis to resolve the patient's need to
please authority figures. As Reich continually probed this need to please,
the young man improved. This dogged attention to focus allowed Reich to
succeed in helping the troubled young man.

The issue of change of focus is a serious one that demands thoughtful
attention. Does the client really want to abandon the original focus? What
does the client know that the therapist does not know that makes the change
of focus necessary? Is the client being influenced by a belief that only
through resolving one (deeper) issue will the other (more immediate) issue
be settled? Such questions help to elicit important new information that
helps to inform and shape the treatment.

Cooperating with the Change of Focus

On the other hand, we can easily see the opposite situation, where patient feels the therapist must pass a test or trial before he will talk about some sensitive or difficult material. If the therapist is certain the change of focus is necessary for therapy to succeed, a rethinking of all aspects of the therapy should be the next order of business. The new focus may require a different set of tools to assess progress. The insurance carrier may have to be notified about the change, so as to allow for time to accomplish the new goal. And, more difficult yet, the therapist must ask himself if he has the expertise to undertake the new focus. Obviously, familiarity with the problem is very helpful. Substance abuse counselors tell many stories of long, unproductive therapies resulting from ineffective attempts to help the patient control drinking or drug use. Similarly, there is some reason to think that treatment of early abuse may be harmful if therapists lack expertise and skill.

If we assume that the relationship and not technical skill is central, the therapist may choose to review what sorts of skills might be necessary to treat this new area. If he lacks experience, reading up on the topic is certainly a good idea. If the therapist finds a treatment protocol that makes good sense, it is quite easy to contact the author of the protocol directly. The therapist can arrange telephone consultation with an expert in the field, and the treatment can be an excellent learning experience for both patient and therapist. I have had very good experiences contracting for telephone consultation from a variety of therapists with skill in a particular area or approach. This approach has much to recommend, since the patient can stay with the trusted and known therapist. The therapist who acknowledges his limitations but is not intimidated by them will find his skills constantly expanding. Conversely, the therapist who will not admit limitations is likely to do harm or at least fail to help.

So a shift in focus is warranted and wise primarily when there is some issue that prevents or significantly impedes progress, such as chemical abuse or character problems. Renegotiating the focus in these instances can actually empower the client and therapist and result in more effective therapy. Renegotiation is also useful for the patient who has tested the therapist with a minor problem before proceeding to the central issue.

CHAPTER 5

The Tasks of the Therapist: Warmth and Surprise

But guns alone are not enough, which is why Texas does not control the world.

— Dave Barry

No matter what theory the therapist holds, it appears universally true that all therapy intends to change the view the patient has of the problem and the way the patient behaves toward the problem. While it is conceivable that merely telling a patient how to handle the problem, without changing how she views the problem, may be enough, it is unlikely. Instead, changing the viewing and changing the doing seem to go together; in many instances, changing the viewing makes it possible to change the doing.

Therapists believe that what they say and how they say it makes a difference. It is likely that there is a common element in what therapists say to clients in therapy to change the viewing, and it is also quite likely that most of what helps (in regard to techniques of psychotherapy) comes from that common element. That is not to say that there aren't some specific and unique aspects of treatment; intuitively, it seems probable that those unique and specific aspects also make some difference. But, as the quote above implies, these techniques are not enough to explain all the changes people experience as a result of being in therapy.

Generally, therapists assume that *what* we say makes the difference; however, *how* we speak may be more important. Recently, my wife and I attended a wedding, where we saw some old neighbors. The woman reminisced about a time she had spent in a hospital, recovering from a "nervous breakdown." She asked me if I knew a social worker who had worked there, saying that, of all her therapists, the social worker was the most helpful. She said, "I always think about the things she told me." I was intrigued and asked what was said that had such a positive effect on her life. My neighbor smiled and replied, "Well, actually, I don't remember what she said, I just remember how she made me feel." The emotional impact of the relationship had stayed with her; in our psychotherapy, it is the element of surprise and emotional shift, from unpleasant to pleasant, that influences the patient.

THE COMMON THEME

What is enough in the psychotherapy session to stimulate positive change? Is empathy enough? Occasionally, but probably not in many cases. Is transference interpretation necessary? No, although it can be helpful (Hill, 1989). When we look at what therapists actually do, we find a mass of confusion! While one therapist insists on individual therapy and makes assertions during therapy that the patient obviously is reacting as if the therapist were a parent figure, another therapist sees the whole family and suggests that the symptoms are actually a sacrifice the patient is making on behalf of the family. The outcomes for the patients are similar. It is as if antibiotics and blood pressure medicine produced the same outcomes with pneumonia!

This is not quite true. There are specific effects from specific interventions. At the same time, there is the confounding effect of the patient's active desire to improve his adjustment and competence in the world. Thus, no matter what treatment is offered, patients tend to get better; they even get better on a waiting list! And when treatments are compared, it is rare for one to emerge as significantly superior to another.

Yet, some research shows that different interventions will yield some different results. For example, doing family therapy, unlike individual therapy, appears to help the rest of the family, as well as the individual patient (Szapocznik, Rio, Murray et al., 1989). It appears that various strategies of focused intervention with PTSD result in similar improvements, while doing "supportive psychotherapy" without the sustained focus is much less helpful (Foa, Riggs, Dancu, & Rothbaum, 1993). But all psychotherapy approaches seem to be more helpful to patients than simply ignoring them or offering them contact but not doing therapeutic interventions.

The Role of Surprise

Examining the interview process, we find that therapists offer both warmth (or possibly, in some contexts, prestige) and novelty or surprise. The surprise consists of a new meaning that helps the client view the problem differently, thus changing the feeling the client has about it. For example, the patient says, "You are a terrible therapist," and the therapist says, "Tell me more about that." Such a response is a surprise to the client (at least the first few times it happens). Because of the surprise, the feeling of anger that might have motivated such a statement is sidetracked and the patient feels uncertain, for at least a moment, about what to do next. If a patient says the same thing to another therapist, she might say, "So imagine I am in that chair, and really tell me off." Again, this response is somewhat unusual and therefore surprising. Yet another therapist might thoughtfully agree, "Well, I do have shortcomings as a therapist. I can sympathize with you. But my limitations are to your advantage, since you will have to work hard to benefit. So when you get better, it'll be your efforts that made you better, not mine, and you should take the credit."

All of these interventions are made in the context of a therapeutic relationship, meaning bond, agreement on goals of treatment, and agreement on tasks or methods. In our culture, the bond and the methods involve interpersonal warmth and caring, although this is not necessarily true in other cultures. The warmth conveys a sense of safety, an invitation to explore alternatives. The surprise is the actual exploration of the alternatives. The therapist offers a change in the meaning of the problem, doing so in a way that fixes attention and makes the change a memorable one.

At the same time, the surprise is not some random event, like an earthquake or winning a lottery. It must be related to the patient (somehow conveying, "This comes from *you*"), the focus, and the patient's goals for the therapy. The focus tells us *where* to create novel, surprising interventions that have the kind of effect the patient desires. For the surprise to be most helpful, the patient must feel the therapist's intervention comes not from some theory but from the patient's own behavior.

Thus, the patient who doesn't expect a transference interpretation finds this is a novel idea. It is conveyed in the context of talking about her problematic relationships, so there is a linking of the feeling of surprise to the context of the problem. It doesn't necessarily mean the transference interpretation is true, in some absolute sense, even if the patient benefits from it. The important thing is that it effects a *change of meaning* about that problem, and with a bit of generalization, we will see a change in behavior. The next time the patient is upset with his boss and feeling persecuted, he has a new resource. He can wonder to himself, "Is this just transference, like the analyst said?" Just by the fact of wondering, his emotional reaction is changed. Now he does not give out the same verbal and nonverbal messages he did before. The boss, his colleagues, and his peers may notice that subtle and significant change. Their reactions are now tempered. He finds people are treating him differently, and this tips the question to "Maybe this *is* just transference?" This may mellow him even more, creating a virtuous circle of beneficial reactions.

Let's say that, instead, the therapist memorized Fritz Perls' motto "I do my thing and you do your thing; you are not in this world to meet my expectations, and I am not here to meet yours." While the client is expostulating angrily, the therapist suddenly offers this intervention, and does it in a warm manner (subtly disqualifying the overt meaning, but never mind that), so that the patient now feels safe and able to apply this new "insight" into his life. When he starts to experience his supervisor giving him a hard time, the same generalization can take place: He calms himself and thinks about how people aren't in the world to meet each other's expectations. His boss notices that he is less prickly and defensive (although the boss may not know she noticed that at a conscious level). She now gives him a bit of room, so to speak. He notices the space, likes it, and attributes it to his application of the motto. He then gives her more room, and a virtuous circle is established!

Are either of the interventions true? Of course not — they are not in the realm of true or false. They are in the realm of opinion. In other words, they are as valuable as the effect they have on people.

My Own Surprise

In 1982, I organized a local workshop on hypnosis, and one of the presenters I invited was Jeffrey Zeig, the director of the Milton H. Erickson Foundation in Phoenix. As we shared lunch, we talked about professional development. I said that for the first five years or so after my Ph.D., I did not do any writing, papers, or anything of that sort. I did not have anything to say, I thought; lately, however, I had been noticing that I had a few things to say and had been doing some writing. Jeff stared at me, and said, "You are a turkey!" What??? "I said," Jeff repeated, "you are a turkey. You always had something to say, you just didn't say it."

I actually disagreed then and do now with the *content* of the intervention. I do not think I always had something to say. But the intervention did fulfill the parameters of a therapy experience. It actually had a positive effect on me: I was stimulated to write and present papers, and when I felt stuck in a writing project, I remembered that intervention and smiled. There was something charming and unique about it, something memorable. Our therapy interventions ought to have a similar effect: something that hooks our clients, catches their emotions and their cognitions at the same time. And the impact of the intervention comes as much from the novelty as from the truth of it. There must be some sense that what the counselor says *could be true*, more than that it *is* true.

Beier (1966, Beier & Young, 1984) has suggested the ideal intervention is one that offers a *one-trial learning* consisting of replacing neurotic certainty with beneficial uncertainty. He argues that the patient must carry out activities designed to satisfy both sides of a neurotic conflict, to continually prove to herself that she is stuck. As an example, he describes a client who feels he must test others' interest in him—love tests, so to speak. The client says to the counselor, "You only see me for the money." The counselor may try to reassure the patient, but this creates a dilemma. Obviously the reassurance comes from the feeling of guilt and anxiety the client has created in the therapist. So the reassurance is not spontaneous; it is elicited, forced, if you will. If the client can create a feeling of guilt and anxiety in the counselor, then he has succeeded in "proving" once again that people don't really like him, that they are being false in attempting to reassure him. His own lack of concern for others and sincerity are justified by his view that the world is a corrupt place anyway, so why be kind to people? And this complex interaction takes place very quickly and at a covert, not overt, level; in other words, the rule, "People don't really like me but they should, and I am justified in testing them to see if they do," is at the level of unconscious processing.

Suppose, however, our therapist is an interactionally oriented strategic therapist and is not engaged or caught up in a feeling of guilt and anxiety, that she has nothing to prove or defend, that she is *disengaged* from the emotional demands of the situation. In that case, she might smile warmly and say, "Of course! Why would anyone see a son-of-a-bitch like you *but* for the money?" Her smile and warmth disqualify the message, so the client is now *uncertain* about how to respond next. That uncertainty is clearly beneficial, since it prevents continuation of the self-defeating interpersonal game. When the therapist responds outside the expected range of behavior, and yet does so with some warmth and empathy, a change of meaning is necessarily promoted.

The alert cognitive therapist might say, "I believe I am guilty of that; being paid makes a big difference. If that is true, what is your objection to that? What does it mean to you?" They are off and running on the task of challenging the silent rules, offering different ways of looking at the situation. The outcome is quite similar.

And if an insight-oriented therapist offers the transference interpretation, tying together the present patient's feelings about the therapist with the patient's feelings and actions toward others in his current environment and the patient's early relationship with a parent, a similar outcome has been achieved. This is why all these divergent theories result in very similar outcomes: They all achieve a shift or change in meanings for the patient through their reframing of the patient's behavior. The therapists all behave in a surprising way, creating the emotional climate in which the change of cognitions can have a positive effect. We change the way the patient views the problem; then we can change the way the patient does the problem.

The Chronically Mentally Ill

Now let's apply this to a more difficult population: chronically mentally ill patients. These folks often try the ingenuity and patience of therapists, since they have created a failure-laden self-fulfilling prophecy. Da Verona and Omer (1992) illustrate it this way: The client first begins to fail by not behaving according to social and family norms. Significant others are frustrated and disappointed; their frustration and disappointment hurt the patient, who probably feels she is doing the best she can. Since both parties are now hurt, they begin to avoid each other, leading to feelings of anger and guilt on both sides. The significant other is led to *label* the patient, and the patient begins to think of herself as being the label, as being hopeless and beyond help. This leads both sides to give up. Now the client tends to act in ways that are consistent with her view of herself, and that leads her to act more and more disabled.

Professional helpers feel engaged or obligated by this behavior and rise to defeat it. They encourage the patient to do more or try harder, thus validating the patient's view that something really is wrong with her and promoting more and more hopeless and uncooperative behavior. She must fail to cooperate since she sees herself as incompetent and as eliciting rejection and disappointment from others when she does try.

Since our "game" in mental health might (sometimes) be "I'm only trying to help" (Berne, 1964), this "lack of cooperation" allows us to feel overtly righteous and helpful, while feeling frustrated and guilty at a covert level. The patient is likely to perceive this frustration and guilt, and feel hurt. This leads her to do less and to avoid us. We feel frustrated, guilty, and resentful ("I'm not helping this patient; this patient is resistant"). And so it continues.

If we are to disrupt this process, we have to behave in counter-intuitive ways: We must behave in a way that is both warm and surprising. If we expect that our temptation will be to encourage the client to do more, we must do the opposite, while simultaneously giving verbal and nonverbal messages of warmth and acceptance. For example, Da Verona and Omer (1992) suggest that the patient's symptoms (which serve to put the therapist on notice that the client cannot do anything effective) be encouraged by being positively reframed: "Of course you act as you do! In your situation it is the only reasonable way to behave. This shows that you are now in the right place!" (p. 358). This "paradoxical acceptance," they argue, changes the usual meaning of the difficult behavior, so that, instead of both sides feeling mutually rejected, the interaction is turned into a corrective one. The patient is surprised in a useful way.

Take the chronic patient who doesn't cooperate in the day treatment

program, standing on the porch smoking instead of coming inside and joining an activity group. His experience is that when he does this, a counselor
will approach him and encourage him to come in and participate. He must
resist that, since he "knows" he is not socially competent, will fail, and others
will feel disappointed in him. But this is a different program. Suppose instead
he is met by a counselor who stands next to him and says she is quite happy to
remain beside him on the porch. She recommends that he spend as much
time as necessary standing on the porch smoking, since this is an excellent
way to feel more comfortable. If he wants to come inside and join the group,
it might be wise to go slowly on that, making sure he has spent enough time
away from the group so as to feel comfortable.

The patient likely feels surprised. Surprise makes him uncertain: What
shall he do now? He may have a good deal of experience of counselors only
trying to help by encouraging him to behave in a more "rational" way. This
counselor does not; she accepts what he does, reframes it as good idea, and
encourages him to continue it. Using this approach throughout a treatment
center has had interesting results, Da Verona and Omer suggest. They
quote one patient as saying that the center was the craziest rehabilitation
place on earth, since in any regular place such as the hospital, whenever he
wanted to leave an activity shortly after arriving, he was encouraged to
make an effort to stay and told that he had to fight his nervousness and his
illness in order to get well. He found the encouragement he received in
the center astounding. In fact, at one point the director thought he was
progressing too fast and should slow down. The outcome for that particular
patient was quite positive.

Da Verona and Omer argue that such positive connotation and acceptance of symptoms are more powerful than usual persuasion. In this way,
they reach many patients who might otherwise be unresponsive to treatment. Their results suggest this approach, of offering surprising degrees
of acceptance and even encouraging what would ordinarily be seen as
"resistance," is a better one than encouraging the patient and thus running
the chance of promoting failure, hurt, and rejection.

Therapeutic Surprise: Restraining the Adolescent

Adolescents are frequently referred to residential care because no one
can make them comply with reasonable rules of social intercourse. While
some adolescents respond well to direct requests for change, coupled with
shifting reward contingencies in the family, many do not. Unfortunately,
many treatment settings continue this ineffective approach. The adolescent
sees this as more of the same theme of adults trying to run his life and
continues to (almost mindlessly) resist those efforts.

It is this virtually automatic resistance that led Morrissette and McIntyre (1989) to describe the vicious cycle of more effort to get the adolescent to comply leading to more effort on the teen's part to resist leading to more effort on the treatment team's part to force compliance. They pointed out that when the patient does show some positive behavior, and when the professionals involved congratulate the patient for some improvement, "the young person typically denies this progress or begins to behave in ways that will prove the professional wrong" (p. 32). Morrissette and McIntyre suggest that this dynamic makes perfect sense. The young person, needing to feel in control, will reject any form of evaluation from the staff, since evaluation per se is felt to be a form of control. They say, "Typically, when evaluative reports are shared by staff they are usually delivered with the child care staff assuming an elevated position in the client-worker relationship. This constructed hierarchy (worker telling young person) tends to perpetuate a power struggle around control. To regain control and the elevated, or at least equal position in the hierarchy, the child must prove the professional wrong or incompetent. To do this, the young person often resorts to oppositional behavior" (p. 32). Thus, restraining — suggesting the patient is progressing too fast too soon — is recommended. The patient is told that too much change is taking place. The patient should slow down, and perhaps consider the disadvantages of responsible behavior.

Morrissette and McIntyre (1989) recount the example of a young man ("Jim") who after 40 placements in residential treatment settings had established a rigid pattern of avoiding daily chores and defying staff. He also had periods of compliance ("exceptions"), during which he seemed apologetic. Morrissette helped the staff create a restraining-based approach, designed to surprise Jim. Whenever he acted cooperatively or "exceptionally," the staff would be puzzled and confused and ask Jim if he had thought about the disadvantages of doing his chores. They worried that if Jim were to continue that behavior, the whole staff would have to begin to treat him differently. His good behavior could throw the whole program out of whack! Jim insisted that he could handle it, but the staff persisted in saying that Jim should go slow and then disengaged from the interaction. Jim was left with some sense of surprise, presumably, and continued to defy the staff, this time by continuing to improve, leaving the staff to mutter worriedly to themselves.

Therapeutic Surprises: Saying No to the Patient

In the early 1970s, when I was a graduate student, a fellow student asked me whether sexual relations should be a part of psychotherapy. He said a patient had asked him for such a relationship, saying she had a hang-up about men like him and thought she could work it out in that way.

He asked me what I thought. We pondered it awhile and decided the only unique thing that therapists have to offer is that we don't try to meet our needs in therapy. Everything we do should be with the intention of helping the client. We did a thought-experiment: If the client were a male, with the same hang-up, would the therapist help him in the same way? My friend said, "Absolutely not"! What if the woman were elderly or markedly unattractive? He thoughtfully agreed that would change things. So the proposed intervention failed the disinterest test: It would not really be for her benefit.

My friend told the patient sex in the therapy would be for his needs and not really for hers, and it would not be a part of their relationship. She was amazed. She opened up and talked about things she had not wanted to discuss in therapy. She felt emboldened by his boundaries. He acted in a surprising way, with support and warmth for the client and not for his own needs. This violated her notion of how men were supposed to behave and created *beneficial uncertainty*, which allowed her to experiment with new behaviors. (While with the 20/20 hindsight we now have about such matters we can see his reaction as the only ethical thing to do, I can assure you that in the early '70s there was a much different climate. My friend reported that one of his supervisors at the agency had even encouraged him to act on the patient's invitation!)

Therapeutic Surprises: Saying Yes to the Patient

Here is another example: Beier (personal communication) told me of a family interview he conducted. The father abusively criticized the son for his lack of respect, his lack of ethics and morals, and his lack of general value. The son became silently more and more full of rage, and the mother was dismayed and embarrassed by her husband. Beier silently summed up the situation, jumped out of his chair, walked across the consulting room, took the father by the hand, and, shaking it vigorously, said, "I must congratulate you. Never have I seen a man more devoted to helping his son! You must really love your son. Your commitment and energy are wonderful!" The man just stared at Beier. As he returned to his seat, Beier mentioned, almost as an afterthought, "Now, your methods could use some improvement." The mother and son laughed; the father smiled, ceased the attacking, and was uncertain about what to do next.

The father's attacking behavior was reframed as helpful in intent, if not in execution, and the reframing was accomplished in a memorable, engaging, attention-compelling way. No one in the family could dispute that the atmosphere in the session had changed dramatically. The father was more open to change, more of a customer; the son's attention was compelled and he also felt more open and engaged in the therapy. Improvement followed.

Using Surprise to Encourage Compliance

Therapists often have ideas about how the patient ought to behave to make the problem disappear. They may believe in asserting oneself, writing down one's thoughts, or making conscious, willful errors. The problem is in getting the patient to comply, to do these useful things. The therapeutic task is somewhat unnatural, at least for the patient, and there may be a natural resistance to going along with this new behavior. Cialdini (1984) points out that surprise is one way to get people to comply. He cites Milgram and Sabini's unpublished manuscript (1975), where they demonstrated that people were more likely to comply with unusual requests when they were surprised than when they were cued as to what was about to happen. Thus, the intervention creates surprise and uncertainty, and the client is more likely to agree to experiment with some new behavior.

The example above, of reframing the father's attacking as helpful, was followed with the suggestion of needed improvement. The surprise opened the father to change in a way that an approach based on education may not have.

CREATING SURPRISE

How do you introduce novelty, especially if you are like me, rather unimaginative and pedestrian in thought? A general model of intervention is *reframing*, which offers a new explanation about a complaint that both fits the facts of the situation and at the same time changes the meaning (Watzlawick, Weakland, & Fisch, 1974). In reframing, we usually interpret a negative complaint in a more positive way, suggesting a change of feeling about that idea. For example, parents may complain about their teenager being rebellious. The therapist can reframe that to point out that, while the teen's behavior is unpleasant, the intention behind it is to become more independent and therefore ready to leave the family. The parents are encouraged to think of the rebelliousness as one of many attempts to get ready to be on his own.

The common way for people to get others to change is to criticize them. For example, in marriage, spouses often try to change one another by attributing undesirable behavior to negative aspects of the personality (Orvis, Kelley, & Butler, 1976). I might tell my wife, for example, that she is acting just like her mother. I generously allow that she is not *like* her mother, she just acts in such a way that this is the impression she gives me and others. I assume that, unless she prefers to be like her mother, she will change her behavior so as to not leave me with that impression (Beck & Strong, 1982).

Oddly enough, though, criticism often produces the opposite result.

Instead of responding positively to my kind diagnosis and changing her behavior, my wife tries to change my attributions. She actually resists me! She argues. When I see how resistant she is to good common sense, I double my efforts to get her to see how stubborn and unreasonable she is, just like her mother. She now sees my behavior as more and more in need of correction, so she redoubles her efforts. We have created a vicious circle, caused by our efforts to correct each other.

Many of our psychotherapeutic interventions are actually negative attributions about the client; for example, the patient's behavior is due to repressed memories of abuse, irrational beliefs, negative self-talk, or unresolved neurotic wishes. These are our own constructions, and as I have pointed out earlier, cannot be true in any absolute sense. Their only value lies in their usefulness (and it may be that our therapy succeeds in spite of what we do and not because of it). The evidence that we do have is that positive connotation and positive reframing are powerful change agents (Beck & Strong, 1982; Cordova & Jacobson, 1993; Jacobson, 1992; Kraft, Clairborn, & Dowd, 1985). Instead of promoting marital change, for instance, Jacobson now advocates a greater promotion of acceptance, something based on strategic therapy principles of externalizing the problem and positive connotation. The patients look for ways to view the problem that allow them to accept their partner rather than changing him.

I am not suggesting that positive connotation is true, only that it seems to be more useful, in that it is more parsimonious. If I can positively reframe symptoms, I seem to produce a useful and positive response in the client, with less resistance and difficulty than I used to get when I was trying to do insight-oriented psychotherapy or behavioral therapy, both of which involved a certain amount of negative attributions. You can already guess what the negative attributions were in the insight-oriented work. The behavior therapy was likewise based on negative attributions, seeing problems as problems in faulty learning, which the therapist was supposed to cure.

Instead of even agreeing with the client that the behavior is bad, I now look for some positive function of the behavior, suggesting that there are some advantages. Oddly enough, when a patient stops thinking about the complaint as bad, the very behavior or problem seems to diminish.

Case Example: A Pain in the Feet

For example, a man recently complained about some symptoms that sounded like anxiety or panic problems, mixed with somatic preoccupations. One symptom was that the soles of his feet were tender and painful to walk on. Convinced his symptoms were completely physical in origin, he had spent much energy and money with medical doctors, without help. He was intelligent and wanted to understand his symptoms, and by the time he came to me he was open to the possibility that the symptoms were psychological, although that was still hard for him to believe. I suggested perhaps the symptoms were actually some sort of a gift, a useful message, but that neither he nor I understood it. I asked him to shut his eyes and meditate on the pain and soreness in his feet.

For two minutes, I encouraged him to simply accept those feelings, without trying to change them, without trying to cure them, without trying to do anything at all. Rather, he could simply be curious about what, if anything, he could learn from those symptoms. As he and I sat quietly, a couple of possibilities came to my mind. He couldn't think of much, he said, so I suggested the pain in his feet related to his work. He had been walked on at work, and the tenderness in his feet reminded him to treat people with respect and to not walk on them.

Another possibility, I thought, was that he needed to decide how much energy to put into doing something about being walked on at work. His feet might be saying, "You must stand on your own two feet, and stand up for yourself, no matter how painful it is."

He liked both of those ideas. Because he liked what we did and found the meanings unique and interesting, we repeated the exercise, this time with the symptoms of fullness and ringing in the ears. After focusing only on those symptoms, accepting them, and making no effort to change them, he reported the meaning he discovered was that the symptoms were telling him he ought to listen to himself and not to outside influences so much. He talked about a conflict at work. He wanted to blow the whistle on some illegal practices, but his peers said to let it go. The ringing reminded him to have integrity and not listen to the peers.

Are these meanings true? How can we know? It may be they existed before we did the exercise. It also may be that they did not exist until we asked about them, and so the act of asking created them. The therapist is not an impartial observer of therapy, and cannot be. Everything the therapist does in the relationship affects the way the client experiences the world; even the act of observing the therapy changes it. But if we cannot know whether we are discovering truth, so what? What we can know is that the change of meaning has a powerfully liberating impact on the client, and that is what we are after.

Reframing and Dialectics

Omer (1991) has pointed out that interventions have a dialectical quality, in that they are an antithesis to the patient's thesis, and out of the tension between them comes the synthesis of new meaning. What is easy to forget is that the patient's position, the thesis, does not really exist until it is created interpersonally. In other words, the therapist is co-creating the reality of the problem all the time. This means that the therapist's position can also be a thesis, and the patient's response can be an antithesis. If the therapist's position is that the problem is really something with value, the patient's antithesis is likely to be that the problem has less value, or none at all. Conversely, if the therapist offers a thesis that the problem is a bad thing, there is an undeniable pull for the patient to offer a counter, that there might be something attractive about the difficulty.

Omer suggests that an effective intervention *"embodies two antithetical moves* in such a way that as the pendulum swings from one to the other, change forces are mobilized and resistances neutralized"* (p. 565, emphasis in original). So rather than see the thesis in the patient and the antithesis in the therapist, Omer suggests the thesis and antithesis are both in the intervention of the therapist. He gives an example of family therapy with two therapists, one of whom is critical and judgmental, the other understanding and supportive. The "bad" therapist says the identified patient will not make progress, but the good therapist conspiratorially suggests the opposite.

In family therapy sessions I often make use of the dialectical intervention even while operating alone. The therapist can refer to the "behind the mirror" consultant when there is one; if not, I can simply say I am of two minds on a question, and cannot decide. In a recent example, the oldest son declared the improvements discussed in the second session would not last, since the family had been in therapy before and had never made an improvement last. As I summed up the session, I said, "I am undecided about whether the family will learn more by continuing the good work, or whether the prediction by Dale about the relapse would be more helpful. When the family notices good progress, we don't know whether being modest and not mentioning it would promote more of the good behavior, or whether it would promote relapse. And I can't decide whether, if you decide to notice good behavior and brag it up, that will promote more good behavior or whether is would promote relapse. You can learn a great deal, no matter what you do."

The intervention at the end of the session was intended to legitimize and positively reframe all possible behaviors, and to incorporate them into a statement I hoped would be memorable and surprising, while doing that within a context of warmth.

All reframing is a subtle dialectic, since at one level the purpose of the relationship is to replace the symptomatic behavior with more functional action. The therapist agrees with the seriousness of the symptom, but then confuses the picture by suggesting the symptoms are actually helpful or positive in some way or another. The two positions of "the symptoms are bad/no, the symptoms are good" are simultaneously held by the therapist, thus freeing the patient to experiment with completely new ideas.

Reframing Patterns

Here are some frameworks for creating positive attributions to complaints and symptoms:

1. Look for a possible good intention behind the "bad" behavior. For example, in doing hypnosis with persons who want to quit smoking, I often suggest that there is a very good intention behind the desire to smoke. I suggest that in hypnosis we will discover that good intention. It usually turns out that the good intention is to feel comfortable or to fit in or both. Since it is reasonable and useful to feel comfortable, and to fit in, the smoking has satisfied a very real need in the client's life. When the therapist accepts the good intention, the patient is often ready to give up the behavior, when a more effective way of meeting the need behind the behavior is created.

2. Look for unintended consequences of the bad behavior. For example, a patient complained that he was married to a woman who ignored his attempts to make the marriage more warm and intimate. I suggested he needed to learn to accept his wife as she was. We began looking for ways in which the wife's rejecting behavior was actually a good thing, and we were actually able to find several ways. For example, living with a woman who is "rejecting" requires him to develop independence and self-sufficiency. Another benefit is that it promotes flexibility on his part, since he is under an ethical obligation, if he is convinced that intimacy is good, to offer it to her whether she seems to deserve it or not. Perhaps when she rejects something about him, it may simply be her way of objecting to his annoying or difficult habits, so he can learn to be less self-righteous and listen better. Similarly, a patient with panic disorder was asked to make a list of how his symptoms of racing heart and sense of doom could actually be helpful to him. When he had any symptoms he agreed to sit quietly and meditate on how the symptoms could have an unexpected good effect. His symptoms rapidly began to abate, which I suggested was unfortunate since we couldn't be sure he had learned as much as possible from those problems.

Some unintended consequences might be beneficial to other people. I reframed a child's refusal to turn in schoolwork as a sacrifice for the benefit of the other children, since if he did not turn that homework in, the other children would gain more attention and time from the teacher. She wouldn't have to spend as much time on him.

Molnar and Lindquist (1989) consulted with teachers to help them change problem behaviors in the classroom. They emphasized how reframing contributed to solutions by helping the teacher view the problem differently. One teacher reported that she saw how talking during class helped a boy socialize, something she had ignored when she was irritated. She told the boy how she could see that talking in class was important to him to help him be friendly, how talking was probably part of his way of learning, how he was sometimes quiet and sometimes noisy and everyone needs to be noisy at times, and how she noticed he tried to cooperate by sitting at his desk when he talked. The student smiled and replied, "Sometimes I know I should be quiet and work, so I will." Her analysis was that "he was showing understanding of my perspective just as I had shown understanding of his" (pp. 21–22).

3. Think of a continuum of attention, from intrapsychic ("Now why did I say that?") or proprioceptive ("Why am I feeling that feeling?") on one end to social and external ("What is she doing now, and why is she doing it?") on the other. Imagine that people may be primarily *internal* or primarily *external* in their attention. An internal person ("I have terrible anxiety attacks") can be helped by focusing on external experience (therapist says, "Notice how much safer and more secure your husband seems to feel when you are having an anxiety attack"). Conversely, the external client ("My husband/wife doesn't do the right things") can be helped by focusing on internal aspects of experience. One man whose wife wasn't interested in intimacies was powerfully struck when we helped him realize that by avoiding those intimacies she was assuring him that he'd never have to face the trauma of inability to perform. It was even possible, we thought, that she might have sensed an unconscious fear of that on his part and was trying to help him avoid that out of love and concern for him.

4. Think about the *locus of control* of the problem, moving from "you have a problem" to "the problem appears to have or control you." While therapists have traditionally thought of therapy as making the patient responsible for the problem, a good deal of research (Seligman, 1990) and clinical experience (White, 1984, 1986, 1987; White & Epston, 1990) suggests that such an approach may be harmful to our patients. Seligman demonstrates that the problem can be that the patient feels *too* responsible for the problem. In fact, it turns out that the more responsible for the problem the patient feels, the less well the patient responds to therapy. We may benefit

from helping the patient see the problem as an external agent, as an "it," as Jacobson says (Cordova & Jacobson, 1993).

White has had good success with such problems as encopresis and schizophrenia by externalizing the problem, thus implicitly internalizing the resistance to the problem. Encopresis can be thought of as a "sneaky-poo" that tries to mess up the patient's life. The patient can develop a feeling of resistance to the "sneaky-poo" and develop ways of combating it. Similarly, the schizophrenic's symptoms can be reframed as external to him, as things wanting to control the patient. But there may be times when the symptoms fail in their desire to control the patient; these times can be explored to see if they can be repeated.

White (White & Epston, 1990) suggests a two-step strategy for reframing the problem as external to the patient. The steps are:

(a) Map the influence of the problem. The patient is asked how the problem influences him/her in all possible contexts. How does it influence self-concept? How does it influence relationships with friends? What does the problem seem to encourage you to think about yourself? What does it keep you from doing? What does it invite others to think about you? How has the problem isolated or distanced you from those you want to be close to?
(b) Map the influence of the person or persons. This phase focuses on exceptions to the problem. Questions might include: What explanation do you give for the times when the problem tried to influence you and you influenced the problem instead? What times can you remember when you didn't cooperate with the problem but cooperated with yourself instead? How do those times invite you to think about yourself? In what ways have you influenced the problem that you may not have noticed?

White argues that this process of externalizing the problem and internalizing the resistance to the problem has the effect of mobilizing the patient into a healthy rebellion toward the problem. The "story" the patient tells changes, and so does the way the patient behaves about the problem.

An article in *USA Today* (1992) gave a particularly touching example of this. Donna Williams has a diagnosis of autism, and has written a book about her experiences (Williams, 1992). In the article, Williams said to her interviewer, "You may say 'Donna is the one with the quirks about the light switches, Donna is the one with the quirks about the doorbell. Donna is the one who won't look at you at the table.' But that's wrong. Autism is the thing that makes Donna unable to look at you at the table. I am Donna who is an optimist and I am Donna who is a fairly happy person and has a funny outlook on many things. And I am Donna who is social, despite it being easier not to be. That's what is me."

5. Simply ask, "That is one way to look at it; can you think of any other explanations?" This is a surprise, since the patient may not be aware of any alternative ways of seeing problems or even that alternatives exist. This sort of question, often used by cognitive therapists, can lead the patient to question his views of problems generally and reduce his emotional reactions to them.

The ABCDE structure (Seligman, 1990) is a useful pattern for thinking about cognitive reframing. Each letter represents a prompt: A = Adverse Act, B = Belief, C = Consequence, D = Dispute, and E = Effect. The client reframes her own thinking by responding to the pattern:

A: What *Adverse Act* has influenced me?
B: What is my *Belief* about that action?
C: As a *Consequence* of my *Belief*, what do I feel or do?
D: How can I *Dispute* (or challenge) my *Belief*?
E: What is the *Effect* of *Disputing* the *Belief*?

6. Ask the client's "parts" to join in therapy. Andreas and Andreas (1994) have developed this model of quasi-hypnotic reframing. It involves assuming that undesirable behavior is the result of misguided "parts" (somewhat like unconscious ego states, whatever *those* are) attempting to help the person or achieve something positive or helpful. The quasi-hypnotic aspect comes from the involuntary responses the patient feels as the therapist follows these specific steps (pp. 16–17; I have edited their version):

(a) Relive the negative experience, noticing all the thoughts, feelings, and visualizations that go along with it. Thank the experience for whatever positive message is being conveyed.
(b) Notice where the "part" of you that is running the problem behavior seems to be located in your body. Is there an inner feeling in some part of your body? Do you hear an internal voice connected with the behavior? Are there inner pictures? Where are they located in space? Andreas and Andreas say, "Gently invite the part into your awareness."
(c) Thank the part for trying to help you even though you do not know what the part is trying to achieve. They advocate, " . . . you can assume that it has some positive purpose. Begin thanking this part of you

for being there, doing its best to accomplish something on your behalf. Shower this part with appreciation."

(d) Ask what the purpose is. This is the hypnotic aspect, since asking for inner responses that tell you something unknown about yourself is a classic hypnotic procedure. They suggest you simply ask what the part is trying to accomplish for you and wait for the response.

(e) Whatever response you feel, thank that part or thank yourself for giving a response.

(f) Continue asking the question, "What do you want to accomplish by doing *that*?" until you get a response that you can wholeheartedly endorse as positive. That may take one step or several. For example, you may argue with a partner "to get even." That may not seem positive, but if you keep asking, "What do I want to accomplish by doing *that*?" eventually you will find something positive, such as "to live in peace." And while the *method* chosen by the part may not be to your liking, the intention can be very positive and something you appreciate about yourself.

This model involves at its core the same type of reframing we have earlier discussed, namely separating the intention from the behavior. For people who are receptive to hypnosis, it can be a highly effective exercise. My own experience is more disappointing. If I have any parts in me, they are mute.

7. Ask solution-focused questions, which tend to automatically reframe problems. These questions have been developed at the Brief Therapy Center in Milwaukee (Berg & Miller, 1992; de Shazer, 1985, 1988, 1991). Ponder how the questions accomplish the task of reframing and changing the emotional climate.

These questions fall into several categories:

(a) The exception frame:

(i) Pre-session change: This frame assumes that patients can and do change on their own, prior to the first session (Weiner-Davis, de Shazer, & Gingerich, 1987) but that the patient may ignore those changes, unless they are attended to.

Ask, "Often people notice a change between the time they call for an appointment and their first session. What kinds of changes have you noticed?" If any positive answer is found for this inquiry, the therapist follows up with many questions about the impact of the change, the degree to which the change was satisfying, and whether the change can be continued or repeated.

(ii) Exceptions: This assumes that there are times when the problem does not occur, and searches to learn if those times can be a foundation for further change.

- "What seems to be different about times when the problem does not occur? What happens instead? "
- "What is different about times when the problem is not so strong or noticeable?"
- "What seems to be causing those exceptions? How do they occur?"

(b) The outcome frame: The therapist learns about the patient's goals.

- "How will you know when you are getting what you want from therapy?"
- "Who will notice that you are benefiting from therapy, *without your even having to tell them?* How will they notice?"
- "If we meet a year from now, and you tell me the problem that brought you into therapy has disappeared, what will you say is different in your life since that happened?"
- "Suppose in the middle of the night tonight, a miracle happens, and the problem that brought you into therapy is solved. But because it happens while you are asleep, you don't realize it. Tomorrow when you wake up, what will tell you the problem has been solved?"
- "What will be the *smallest* sign that this is happening?"
- "What will be the *first* sign that this is happening?"
- "I am not quite sure what you mean when you say (happy, light-hearted, or any vague term the client uses to describe the desired outcome). How will others know you have those feelings?"
- "If I had a video camera and followed you around when you (were feeling better, had solved this problem, etc.), what would we see you doing on the tape that would tell us that this problem had been solved?"
- "Where will you be when you first notice this happening?"
- "Who will be the first to notice that this is happening?"
- "What will be the first thing others notice is different about you that will tell them this is happening?"
- "What do you know about (your past, yourself, your situation, others, etc.) that tells you that this could happen for you?"

(c) The coping frame: When there are no useful exceptions and the patient cannot respond to the outcome frame, the therapist should be quite concerned. There may be suicidal thoughts or plans, since hopelessness is directly measured by how well the client can think of a positive, realistic outcome from therapy.

When conditions are so bad, or when the patient feels so hopeless that no reasonable outcome can be found, the patient's coping strategies must be explored. As we explore the strategies, the patient's life is indirectly reframed as one of heroically coping with difficult outside influences.

- "Things are quite difficult and hard, very bad for you. How do you manage to keep yourself going?"
- "What kinds of things help you cope with the terrible conditions you must face?"
- "If you hadn't gone through it, would you ever have expected you would cope as well as you have with these troubles?"
- "This sounds like a very serious problem. How have you managed to cope?"
- "Given how (depressed, anxious, etc.) you have been, how do you manage to keep going every day?"
- "What have you been doing to fight off the urge to (let yourself be depressed, feel worse, commit suicide, etc.)?"
- "How have (you, others) kept things from becoming even worse?"
- "What are you doing to keep (anxiety, depression, etc.) from getting the best of you?"
- "How did you (know, figure out) that would help?"
- "How did you (know, figure out) that was the right thing for you to do?"
- "If you hadn't been through this experience personally, would you have ever thought you had the strength to survive like you have?"
- "Given how bad things have been, how come things aren't worse?"

(d) The scaling frame: Patients benefit from looking at their problems as continua rather than dichotomies. Scaling questions help the patient and the therapist map the strength of various aspects of the problems or the solutions. The general form of the question is:

- "On a 1–10 scale, with 10 equal to the most problem you could have and 1 equal to the least, what would you rate the current problem?"

The application of this frame is limited only by the imagination of the therapist. For example:

- "On a 1–10 scale, with 10 meaning 'I will do anything including walking on hot coals in my bare feet' and 1 meaning 'I really couldn't be bothered to do anything,' what rating do you give yourself today about how motivated you are to solve this problem?"

- "What would make your motivation go up one point?"
- "What could make your motivation go down one point?"
- "If your wife/husband/teacher/probation officer were here, what would he/she have guessed your rating would be? How do you account for any difference?"

Ask both persons in a marital relationship to rate their hopefulness about how likely the problem is to be solved. Then encourage them to account for differences in their ratings:

- "What is it that you, Joan, know about the marriage that John doesn't know, that makes you more hopeful the marriage can be improved?"
- "What is it that you, John, know about the marriage that Joan does not know that makes you less hopeful the marriage can be helped?"
- "On a scale on 1–10, with 10 meaning you have totally achieved the goals you came to therapy for, and 1 meaning you haven't started yet, where would you rate yourself today?" ("4") "OK, that's great! Now what do you need to do to move from a 4 to a 5? What would be the next thing to do?"

(e) Positive description frame: Patients often frame their goals in negative terms, meaning they describe what will be *missing* when they have achieved what they hope for. "I won't feel so bad all the time." "I will stop drinking." "My husband will stop being so angry and insulting."

In this situation, the therapist must ask, "What will you/he/she/it do instead?" The word, "instead" is the operant term here. A positive, achievable replacement must be found for negative goals.

- "What will you be doing instead of drinking?"
- "What kinds of feelings will you notice instead of the depressed, bad feelings?"
- "What will you do when you feel those more positive feelings?"
- "What will your husband say when he disagrees instead of his present insults?"

(f) The relevant effects frame: the therapist asks for the impact of positive and negative experiences by asking:

- "How is that a problem to you?" Rather than assuming the therapist knows what a patient means by labeling a problem state ("I have panic attacks"), the therapist carefully maps out with the patient how the complaint interferes with the patient's life.

- "How did that help?" Whenever a patient is pleased about something, the same mapping process enlightens both therapist and patient about the effect of the positive event.

    These questions resemble White's mapping the influence of the
problem and mapping the influence of the persons. The question,
"How does that help?" is quite useful when something positive has
happened. For example, a patient reported he was able to get out of
bed and do something instead of lying there feeling depressed. The
therapist's comments are in italics.

    "How did that help?"

    "Well, I just felt better about myself."

    *"Yes, you felt better about yourself. How does it help you to feel better about
yourself?"*

    "Oh, I kept doing a few things. I did a little work in my garden,
and I smiled more at my wife."

    "That's great! How did it help when you smiled at your wife?"

    "You know, she was quite pleased."

    "I can imagine. What did she do when she felt pleased?"

    "She was nicer to the kids, you know, more patient. In fact, now
that I think about it, the whole day seemed to go better after that."

    "How did that help the kids, when she was more patient?"

    And so it goes. Positive descriptions emphasize the power and
strength of the patient's own behavior by linking it recursively with
all sorts of responses from others.

(g) The individual and the relationship metaframes: Each question from
the preceding frames can be asked from the *individual* perspective or
from the *relationship* perspective. The relationship perspective helps the
client to feel empathy for other persons and to see him/herself as others
see him/her. For example, the individual frame of the scaling question
might be: "On a scale of 1–10, how ready do you feel you are to stop
your drinking?" A relationship question would be: "If your wife were
here today, and I asked her to estimate on a 1–10 scale how ready you
are to give up your drinking, *what do you think she would say?*"

    You can practice varying the solution-focused questions, asking from
both a relationship and an individual perspective.

8. Identify times or areas when the client is competent or capable and
generalize that to other contexts (O'Hanlon & Beadle, 1994; O'Hanlon &
Weiner-Davis, 1989). For example, a woman who trained horses for a
living and complained of how her husband would not cooperate could be
asked how she would design a training program for a stubborn horse.

This approach has two aspects. First, when the patient is talking about a problem area and the therapist (perhaps using a Colombo-like confused tone) asks about an area of strength, there is some surprise because of the juxtaposition of two incompatible associations.

Client: "I feel helpless to change his mind."

Counselor: "Your job as a teacher involves changing minds everyday. Do you usually feel this helpless when you need to change the mind of a student?"

Directly link the association to competence to the new situation.

Client: "She just won't talk about the problems in the marriage."

Counselor: "As an attorney, you are used to setting up times when people are going to talk about areas they disagree on. Can you use some of those skills to set up a specific time to argue about this problem?"

We can see that changing meanings and understandings, regardless of how that is achieved, is a common theme in all psychotherapy, and perhaps we can now agree that *reframing* is a reasonable label for that activity. Here is a final example.

Case Example: The Stubborn Pianist

Years ago my son was taking piano lessons. He was given a piece to play at a Halloween recital. It was in a minor key and was supposed to be played slowly. He played it rapidly, in spite of what his teacher and his mother said. They couldn't get him to slow down.

I listened to him practice one day, and told him I thought it was good he played it fast. He asked why.

"That is a scary piece of music, and the faster you play it, the less people who listen will be scared!"

"Dad," he said scornfully, "it is supposed to be scary."

"Oh." I paused. "Well, maybe if you played it slow, it would be too scary. Try it both ways. I think you will feel more comfortable if you play it fast."

He began playing it slowly. I was pleased and told my wife what I had done. She ridiculed me, saying it was because he finally decided to listen to her, and it had nothing to do with my reframing. I am sure she is right.

Avoiding Danger

There is some risk to seeing surprise as a common element of therapy. A therapist who is undisciplined or wild in his or her interventions may say things for the shock value and may actually harm the patient. Confrontation is not a therapeutic surprise. While it may occasionally be helpful, it is often not useful, and is probably overused by therapists, including myself, with little imagination and empathy. Therapists must constantly bear in mind that a positive therapeutic relationship is the basis of all interventions, and when this is lost, the treatment may become psychonoxious and harmful.

CHAPTER 6

The Tasks of the Patient: Utilizing Homework in Psychotherapy

There is a folk story of a wise old man who is revered by the people in his village. Each day he sits in the town square and the citizens ask for his thoughts and observations on their problems. He loves them and helps them, and they cherish his help and love him.

In this village there is a young tough who leads a group of adolescents, rebels without a clue. The youth is jealous of the old man and the respect he is given. He hatches a plot to discredit the elder. He tells his gang, "I will put a bird in my hand, and close my fingers around it. I will say, 'Old man, there is a bird in my hand. Does it live, or is it dead?' If he says it is alive, I will crush it and open my hand to prove it is dead. But if he says it is dead, I will open my hand and it will fly away. He will be wrong no matter what he says."

So the gang proceeds to the town square, and the young man says, "Old man, there is a bird in my hand. Does it live or is it dead?"

The old man smiles sadly at the youth and replies, "The bird lives or dies according to your will, for it is in your hand."

Effective therapy conveys a similar message. Our own destiny is much more in our hands than we may think. While we cannot control what happens to us, due to outside forces, random happenstance, or fate, our reactions to what happens is in our control, to a greater or lesser degree.

It is clear that patients who actively carry out homework benefit more than those who do not (Burns & Nolen-Hoeksema, 1992; Gelso & Johnson, 1983). The Gelso and Johnson analysis suggested that patients who continue to benefit from therapy after formal termination are those who are actively involved in therapy, seeming to see themselves as the dynamic factor and not depending on passively attending therapy to make them different.

It appears that client factors (including activity, openness, motivation to change, ability to form trusting relationships) contributes about 40% of the variation in therapy outcome, while therapist technique only contributes 15% (Lambert, 1992; Miller, Hubble, & Duncan, 1995). This leads Miller, Hubble, and Duncan to suggest that therapists be reluctant in making claims for the superiority of particular therapy technique, compared with influence of client factors, therapy relationship, and expectancy and placebo factors. In my view, this is far too pessimistic. Wise therapists learn to impact client expectations, improve the therapy relationship, and fit in with the factors a client brings to the session, assigning homework that fits with those factors.

Not all therapists utilize homework. I once asked a skilled psychodynamic brief therapist why he didn't use homework assignments. He said he thought it would infantilize the patient and create dependency. He did expect spontaneous behavior change on the part of the patient, but wouldn't provide the direction that assignments would require.

I disagree. Well-designed homework reduces dependency on the therapist and increases the patient's feeling of personal responsibility for therapy outcome. In part this may be due to the increase in self-efficacy. The patient sees he has made a difference; he then feels more powerful and competent.

But another reason for a diminishing of dependency is that homework takes some time to do, so a therapist will seldom schedule a follow-up session the next week (see Chapter 7). Usually, when the homework is well-accepted and seems to make sense to all concerned, two or three weeks are allowed to complete that homework assignment. Unhealthy dependency doesn't develop, since the patient's attention is away from the relationship with the therapist and on the responses she elicits from the environment.

In consulting with therapists having trouble with homework, I have noticed some patterns. Here are some suggestions in regard to homework that may be helpful.

GENERAL SUGGESTIONS ABOUT HOMEWORK

Take Small Steps

Is the client a customer (see Chapter 3) for a change of behavior? Some are not. A person may be only a customer for understanding, insight, or exploring the past. Initially, at least, such patients will resist homework, since they see the problem as existing in the past or in other relationships, such as "my family of origin," not within themselves, not in the present or the future. These patients may have been in therapy with counselors who have socialized them into this view.

Now assume there is a true customer in the office, someone who both acknowledges a problem and wants to work hard to change it. When we do decide to assign homework? It is good to go rather slowly. Effective brief therapy is usually very small steps done slowly. Two homework assignments in a single session are too many; likewise, complicated homework assignments may do more damage to the therapy relationship than any good that might come from them. Give small homework assignments that you are sure the client will be able to complete. Assign a person to do something once, twice at the very most, and you have a chance of their doing it more. Since a small homework assignment that they will do a few times is easier to succeed at, this gives the therapist many chances to compliment the client on progress.

If your assignment is "do this from now on," clients are likely to fail. This might be positive for some patients, as you give them a chance to learn to tolerate failure. Some people learn more from failure than others; however, it is wise to limit the patients to whom you offer this particular gift.

Some of the desire to give large assignments comes from watching certain famous therapists who give comprehensive homework that does not allow for exceptions. I am sure they have a rationale for this, and it may be they can summon up the emotional climate to motivate clients better than I can. I frankly do not know how these therapists manage the problems I find from this style of homework. If you get good results from the all-or-none homework, then keep up the good work. But if you are like me, you may want to take smaller bites of the problem.

Accept and Utilize the Patient's Goals

The therapist who is grimly focused on solutions or behavior change will have difficulty with patients who are seeking self-understanding. We might call these people complainants, but this is not quite accurate. They are customers for a certain kind of relationship ("My therapist should understand me") and certain goals ("I should understand myself"). They might insist on a global view of their problem ("I am codependent"), which makes small, concrete changes in viewing/doing unlikely. We can accept and work within their framework but carefully, gradually, and respectfully change their views of the temporal and interpersonal location of the problem. Such patients are appreciated by the wise therapist, since she realizes they are a chance for her to become more skillful at reframing. Here we might want to dust off our skills at making defense and transference interpretations, since that is what the client seems to value.

Another approach is to reframe their focus on self-understanding as positive, since it makes change happen more slowly. Change can be dangerous and unpredictable. Homework might be symbolic or ambiguous assignments, asking the client what he learned about himself with each assignment. This accomplishes a similar result to the dynamic interpretations, namely, to give one the experience of learning about oneself. The specifics of ambiguous and symbolic assignments are explored later.

Remember, if the therapist cannot see a truth behind the reframing, and offer it with sincerity, it is better left unsaid. If the therapist fails to recognize the danger of change, perhaps the therapist has led a charmed life safely devoid of many changes, or is a rare individual for whom change has been only positive. In any case, a naive person might offer that reframing in a sarcastic way, undermining the therapy relationship. The patient who does not want behavioral change, who only wants understanding, may have an unknown reason for fearing change; the implicit wisdom of the patient should be assumed and validated.

Follow Up and Maintain Focus

The patient who requests change in behavior, relationship change, or simply self-understanding should receive homework experiments consistent with those goals, and this focus should be maintained. In other words, each session of accountable therapy will include a section where the patient reports on what has been done with the previous session's work. Rather than ask, "What do you want to work on today?" inquire, "What was your reaction to last session? What did you do and how did it work?"

If the therapist begins the session with an inquiry about how the homework went (and obviously has written down what the homework was, so the inquiry is accurate), there is a powerful communication that the homework is an important, even essential aspect of the therapy. Occasionally, I have consulted with a therapist who designed a useful bit of homework, but began the subsequent session with "What do you want to talk about today?" Not only was this the wrong question, but it was also disrespectful to the therapy and to the patient. If the patient did the homework, there should be a time to talk about that; if the client did not do homework, some time should be spend finding out why. Further therapy work should be put on hold until this question is thoroughly investigated.

It is not unusual for the homework to be rejected by the patient in favor of something that works even better. If at first it appears the homework was not done, it is useful patiently to inquire about what the patient has done differently in the intervening time. If a better coping is discovered, of course the client is heartily congratulated for her insight into the problem. The therapist ought to inquire into how likely the patient is to continue that good behavior, helping the patient to troubleshoot her own solutions.

Be Sensitive to Client Values and Abilities

Therapists might inadvertently assign homework that violates values or perceived abilities of the client. It is useful to carefully question the client about his reactions to the homework assignment, and to troubleshoot any problems the client can anticipate. Can the client think of specific times to accomplish the homework? Can he think of how to overcome any resistance or reluctance? Does the patient think he can accept the reactions of others to the homework assignment? Does the client think he will feel pride or a sense of accomplishment from the homework? All of these sorts of questions help the client to reframe and rethink objections. It seems quite likely that we will find some problems as we ask the questions. I would rather learn about these problems there in the session than discover them later.

Keep a Souvenir of the Problem

It is important to retain some part of the problem behavior in a literal or symbolic fashion when assigning homework. For example, the client can do homework on odd numbered days and continue to do the old behavior on even numbered days; then he can compare how the two strategies work. Some clients insist on keeping much of their old problem behavior. Milton Erickson once treated a man who was very resentful and angry. Erickson used hypnosis to transfer that resentment onto shrubs which were closer than 18 inches from the sidewalks. All his resentment was focused on shrubs.

Very few people have the kind of motivation and self-discipline to abandon an old habit or behavior completely, so it is foolish for us as therapists to give a homework assignment that presupposes such an abandonment. Make space for the client to be ambivalent about leaving that behavior.

Make Homework Concrete

Homework is a physical, behavioral task, a change in a pattern of action, not a change in thinking. Less experienced therapists will often tell me their homework assignment to a client was to "think about such-and-such." This is not homework, and unless the client is that rare person who never thinks about anything, such a suggestion does not even constitute a shift in client behavior. As such, it is an eloquent testimony to the exceedingly high self-esteem that many new therapists seem to possess, in that they think that a simple suggestion to think about some rather pedestrian observation will bring about a profound change in the perceptions and behavior of the client. Giving such homework is an opportunity to develop a sense of humility and appreciation for our limitations as therapists.

Attend to Motivation

Think carefully about what will motivate this particular client to carry out a homework assignment or behavioral experiment. Some clients are motivated by family presence, so that an assignment given in the context of the whole family is more likely to be carried out than one given to the client alone. Other clients are motivated by the therapist's reviewing all the ways they have failed to solve the problem, while some clients find their motivation suffers with that strategy. In other words, there is no universal motivational strategy, since persons vary so much.

Use a scaling question after offering a homework assignment. How likely is it, on a 1–10 scale, that the patient will carry out the homework? One equals totally unlikely, and 10 equals totally likely. The patient can often give a very accurate estimate. The therapist can then simply ask, "What would have to change in your thinking or feelings to move that up one step?"

It is also useful to ask the patient, "What would make your commitment to do the homework move down one step?" They can then find ways to inoculate against that possibility.

Cialdini (1984) offers suggestions from social psychology to enhance compliance, including the ploy of asking the patient to do something rather small at first; then ask for a larger commitment to something more difficult. Barlow's (1988; Barlow & Craske, 1990) protocols for panic unintentionally follow this: He requires some very difficult homework, namely paradoxically creating the very feeling the patient has always fled. He achieves this seemingly impossible task by asking the patient to do smaller and easier homework assignments first.

Cialdini (1984) also points out the importance of consistency in people's self-concept. He suggests that if a person writes down and signs a small document about the importance of performing an act, that person is very likely to carry out a much more difficult act.

So therapists ought to (1) structure their sessions so the patient makes and keeps commitments within the session that serve as patterns for later cooperation outside; (2) give homework in small, graduated steps over several sessions; (3) ask the patient to make some sort of public commitment to small acts (e.g., the signing and sharing of a small pledge or commitment).

Motivation is affected by how the therapist gives the homework. If the therapist is earnest and sincere, the patient will take the homework more seriously. Some therapists convey a sense of inattention or insincerity when they give assignments and then are surprised when the client does not carry out the experiment. I vividly remember Milton Erickson sitting in his wheelchair, outside his office, talking earnestly and intensely about some homework he wanted me to do. I was struck with his power and sincerity. Because of that heartfelt desire on his part that I do the task, I felt a mighty commitment to do so.

The specific tasks of homework flow naturally out of the way the therapist conceptualizes human difficulties. Cognitive therapists tend to locate and assign homework that focuses on the individual's thinking processes; behavior therapists create homework that changes contingencies; strategic therapists tend to focus on reversing the attempted solutions; systems-oriented therapists tend to shift family structure and hierarchies. A coherent theory of human behavior is useful in generating homework. The sections below emphasize only those approaches to homework with which I am familiar. I am certain there are many more that are just as (or even more) useful and valid.

COGNITIVE-BEHAVIORAL APPROACHES
TO HOMEWORK

Cognitive-behavioral approaches are a rich source of ideas about patient involvement. For example, Barlow (1988) proposed an avoidance-learning-based theory of panic disorder, suggesting that the core avoidance was not to external stimuli, such as grocery stores, but to internal stimuli, such as rapid heartbeat, paresthesia, and so forth. Thus, his interventions center on helping patients desensitize to their own fears. (This homework comes only after the patient has done other, less threatening homework for several weeks.)

During the session, the client and therapist target a specific panic symptom, such as dizziness, and the client is asked to produce that symptom. The notion behind such a paradoxical task is usually easy to explain, focusing on the role of avoidance in maintaining the symptom. Dizziness can usually be produced by asking the patient to shake her head back and forth or to spin around in the office swivel chair. After the patient spins around for one minute, she will feel quite dizzy, and that feeling may trigger nervousness. The patient rates (on a 1–10 or 1–100 scale) how nervous she feels. Then the therapist discusses the meanings the patient attributes to being dizzy, and reframes or restructures them. The patient again spins around in the chair, rates her level of panic, and discusses the thoughts underlying the fear. The patient spins again. Usually each iteration of the process results in lower ratings of panic, and dizziness begins to mean something less threatening.

Having established in the session that the patient can reduce symptoms by voluntarily creating them over and over, the therapist gives the patient the homework assignment of repeating that process at home. Several times during the week, the patient will induce dizziness in herself and scale how fearful she feels after each time.

For a patient who is fearful when his heart begins to pound, the therapist can (with proper medical clearance) help the patient induce elevated heart rate through mild exercise. For example, the patient can step on and off a 12-inch step. After one minute, the patient's heart will be beating vigorously, and he can be quizzed about his level of fear and his cognitions. Once his heart rate comes down, he again exercises and elevates the heart rate.

A patient who is reactive to feelings of being hot and closed in can sit in a sauna or ride in a hot car with windows rolled up. After a short time the patient can step out of the stressful environment and scale the fear, then step back into the provocative situation.

A patient who has any of the many symptoms of hyperventilation (such as a tight chest, paresthesia, and shortness of breath) will be encouraged to hyperventilate for a minute or two. The same process is followed, with the patient inducing the symptom over and over.

Barlow's belief is that, once the patient desensitizes him or herself to the physical symptoms, there will be little or no reaction when the symptoms occur spontaneously. The homework, the desensitization paradigm, emerges directly from the theory he espouses.

Barlow's approach also exemplifies the rule about going slowly and asking for small changes before asking for big ones. Usually, the patient has done several easier things before these difficult homework assignments are offered. First, she has tracked her symptoms, producing a record of when she has the panics, how they start, what her thoughts and theories are about them, and how long they last. She begins to see a relationship between her thinking and the panic symptoms.

Next she practices stress management skills, such as progressive relaxation and controlled breathing. The controlled breathing homework consists of pacing breathing to teach the patient not to hyperventilate. I have also used diaphragmatic breathing, extending the out-breath so it takes longer than the in-breath, and following a rhythm so as to counteract any tendency to hyperventilate. After the patient is skilled at supportive self-talk, at physical relaxation and breathing control, she is ready for the proprioceptive desensitization.

Case Example: Take a Deep Breath

I recently saw a woman who complained about panic attacks. She had done breathing and relaxation homework, but this was insufficient to reverse the panic attacks. Her symptoms of the panic were a feeling of pressure and "fuzziness" in her head, cold feet, and dizziness. She believed that she would "fall apart" in front of a group she had to speak to, meaning she would faint or have a heart attack.

It seemed likely to me that she had been hyperventilating to cause the attack, so I suggested she hyperventilate in the office. I gave her a target of hyperventilating for one minute. After she understood the rationale, she began to pant and breathe rapidly. Within 20 seconds, she felt the pressure and fuzziness in her head and noticed her feet were going cold. As she continued, I asked her to describe and counter the mental processes she was noticing, such as the theory that the feelings were because of a stroke or the fear she would lose control in the office.

After a minute, she stopped and I asked her to do her controlled breathing. She did, and immediately all her symptoms dramatically reversed. We repeated that process several times, and by the end of the session she was committed to performing the homework. As a result of that homework, she gained confidence in her ability to notice and respond to hyperventilation and she lost her fear of the symptoms, seeing them as helpful signs that she had begun to hyperventilate. She had no more panic attacks.

Similarly, Beck's (Beck et al., 1979) theory about depression suggests the central importance of thinking patterns. The homework that emerges from that involves tracking and challenging cognitions. Beck suggests writing down thoughts in a diary and assigning labels to the thoughts to identify irrational patterns. The patient may choose from a list of faulty thinking patterns, such as using a mental filter and all-or-none thinking. Then the patient generates an alternative cognition to challenge the dysfunctional thought.

Another homework assignment is the prediction task. The depressed patient may not involve herself in activities because she predicts she will not enjoy them. The patient is asked to predict, on a 1–10 scale, how much she will enjoy the activity, with 1 = no fun at all and 10 = more fun than allowed in most states. Then she attends the activity and *postdicts* (i.e., rates after the fact) how much fun she actually had.

Now Beck's theory, that faulty cognitions underlie the depressive process, is not really any better than the theory behind interpersonal therapy (Klerman, Weissman, & Rousaville, 1984), which suggests that depression is an interpersonal process arising out of a client's reaction to one of four general content categories: grief, interpersonal disputes, role transitions, and interpersonal skill deficits. Each category has particular homework assignments, designed to help the patient address those stressors in an integrative way. Both cognitive and interpersonal therapy focus on changing the patient's views and increasing his activity.

Homework from the cognitive-behavioral approaches has a good deal of appeal to therapists. It is based on a learning model, something which therapists understand. There is a nice step-by-step feeling to the approach, which allows the therapist and the client to assume they are following a reasonable, rational approach. There are many treatment protocols available that are based on cognitive-behavioral theory (Barlow, 1993; Giles, 1993). All in all, there is a good deal to recommend in these approaches.

STRATEGIC APPROACHES TO HOMEWORK

In contrast to cognitive-behavioral approaches, strategic approaches emphasize homework that has more symbolic or systemic impact. The strategic view is characterized by exquisite sensitivity to interpersonal meanings and attributions. For instance, homework for a rebellious teenager might include a suggestion that he actually do what his parents are asking him to do, but at the wrong time or in the wrong place. He might decide to work hard on his homework at 11:00 p.m., or on the kitchen table on Sunday morning when the family wants to have brunch. Another example: a 12-year old patient objected to being forced to practice the piano. I agreed that would make anyone angry, but suggested life has many such obnoxious tasks in it. Why not make it more pleasant? He was curious how. I suggested that he had to practice, but he could choose the time. He ought to choose a time inconvenient to others in the family, to see whether that made his practice more pleasant.

Strategic views also incorporate a flavor of hypnosis, expecting spontaneous elaborated change from simple interventions. Strategic homework may also appeal to an artistic or symbolic aspect of the patient. Thus, a patient who feels he has hit a wall in his life might be assigned the task of seeking out walls and fences and figuring out how to climb over or get around them. He might be told to investigate how walls are useful, and perhaps to write an essay on the positive features of walls.

Strategic therapy arises out of the work of Milton H. Erickson, the legendary psychiatrist and hypnotist, and out of interpretations of his work by two men who studied intensively with him in the 1950s, Jay Haley and John Weakland. Much of what we know about Erickson, and many strategic techniques of treatment (such as the solution-focused questions of the Milwaukee group, the use of hypnosis advocated by Budman and Gurman, many family therapy techniques, and the use of symbolic homework assignments) arise from them. Quibblers will argue that there are other sources for paradox, assignments, and family intervention, but pragmatically, it is through the publications and workshops of the groups which coalesced around Haley and Weakland that we know of these techniques.

I have arranged strategic and systemic homework into five categories: (1) ambiguous function assignments; (2) paradoxical assignments; (3) symbolic assignments; (4) pattern interruption; and (5) solution-focused assignments.

Ambiguous Function Assignments

I corresponded occasionally with Milton Erickson in the mid-'70s, and he was quite kind and encouraging of my efforts to master hypnosis skills. Finally I screwed up my courage and asked if I could come and watch him work. Soon I was heading to Phoenix with a colleague and friend, Jay Wilimek. The two of us spent a week meeting with Erickson every day.

At the end of our first day with Erickson, he assigned us the task of climbing Squaw Peak, a small mountain in Phoenix. However, we had been on the road for 13 hours, had been through a ferocious winter storm in northern Arizona, and had been in a minor fender bender. Exhausted, we decided to head to a cheap motel and get some sleep.

The next day, Erickson listened to our report (we hadn't done our assignment). He started to talk about all the things people can learn from climbing Squaw Peak, and went on and on for what seemed like hours on the growth someone might achieve from carrying out the assignment. I thought he would never let up. At the end of that day's work, Erickson told us to visit the botanical gardens. We did.

Not complying with Erickson's first assignment bothered me so much that, years later, after his death, I went to Phoenix, got up very early one morning, and climbed Squaw Peak. I passed a lot of people who were going down and strolling up. I noticed a couple of places where I could have stopped, but I kept going, reached the peak, and clambered up some rocks to stand on the very highest point. Phoenix is a beautiful city, early in the morning and seen from a high point. I cannot say I achieved anything from doing it. While it was an interesting climb, it certainly was not a "peak" experience. But the fact that I felt I had to do it illustrates one of the great advantages of an assignment with an ambiguous function: It intensifies the relationship between the therapist and the patient.

The assignment is like a Rorschach card, something in which the client will find personal meaning by projecting his or her own experiences. Lankton and Lankton (1986) emphasize that the well-constructed ambiguous function assignment does not have a symbolic meaning of which the therapist is aware. They assign elaborate ritualistic activities for patients, such as carrying around the block buckets containing different cargos (such as feathers one time and water another), or going to the top of a tall building and gazing at the sunset through one's wedding ring, framed by two sterling silver spoons. They emphasize that they attach no secret symbolic meaning to such rituals; the patient will be responsible for assigning meaning.

The notion behind the ambiguous function assignments is that, since the therapist truly does not know what meaning will result, there will be a symbolic shift of responsibility from the therapist to the patient. Erickson had no way of knowing what sorts of personal meanings Jay and I would take from looking at boojum trees, creeping devils, and other bizarre Sonoran life forms at the botanical gardens. When we questioned him about those assignments, his rationale (at least the rationale he was willing to share) was that they provide a rich variety of stimuli to foster new interpretations of ourselves and our world.

But the fact that the therapist doesn't know the meaning of the assignment doesn't obviate the need for careful planning. An ambiguous function assignment must be quite specific, involving some particular behaviors, to be done in a certain place, and likely at a certain time. The Heard Museum, the Botanical Gardens, or Squaw Peak are all specific places Erickson sent us. There was some expectation that the time would be in the afternoon, after we had left his office. There was a particular sequence implied (e.g., one goes into the museum, travels around the display cases, and lingers over the ironwood carvings).

Lankton and Lankton recommend that the client be strongly encouraged to create a meaning, so the therapist questions the client after the homework is done, asking, "What did you learn from that? What did you notice? What did you think? How does that relate to the problem you came to see me about? What else might that mean? What else? What else?" They recommend that the therapist appear to the client to have a secret meaning; whatever meaning the client constructs, the therapist says, "Yes, that's right. And what else?" Thus, they imply there are many ways to interpret any particular situation.

I have experimented with ambiguous function assignments, but they don't really fit my personality or approach, and I seldom use them. They are not for everybody. But there are versions of ambiguous function assignments which I often do assign, with good results. These are called "skeleton key assignments."

A skeleton key is a key that will fit many different locks (de Shazer, 1985). Rather than matching homework to a unique problem (e.g., *in vivo* desensitization to phobias, and diary of cognitions for depression), one can choose a skeleton key assignment with the capacity to unlock many different problems. The assignment is not quite ambiguous, since many of the advantages are immediately apparent. The ambiguity lies in the fact that it focuses away from the presenting complaint and stimulates independent thinking on the part of the patient.

De Shazer suggests that when nothing else can be thought of, a *formula first-session task* can be assigned. This task is an information-gathering task. The patient is instructed to pay close attention, between this session and the next, to what happens in his life that he wants to continue. The therapist promises to ask about those perceptions in the next session and, in fact, does so. This attention to what was learned and how that helped can be powerful. By expecting a client to see something, and then searching until the client does report something of value, the therapist indirectly conveys a helpful meta-learning: Life's meanings consist not of what happens to us, but what we look for and choose to notice, and how we interpret those perceptions.

Paradoxical Assignments

Paradoxical assignments have attracted a good deal of attention, but few therapists actually use them. Paradox changes the problem by encouraging it, so the therapist must find some reason why the patient should do the very thing he wants to be rid of. The result is that the problem disappears, either because the patient rebels against the therapist's injunction or because the problem itself is dissolved by the act of cooperating with it.

The patient's rebelling against the therapist is seen in the treatment of anorexia in family therapy. The counselor reframes the symptoms of anorexia as serving a useful function in the family, and therefore the patient is making a noble personal sacrifice to aid the family. The family is asked to thank the patient for this relinquishing of her own interests. The patient and family usually appear to coalesce against the therapist, losing the symptoms in the process. But this may be one of the reasons that this type of paradox, which depends on the patient resisting the therapist's instructions, is so unpopular. The therapist may not be able to see the deeper truth behind the paradox, and thus feels tricky. This will inevitably "leak" in communication with the client. Therefore paradox will fail, and the patient will feel angry and alienated. These are high stakes, ones which many therapists cannot tolerate, and which they wisely avoid.

But there is a deeper truth in paradox, and if the therapist can think deeply enough so as to find it, then the intervention becomes the only reasonable one. I have seldom used true paradox, but have done so occasionally, and with very good results.

Case Example: Help Me And I Will Kill Myself

A man came to me weighing over 450 pounds. He owned a restaurant and ate compulsively. He drank a quart of whiskey a day. And he felt constantly suicidal.

He had been to see several therapists in the area, who had told him it would be necessary for him to stop overeating and stop his abusive drinking before they could treat him for the depressive feelings and suicidal thoughts. However, when he tried to carry out their instructions, he became dangerously suicidal. The more good advice they gave the more suicidal he became.

There were few useful options open to me. It seemed to me quitting his overeating and his drinking would be necessary before he could feel better, but this was precisely the thing I could not say. In fact, in a certain way, he rebelled against the previous therapists, saying, "See, you are making me worse." Since he had rebelled against some very fine therapists, I had no hope he would not rebel against my good advice.

My only intervention seemed to be paradox. Accordingly, at the end of the first session, I told him I did not understand what was going on, but it seemed to me that there was a great deal of danger in his trying to improve. (This was obviously totally true, since he did become acutely suicidal when he tried to improve.) I told him that it seemed to me that somehow his overeating and his drinking were necessary in ways I did not understand. Since neither he nor I understood them, it seemed to me we should just assume they were some sort of crutches which he found indispensable. I didn't know if I should even tell him this, but it occurred to me that if he were to throw away those crutches, he would likely fall flat on his face. I advised him against making any changes. My use of "paradox" here was based on my understanding of the situation, *from his point of view*. I attempted to put myself into that point of view and make recommendations based on his experience of the world.

The man returned the next week and informed me he hadn't had a drink for a week and was feeling somewhat better. I thought about how my consultant, John Weakland, had often said, "Never change a winning game," and realized I had to continue on the same track. I told him I felt rather worried about this sudden change (quite true, since he had recently been suicidal), and I was still convinced there was a deep need in him for these self-damaging behaviors (How could the need for them disappear so soon?). Perhaps he should be careful about such rapid change. At the very least, I suggested, he should continue to overeat during the week. He rebelled against that instruction, and thus therapy progressed. After ten or so visits, when we had discovered what his hopelessness was about, he mentioned that he liked talking to me better than other therapists. I was surprised and asked why, and he said, "Well, when you say things, I really have to think about them." He remained sober and lost over 250 pounds. He also quit the restaurant industry and opened a weight-loss business. He would show his clients his "before" pictures, and let them try on the pants he used to wear. It was very motivational for them.

For me successful paradox always involves this quality of a patient feeling some kind of compulsion to resist good advice. Since I don't find such people very often, I seldom use paradox. It is a valuable tool that needs to be used only occasionally. Note that if I had not practiced some flexibility in my own thinking, I would have become another in a string of therapeutic failures for my patient. It is clearly not the case that I am smarter than the other therapists; I recognized some of them and knew them to be my intellectual superiors. Rather, I had the advantage of some training and supervision in paradoxical intervention, so I was able to use it when it was useful.

Much work that sounds paradoxical is not. Rather, it is paradoxical intention, where the patient does not rebel but rather performs the symptom he had been resisting so as to gain control of it. For example, see the work of the Mental Research Institute (MRI) group. Most of their homework is designed to be obeyed (Fisch, Weakland, & Segal, 1982). As they say, "in our own view the use of paradoxes as interventions is relatively rare" (p. 127). Their view is that the problem is being maintained by ineffective or self-defeating efforts to solve it. Some good examples are depression and anxiety. In both, the patient is usually trying to control her own feelings, and the harder she tries, the more she fails. The anxious patient tries not to feel jumpy and monitors herself moment-to-moment for any evidence that she is failing in that quest for control of involuntary symptoms. However, if the patient tries to produce rather than avoid the symptoms, the problem can be rapidly dissolved.

Case Example: Paralyzed with Depression

A young man consulted me for episodes of incapacitating depression. The symptoms were worst during his workday, so that often he would flee to the men's restroom and sit in a stall for an hour or two at a time, avoiding work. Sitting in the restroom was an attempt on his part to avoid feeling the depression, supposing that if he were to try to accomplish something at work, it would only get worse.

It seemed to me that there was something mysterious about this depression, and that there might be some valuable information embedded within it. I suggested that, as the poet says, "the way out is through," and mentioned that the depression came at inconvenient times, since work was not a helpful place to try to understand oneself. I suggested he schedule the depressions in the evenings, when he could concentrate on them. I suggested he take between 30 and 60 minutes to try to be as depressed as possible; during that time, he should resist any cheering thoughts. He should keep a diary of his feelings and thoughts. We decided that from 8 to 9 p.m. would be the ideal time for him to experience his depression.

After a week he reported that the daytime depressions had vanished, and when he felt a depressed feeling coming on, he would make note of the thoughts and feelings in a small notebook so he could concentrate on them during his depression time. He was productive at work and felt better. However, he did have something to talk about which he had hoped to avoid, and he proceeded to do that.

Symbolic Assignments

Here is something that many patients genuinely enjoy. The assignment addresses something symbolic about the presenting problem, and feels to the client like a ritual that allows for a resolution to the problem. If you have an artistic flair and enjoy drama (I have little of the artist and don't enjoy drama), you may do well with this style of homework. When I have opposed my natural tendency and assigned symbolic homework, it has had excellent results, and I do recommend it.

In constructing symbolic homework, we emphasize how the homework will serve as a *transition* from one state to another. For example, strategic therapists like to use the write-read-burn assignment with patients who have experienced abuse. They encourage the patient to write down the terrible things that have happened to her. A day later the patient should read the description to another person, a trusted confidant. Then, in the presence of that witness, the client burns the description. This homework is repeated several times, until the patient feels the incident is being healed within her.

Here there is an emphasis on the irrational quality of human construction of reality. There might be some desensitization effect from reading the description of the client's experiences and reactions, but the burning is another matter entirely. Why does that have such a liberating effect on the client? What is it in our makeup that loves ritual and symbol?

Case Example: Please Release Me

A woman felt a sense of bondage toward a powerful person who had once played a large role in her life. Feeling a need for the approval of this man, she would still compulsively explain what she was doing in her life when she would encounter him in social or professional circles. He did not seem to require this, and the patient thought of it as an internal problem, not one between the two of them. I asked her to write about her dilemma in the form of a letter to him, and bring her letter and an envelope with her to the next session. We might or might not send it.

During the session, we cut parts of the letter out, making one pile for positive experiences and another pile for negative experiences. We put the positive experiences into the envelope and then took the negative ones out into an empty field and burned them. We then buried the ashes and marked the spot with a small stone. We returned to the office and she agreed she would do anything to be rid of this compulsion. So we mailed the other part of the letter, the positive experiences, to her former superior, as I extracted a solemn promise that she would never explain why she had done that. This was easy for her to promise, since she didn't quite know why she had done it herself.

She later found she felt a remarkable sense of liberty around this man, and to her surprise he never asked her about the letter. (He might not have known who it was from.) Her compulsion never bothered her again.

If you have a flair for this, it won't be hard to construct transition rituals, but if you want to incorporate rituals but don't seem to think them up easily, here is a suggestion: Ask patients to search for a symbol of their current life. This symbol should be something that appeals to them, but they don't know why. They might find it in a flea market or an expensive store, it could be old or new, it could be something from the attic or something they get from a friend. They are to call for an appointment when they have located this symbol. They bring it to a session and discuss it, and they then dispose of it in some symbolic way.

Next, they seek a symbol of how their life will be after therapy has completed the changes they want in their life. They bring this future-oriented symbol and discuss that. Patients find this an invigorating and motivating experience.

Reframing or change of meaning is intimately associated with the home-work. For instance, a therapist was seeing a couple who bickered and argued constantly. After observing this, he suggested a particular way to see their bickering as being like children who say, "Did not!" "Did so!" "Did not!" "Did so!" The spouses were willing to admit that there was truth in what he said. He then suggested that this childish pattern was actually a desire on both their parts to bring youthfulness and childish enthusiasm back into their middle-aged lives. They agreed with some surprise that it was a possibility. The homework for them was to shop for convertibles. Not only did they do so, but they bought a classic restored convertible and greatly enjoyed driving around in it. They felt the homework reduced their arguing significantly and driving around in the convertible gave them a common activity to enjoy.

Pattern Interruption

Many of Milton Erickson's assignments disrupted patterns in patient's symptoms. Pattern interruption follows his lead by asking the patients to perform certain behaviors in a different way and notice the result. This homework is based on the notion that people are quite patterned in their lives, and when a pattern is disrupted, there is space made for a new behavior to emerge. The patterns can be discerned by an alert therapist who asks about when the problem occurs, in what context, how long it takes, how the patient attributes meaning to the symptom, how the patient responds to the symptoms, how others respond, and so forth.

For example, suppose a couple argues vehemently. The pattern we discern is for each person to interrupt the other to correct some misperception. It can be predicted that each partner has a unit of time during which he will allow the other to speak without interruption, and when that time is up, the partner interrupts. If the amount of time is changed, so that the uninterrupted time is doubled or tripled, a change in the relationship is likely to result.

Some ways to intervene in patterns (O'Hanlon, 1987) are to change:

- time of occurrence, duration, or frequency
- location or setting
- sequence, so that what happens late in the pattern now happens early
- composition; add an element, such as ordeals where you add an unpleasant element, or subtract an element, so that some aspect of the problem is removed
- the players, so that people who were excluded from the problem are added, and people who were involved are excluded or their roles are changed,
- anything, by introducing a random variation, with the assignment the patient do something different, with almost any change being possible

Time can be changed by altering when the problem occurs, how long it lasts, or how often is occurs. For example, a panic attack may have a predictable range of time it occurs. The intense portion may last thirty seconds, two minutes, or five minutes. This might randomly vary (making it difficult to disrupt the pattern), or it may be fairly consistent (making disruption easier). Suppose the patient is encouraged to view the anxiety as being like a bully who intimidates her. If she stands up to the bully, it may leave her alone. She agrees to try to lengthen rather than shorten the time the anxiety and panic last. If the panic lasts for two minutes, the patient will try to lengthen it to three minutes.

When a problem occurs can also be shifted. Consider a patient who has depression in the morning and feels better in the afternoon. The afternoon times are likely to be when the client is more active. The behavior of more activity can be assigned in the early morning, and the depression-like behavior can be assigned to the late afternoon, with the instruction to try to remain as depressed as possible for 30–60 minutes, so as to learn if there is any possible value in the depression. Since the patient is at his best in the late afternoon, that is the ideal time to study such a question.

Location or setting: A woman who was depressed at her work (feeling her coworkers did not appreciate or like her) was asked to go to other settings and notice whether she could make the feeling happen in those settings, such as at the mall. She found that she could cause her feeling in other settings, which made her think she didn't need to feel it at work.

Sequence: Milton Erickson once intervened with a couple who would arrive at their family-owned restaurant together, and would bicker and fight all day about how to run the restaurant. He arranged for the husband to arrive one-half hour earlier than the husband, and this ended the fighting. He had changed the sequence, so the husband was a step ahead of his wife at their work. Instead of the two of them competing about who was right, the husband did some things and the wife did others.

Add an element (ordeals): I had a patient who wanted to overcome bulimia behavior. I found she thoroughly hated housework, although she admitted she ought to do her share in the house she shared. Her goal was to get an education and a job that would give her enough income to never do housework.

One of the interventions in this case was to ask her to agree that she had a right to binge and purge whenever she chose to do so; however, when she did, she would have to do two hours of housework. She was appalled, saying, "Two hours! I'd never vomit!" Since that was a goal, we decided that would be a useful outcome. She carried out the homework and stopped purging.

I have occasionally used ordeals with myself. Once I was building a new home and running my private practice at the same time. I would work on the home in the early morning, rush to work, come home and work on the house until dark. I started getting overstimulated and would wake up every night at 2 a.m. with all kinds of house and practice problems running through my head. I determined a good ordeal would be to read the Old Testament, something I didn't want to do. If I wasn't asleep in 15 minutes, I had to get up, stand in the hall and read until I felt sleepy. I could go back to bed if I was sleepy, but if I wasn't asleep in 15 minutes, I would repeat the process. After a few days of this, I had finished Genesis and started into Exodus, but I didn't finish because I started sleeping through the night.

Adding and subtracting an element: In the eating problem above, another aspect of the bulimia was fasting and restricted eating as a weight control strategy. We *subtracted* the element of fasting/restricted eating and *added* small, frequent meals, which helped the patient to control weight without the terrible urge to binge.

Changing the players: The easiest way to do this is to include family members or even significant others. When working on an "individual" problem, such as phobia or depression, I like to invite family or friends to attend the session with the patient. Including those other people in the problem has a powerful effect. For example, a man who had anxiety and panic symptoms believed he could not show his feelings or symptoms to others. In the family session I asked who noticed when he is suffering from symptoms, and how they knew. I engaged the family in a discussion of what it meant to others to know he was suffering, and framed his problem as being controlled by an irrational fear that if people knew he was in pain, it would be awful. I convinced him to test that hypothesis, by randomly exaggerating the symptoms on certain days, by suppressing the symptoms on other days, and by noticing *what difference that made.* He was surprised to learn that on the days he exaggerated symptoms, he actually felt much better. His family felt more comfortable when they thought he was being more honest about the symptoms, so the exaggeration days were helpful to everyone in the family.

Random variation: A woman brought to therapy her teenage son, who had adopted a "punk" dress style and was generally uncooperative around home, possibly using marijuana, and doing poorly in school. Since he was a visitor, I tried to give him some compliments and dismissed him, focusing on the mother, who was definitely a customer. We talked about shifting her style from one-up (which didn't work) to one-down.

Along with the one-down position, we talked about the usefulness of creating beneficial uncertainty in the son's life. I suggested his problem stemmed from the fact that he was too confident, and that a certain amount of doubt or even fear in life is quite healthy. She could do this by surprising him (Beier & Young, 1984). She would devote some time each week to brainstorming some ways to surprise her son, giving random unusual responses to his provocative behavior. Each week she would proudly detail the ways she had surprised her son, who was more and more puzzled. He began to behave better and better.

Solution-focused Homework

One of the great strengths of solution-focused treatment is its simplicity. This is true also of its homework. The solution-focused intervention questions described in Chapter 5 lead directly to useful homework prescriptions. The reader should consult de Shazer (1988) for a more extensive discussion of these patterns.

(a) The exception frame:

   (i) Pre-session change: If there are pre-session changes, if they are under the control of the patient (that is, the result of her making some voluntary effort), and if continuing and expanding those changes would be enough for the patient to feel therapy was successful, the assignment is to continue to do what has been already done, and see what difference that continues to make. For example, an adolescent I recently saw had been in a good deal of trouble at school; however, when told her parents were taking her to a therapist, she began to behave much better. The session was spent negotiating whether and how she could continue to keep up that good work. Since she did not like seeing a counselor, she did keep it up, and with some renegotiation of some family communication patterns, the problems were solved.

   (ii) Exceptions: A 21-year-old man had suffered for several years from depression. One exception was when he played basketball with some friends. He seldom played, however, thinking he would not have fun or they would be "brought down" by his depression. He agreed to test those notions scientifically, by flipping a coin each day. If it was heads, he had to seek out a basketball game, get involved, and keep track of how it went for him. If it was tails, he had to stay at home and see how that affected him.

He learned that his friends did not seem as affected by his depression as he thought they would be, and he felt much better. Therefore, we looked for ways to expand this pattern, and found there were many other times he did not do something because he predicted it would not go well. The exception became the foundation for his recovery.

(b) The outcome frame: By asking the miracle question and then specifying smaller and smaller components of the miracle, very useful homework can be derived from the patient herself, rather than from the therapist's model. For instance, a woman said if the miracle happened, and she was feeling better, she would feel happy, for a change. When asked how others would figure out she was feeling happier, *without her even having to tell them*, she replied she would smile more. Her homework was couched in terms of asking if she would be willing to help get the miracle started by smiling more on odd numbered days, and noticing what difference that made.

(c) The coping frame: A patient can be encouraged to increase her coping with a problem which cannot be changed. For example, a patient had a stormy and difficult relationship with her brother, who would verbally abuse her from time to time. After repeated attempts on my part to intervene had failed, we adopted a strategy of "bouncing back" from these arguments by treating herself extra nice. She bought some expensive bubble bath, and after an argument, took a long bath and treated herself to some nice lotion. While the brother continued to be cranky and obnoxious, she felt much better and less affected by his moods.

Voluntary versus involuntary: Some exceptions and coping are seen by the patient as *involuntary* and occuring randomly. In this case, ask the patient to simply predict each day whether an exception will occur. For example, I have had good success asking young men with bedwetting problems to predict each night whether, when they wake up, *they will discover a dry bed*. They then keep a diary of their predictions and which ones come true. What they generally find is that the more they try to predict, the more dry beds they discover.

Dangers of Strategic Therapy

There is a certain political danger to strategic therapy, in spite of the fact that strategic approaches appear to be at least as useful and effective as behavioral approaches (Szykula, Morris, Sudweeks, & Sayger, 1987). While these techniques offer the integrative therapist some useful skills and views, they are anathema to the insight-oriented therapists, and a therapist using them must make sure he knows who is doing the review process for the managed care companies. To present a strategic formulation to a case manager who is a true believer in psychodynamics is professional suicide. Fortunately, the majority of case managers are fairly integrative and open-minded.

Another danger is that occasionally (not always, by any means) a paradoxical or strategic assignment seems to work a miracle, and the therapist becomes so enamored of strategic therapy, that he becomes a bore. All he can talk about is strategic ideas, and his supervisors and peers can barely stand him. So a therapist who experiments with strategic work would be wise to keep his successes a secret.

OTHER HOMEWORK POSSIBILITIES

Time-sensitive treatment can benefit from patients' involvement in natural activities. Therapists need to be aware of many activities, groups, and locations around which they can plan their homework assignments, and can use a variety of community resources to design helpful and cost-sensitive assignments.

Many clients benefit from assertiveness training, but to conduct it within an individual session is both wasteful of therapist time and less effective for the client. The preferred way to accomplish assertiveness is to ask the patient to read a book on assertion and enroll in a class, often offered through school districts and social agencies.

Assigning the task of joining clubs, interest groups, church congregations, and social organizations is helpful for the more isolated client. Other helpful tasks include stress management tasks, career development classes, and meditation, to name only a few. Nearly all patients can benefit from such assignments, and they are widely available. Some support groups are not useful, and actually become pathogenic. A few 12-step programs, for example, have become perversions of a very fine philosophy, promoting victimhood rather than health. Those who join them center their lives around the descriptions like "codependent" (or some other label). I have seen some become so enmeshed in self-help groups that they are unable to relate in a natural, comfortable way to anyone. The therapist must know the group well before recommending it to clients, and should bear in mind that some cures are worse than the disease.

SECTION II

Supportive Concepts

CHAPTER 7

On Time in Psychotherapy

When I was a sophomore in college, I attended a weekend leadership training as a minor officer in the student government. A speaker there talked about Lao Tzu and the Way of the Tao, and quoted, "As for the best leaders, the people say, 'We did it ourselves.'"

Later, as I began to study psychotherapy as a graduate student, Lao Tzu rang in my ears. It was clear that psychotherapy emphasized the essential role of the therapist. It seemed unlikely the patient could say, "I did it myself." I questioned whether the long, intense relationship in traditional psychotherapy might be dangerous or disempowering for some clients. I wondered whether there were a better way. Throughout my career as a therapist I have asked, What are the better ways and how I can find them? Judging that I was rarely as efficient and effective as I might have been, I sought to do therapy as parsimoniously as possible. My hope was that at the end of therapy, the client would say, "Never mind, I got over it by myself."

In both private practice and public work, there is an increasing need to become sensitive to resources. While funding for public mental health has remained flat, agencies are being required to assume more and more responsibilities. At the same time, in private practice we face managed mental health plans that require more and more paperwork and reporting and allow fewer and fewer benefits. While all of this is naturally distressing to thoughtful clinicians, we can't help but notice it has an "up" side. Just as the environmental movement helps us become sensitive to using less and living with less impact on the earth, so also the limits of reimbursement help us become more sensitive to the need to work more powerfully and efficiently. Since our patients want to get better as soon as possible (Pekarik & Wierzbicki, 1986), working more briefly will primarily benefit clients, not insurers or funding sources.

And just as becoming better conservationists helps us come together and live more spiritually and less materialistically, so also does this new emphasis on limited resources help us become better at what we do. If we do have limited resources, we can take advantage of this to become more skilled and to better meet needs of patients even when resources are not limited. After all, to fail to help when someone needs our aid is unethical; so also, to take longer to help than is necessary should be unconscionable. To do therapy slowly when quicker help is available is as unethical as a medical doctor withholding antibiotics because he believes it is better for our character to overcome the infection by ourselves.

TIME LIMITS AND TIME SENSITIVITY

Perhaps "brief" therapy is an unfortunate term, since it suggests a time limit. Some models do set definite time limits; others do not. Mann (1973) and Horowitz, Marmer, Krupnick et al. (1984) set a limit of 12 sessions, deeming that number sufficient for intense working-through of a single, limited focus. Other models allow for more flexibility, such as those of Sifneos (1979) or Malan (1976). Hoyt (1990, 1995) tells of visiting Malan in London. Malan said, "Here at the Tavistock we allow trainees 35–40 sessions. It allows for wasting time and making mistakes." Hoyt replied, "Well, in America we're more efficient. We find that we can waste time and make mistakes in 12 sessions."

All brief therapy models are aware of time (Fuhriman, Paul, & Burlingame 1988; Hoyt, 1990). This may take the form either of setting time limits or of trying to do the most in the least time without an explicit focus on time limits. Time limits are helpful since they help create unity among a diverse group of mental health professionals. For example, at the University of Utah, there was a program developed by Fuhriman and colleagues to create a time-limited treatment program at the counseling center. Since some of the therapists were behaviorists and others were insight-oriented, a common model was developed, with a limit of 10 sessions, plus two for follow-up. While they had divergent views on the mechanisms of change, all the counselors could agree on this time limit.

If we use time limits, we must inform the client at the beginning of those limits; we then structure the work around those limits. The first task is to establish a focus, an agreement on what will be accomplished. The middle phase is the working-through of the issues connected with the focus. And the final sessions consist of consolidation and working through of reactions to termination. The therapist mentions the session number each time, e.g., "Today is the fourth session; after today we have six sessions left." She encourages the client to talk about reactions to that.

At the MRI in Palo Alto, therapists adhere to a 10-session model, not because it is intrinsic to their theory but for research purposes and to keep therapy homogeneous. Often clients seem to have achieved their goals short of the 10 sessions, and their therapist will encourage them to "put the extra sessions in the bank," keeping them for possible follow-up. John Weakland (Weakland, Johnson, & Morrissette, in press) has pointed out that in their private practices, the MRI therapists do not adhere to a 10-session limit. He ruefully confesses, "While I am known as a brief therapist, sometimes I do extended brief therapy! I usually blame myself when that happens, but sometimes I can blame the patient."

While agencies often set time limits, independent practitioners are likely to use a time-sensitive approach. Managed care programs typically set time limits that force the independent therapist to adapt to constraints similar to those in the public centers. There are advantages and disadvantages to both time-limited and time-sensitive (but unlimited) approaches. In my own practice I use the techniques of time-limited therapy even when there are no external constraints on my time. I will suggest we meet together for six visits. At the end of that time, we will evaluate our progress and decide whether to go forward. I propose, "If you have made some progress, then we should continue or perhaps take a break. You may say at that point you want more treatment, or you may say that things are pretty stable and you would like to break, keeping further sessions for whenever you need them. But if you haven't made any progress in six sessions, they you should probably not spend any more effort with me, since if I can't be of help in six sessions, I probably couldn't help in sixty or six hundred."

My choice of the number "six" is arbitrary but informed by the fact that most studies suggest that six is the average number of sessions. And I do have every expectation that some change or improvement will have happened in that time, although it may not be enough for that particular patient.

TIME-LIMITED PSYCHOTHERAPY MODELS

The time-limited models have an advantage for an agency trying to make therapists more resource-sensitive. By putting an upper limit on treatment, providing either an absolute ceiling (something which is hard to justify) or preferably a review ceiling (meaning that after 10 or 12 sessions, you must review the case with a supervisor), the agency assures that the therapist is focused on effective treatment. Especially within an agency where the motivation for brief therapy is mixed, some therapists believing in it and some not, a time limit is very helpful. It levels the playing field and provides an outside motivation to adhere to a brief model. Then the treatment is likely to be more effective and focused.

One disadvantage is that some therapists will resent the time limits and convey that to the patients, fostering an "us against them" mentality, like Berne's (1964) game, "Let's you and him fight." In this game, the therapist achieves gratification from seeing a fight happen, at the therapist's instigation. A counselor must avoid such exploitation. It is helpful to remember how all of life involves limits and barriers, and living with them graciously is the mark of a cultured individual.

Occasionally a therapist will take advantage of the time limits to justify an aggressive approach to patients that drives them out of therapy too early. Here the therapist and the team need to monitor ratings the therapist is receiving from patients. Therapists who have a high number of second-session "no shows" ought to look at their relationship skills.

Another disadvantage is the "therapeutic dose" effect. Therapists begin to think of therapy as being a 10- or 12-session proposition. They may suggest (overtly or unwittingly) to the client that using less than the full course of 12 sessions is like using less than a full dose of antibiotic; it won't do any good. Thus, a problem that might be dealt with in one or two sessions expands to fill the 12-session dose.

To the contrary, Talmon (1990) has provided convincing evidence that the single session should be the prototype for brief therapy. Since 30% (or more) of patients will be seen only one time, it is essential that the therapist attempt to meet patient needs in the first session. It is a mistake for a therapist to view therapy as being a "dose" of a certain number of sessions. Rather, in an agency with a time limit, the session limit should be viewed as a ceiling, and two or three sessions, one session, or even no session at all (e.g., telephone contact only) as acceptable options. Patients may benefit from being told they can keep the unused sessions "in the bank" for future needs (cf. Watzlawick, Weakland, & Fisch, 1974). Therapists can be rewarded for having good averages (the average patient comes four to eight times) and good patient ratings (the therapist is seen by patients as sensitive, thoughtful, caring, honest, and helpful).

Because of the potential for difficulties with time limits, I recommend that they *not* be imposed from above, by administrative fiat. Rather, limits should be discussed by all members of the organization, from the B.A. level case managers up, and then circulated up the organization to the top. It is necessary for the entire organizational climate to change for time limits to be helpful in improving quality of care to the patient.

Nevertheless, time limits can be very helpful in uniting an organization behind one common standard. The limits "level the playing field," so to speak, and help therapists who might otherwise prefer to conduct longer treatments. Patients who tend to attend interminably can be helped to focus their efforts when the therapist explains that the upper limit for individual therapy is 12 sessions, and that beyond that the patient will be referred to group therapy.

TIME-SENSITIVE MODELS

Models without a time limit focus on intrinsic factors that make treatment briefer, such as careful selection of focus, maintenance of focus, limiting goals within the focus, and avoiding therapeutic perfectionism. Time-unlimited models are more appropriate for an agency where all the therapists share a common model or commitment to brief treatment and so are motivated by a desire to learn how robust and valid the treatment philosophy is. A resource-sensitive model is likely to advocate *intermittent* therapy rather than courses of continual therapy (e.g., Budman & Gurman, 1988; Cummings, 1991). The older model was to continue with a patient until he or she was analyzed or cured, with an emphasis on a complete working-through.

The intermittent model suggests that patients may need interventions from time to time throughout the life cycle. A patient may be seen until there is some sense of progress and stability and then encouraged to break from therapy. There is no effort to "finish" therapy, but to get the patient moving in the right direction. The counselor sees the client as likely to continue to make progress outside of therapy, rather than making progress only when in active treatment. Termination work is generally not done, since there is no plan for termination. The patient can return at any time, just as a patient of a primary care physician can return when a symptom is troubling.

The disadvantage of the time-sensitive models is mostly with the problem of control: The administration of an agency or an insurance company needs to feel powerful and needed, and making rules and imposing limits are ways to achieve satisfaction of that need. With the time-sensitive model, there is always a nagging fear in the hearts of management that someone somewhere is doing long-term therapy, and perhaps even enjoying it. With a time-sensitive approach, there could be counselors in an agency who do not accept the model and stubbornly continue to see patients in long-term therapy. It seems hard to justify time limits only on that basis, however. Quality in treatment cannot be improved by trying to punish "outliers," that is, persons on the margins of the distribution. Rather, quality is improved by improving skills and creating feedback loops for all the therapists in a system, and by working individually with the outliers in consultation/ supervision.

The advantages of resource-sensitive models (compared with time-limited models) lie in the attitude of the therapist. If there is no strict time limit, the therapist may be much more sensitive to what the client wants rather than what the model claims the client needs. The therapist then may be satisfied with a three-session treatment or with a 20-session treatment, as long as client needs are met. The disadvantage is that therapists tend to overestimate how much therapy the client needs or wants.

Pekarik and Wierzbicki (1986) found a remarkable relationship between the number of visits a patient expected when applying for mental health services and the number of visits actually completed. Table 7.1, reprinted from their article, summarizes their findings.

It should be noted that this study revealed that, while 65% of therapists preferred more than 15 sessions, only 12% of clients preferred that many. The patient expectations were essential; therapist expectations were unrealistic. In other words, therapists cannot keep people in therapy much beyond the time they want to be there. Pekarik and Wierzbicki found that no combination of factors was able to predict length of treatment duration as well as client expectation alone. Therapists sometimes claim that the patient is being unrealistic and that we need to find ways to keep people in treatment longer. This may be an error. Perhaps therapists should pay more attention to meeting the patient's needs, instead of forcing them to fit a model. For time-sensitive therapy to function well, therapists must be respectful of the patient's expected length of treatment.

Gelso and Johnson (1983) point out that, while much therapy is pragmatically brief (e.g., the patient terminates after a few sessions), this may be planned or unplanned. Most brief therapy is of the unplanned variety,

Table 7.1 Expected and Actual Therapy Duration

| Visit Category | Expected* | | Cumulative % | Actual** | | Cumulative % |
	n	%		n	%	
1–2	30	20.3	20.3	69	35.4	35.4
3–5	42	28.4	48.7	35	17.9	53.3
6–10	36	24.3	73.0	39	20	73.3
11–15	11	7.4	80.4	16	8.2	81.5
16–25	11	7.4	87.8	22	11.3	92.8
26+	18	12.2	100	14	7.2	100

*Clients who completed the survey
**All consecutive admissions
Reprinted with permission from Pekarik and Wierzbicki, 1986.

since the therapist may hold to a model of treatment that requires a long period of working through conflicts and defenses. In that case, the termination of treatment would be thought of as "premature." However, it is possible that from the point of view of the patient, the therapy actually lasted sufficiently long or met his goals. Certainly, the Pekarik and Wierzbicki study, as well as studies of single-session therapy, suggest that the client may be wiser than the therapist in such matters. Since patients often feel quite positive about their brief therapy, it may be that the therapist who deems the termination premature is trying to accomplish something the patient doesn't want to achieve. Perhaps the therapist is aware of how much better patients could be, and wants them all to achieve that level of mental health. Unfortunately, many patients are unwilling and want only small improvements.

It reminds me of a physician who once cared for me. He was quite a perfectionist, and when my cholesterol was 170, he talked about getting it lower. If my body fat percentage was in a normal range, he talked about how to get it down to 5%. I thought, "Leave me alone! I exercise and eat carefully; I don't want to be any better than I am, or at least I don't have the energy to exercise an hour a day or avoid absolutely all fats. I pretty much like my life as it is." It may be I would live a bit longer if I did even more exercise or ate even less fat. Or maybe it would just seem longer. But that was my decision, not his.

We take the position that brief therapy is not only pragmatically the norm but also the ideal, since in the best type of therapy the patient is helped in the least amount of time. In this brief therapy model, the intense relationship of a therapist and patient is sacrificed in the vast majority of cases, but in return the client is empowered and invigorated. Possibly an occasional patient will say, "Never mind, I got over it myself."

SINGLE-SESSION THERAPY

It shocks some therapists to consider that a single session may be an ideal use of time for some patients, yet that is the case. Malan, Heath, Bacal, and Balfour (1975) reported that of 45 patients seen one time at the Tavistock clinic in London, 25 were symptomatically better, and what was more surprising, 11 were considered improved on dynamic criteria. In other words, as the result of one session, plus the independent actions they had subsequently taken, these patients had changed in just the ways that the researchers would have expected as a result of intensive psychotherapy!

Malan et al. (1975) referred to these patients as "untreated," but that is not fair or accurate. Rather, they were treated one time by a therapist trying to do effective brief therapy. In the first session, the therapist formulated the case and made transference interpretations, Malan's so-called trial interpretations. Those were designed to test whether the person was appropriate for the Tavistock version of brief therapy. The assumption is that only by attempting brief treatment can one determine which patients are suitable. Some of Malan's patients were not judged to be appropriate but nevertheless were found to have improved on follow-up. The single interview seemed to crystalize their dilemma, shift responsibility to them, or in some other way mobilize their coping efforts.

Talmon (1990) surveyed patients seen one time by a therapist who was attempting to do single-session therapy; as pointed out earlier, he found that 79% were satisfied with their single contact with the therapist and considered themselves improved or recovered. They were likely to return for help in the future and were likely to refer their friends for counseling. Talmon's approach reminds us of Eric Berne, who used to start each therapy group saying to himself, "What can I do to cure every person in this group today?"

Therapists are often pessimistic about the probability that a single session will have a positive impact on a client. They tend to remember all the people who needed many sessions and forget those who were seen once or twice. I once had a patient who was trying to become more optimistic in her outlook. One day she came to a session and announced that she had been practicing golf. She said, "I have been practicing holes-in-one." I was impressed and asked her how many she had gotten. She said, "Well, none today." Our challenge is to plan so as to make it possible that each session could be the last. If it is, we have hit a hole-in-one; if not, we go ahead and play the ball as it lays.

Hoyt, Rosenbaum, and Talmon (1992) and Talmon (1990) offer some helpful suggestions about how to conduct planned single-session therapy. They point out that a single session is possible when the patient is highly motivated and the therapist offers a novel and helpful way of looking at the problem which effects a marked change in its viewing or doing. The patient may end the session feeling that the problem isn't so much of a problem as had been thought or knowing how to handle a problem in a new, more effective way. But the new view of the problem is essential.

The first contact is an essential time to set the stage for single-session therapy. The initial contact must be carefully handled. A counselor should contact the patient before the first session. In that telephone contact, the counselor can seed some questions or an assignment to lay groundwork for a single session. For example, the client can be oriented to look for strengths rather than problems as the therapist asks, "Between now and the time you come in for your appointment, will you please watch carefully in your life for things you feel good about and approve of, so your therapist can learn about strengths that can be used in the counseling session? Your therapist will want to know what the things are you want to have continue in your life."

Other times, a small therapeutic task assignment can be given, based on the telephone contact. For example, a parent reporting she fights with her child a great deal can be asked to write down everything the child says (Talmon, 1990), thus obtaining good information and simultaneously de-railing the fighting (since the parent can't fight while writing down the child's language). A patient thus encouraged to make some new effort between the initial contact and the first session is more involved in the treatment and more likely to benefit quickly.

FIRST SESSION TASKS

During the first session, the therapist must listen and interview for a way to respond in a single session. This is a marked departure from stan-dard practice, where the therapist is expected to assess the patient in the first session, with treatment coming later.

Assessment (in a traditional sense of a structured, problem-focused his-tory-taking and mental status interview) may actually make a single-session treatment less likely. When the therapist feels an obligation to cover a checklist of issues that must be addressed in the first session (was the patient a full-term baby; at what age did he/she walk, talk, toilet train, and so on; is there a family history of mental illness or substance abuse; is the patient dangerous to self or others; abusing drugs or alcohol, experiencing delu-sions, hallucinations, or thought disorders, disoriented or with impaired attention), the patient's issues and desires for the session may take a back seat to the therapist's agenda. While these issues are both interesting and helpful to the therapist, the patient may not want to discuss them in the first session. Thorough assessment raises complicated and difficult issues. They distract the therapist from the essential issues of the first session, namely searching for a pivot point, a combination of motivation and change of meaning that will redefine and change the problem.

It seems likely that the sensitive therapist can quickly obtain the essential parts of the evaluation while at the same time listening primarily *not* for what is wrong with the patient but rather for what is wanted by that patient.

There is an apocryphal story about some family therapists who seek consultation from a well-known family therapy supervisor. They say to the consultant, "This mother and daughter are enmeshed in a symbiotic relationship, and we can't get them to differentiate. What should we do?" The wise old therapist says, "Well, first of all, I would never let *that* be the problem!" The therapists think they have discovered the problem and feel an obligation to treat what they think they have discovered. The consultant suggests the problem is an invention that takes place between the client and the counselor. We may be empowered when we see "problems" as not things we diagnose but as things we co-create with the help of the patient. Together our task is to find some definition of the problem that enlivens our client to do something different.

During the first session, the therapist should try to make the problem as simple and easily solved as possible. This contrasts with a common practice in the first session of discovering all possible problems. Often, in supervision a game of "I will discover what you have overlooked" is played. The dynamics of the game seem to involve humiliating the student and proving the supervisor wiser and more insightful. The result is that we produce counselors who are perfectionists, striving to control everything so as to never be caught missing something.

Instead, we might try to oversimplify the problem and offer hope rather than comprehensive evaluation (Frank, 1974). It is certainly not true that the comprehensive evaluation has proven itself in comparative studies, and clinical experience and evidence suggest that the opposite is true: The simple view is very often more useful than the most complex one. The problem may be solved by focusing on nodal change points in the first session. If it turns out to be harder to solve than was originally thought, and the patient returns for additional sessions, the additional information can be obtained at that time.

This is not to imply that therapists should ignore central issues of suicidality, dangerousness to others, or chemical abuse, only that they should briefly assess those and move quickly into the areas of vital concern to the client. Client interests are well addressed by using the solution-focused questions discussed earlier (exceptions, outcome, coping questions) and by focusing on what the patient wants rather than what the therapist thinks is wrong in the patient's life.

In the first session, I tend to ask those questions repeatedly, looking for a central focus or theme around which we can base our interventions. I want to know if the patient has noticed any positive changes between the first contact and the first session. If she has, then we want to see if those changes can continue, and if so, will that be enough to satisfy her that the problem is on its way to being solved? If that is the case, the first session may well be the last one, and the therapy may consist of negotiating ways to "keep up the good work." Even if the client would not be satisfied with continuation of the pre-session changes, then at the very least we have evidence that the client can change things for the better, or that things can spontaneously change for the better, and this is to be congratulated.

If exceptions are occurring, I want to know whether the client can produce those exceptions at will. In the case of depression, suppose the client says he is less depressed when he goes for walks with his wife. I can congratulate him and ask questions about how those walks helped him, how he behaved when he felt better, how his wife reacted when she noticed him acting differently, and how it helped him to notice her noticing him. If the client can make the exception happen by his own efforts, then I will assign "more of the same" to him. The client is congratulated on being observant enough to notice a significant change in the problem and is encouraged to continue those good efforts and *notice what difference they make.*

If the exceptions are not the result of client efforts and are outside of his own efforts, the client should be encouraged to *predict* each day whether the exception is going to continue to occur. The practice of predicting exceptions seems to make them happen more often. Consider a mother complaining about her son's bedwetting. Some days his bed is dry (an exception is present), but both he and she deny that they can do anything to make it happen (it is involuntary and spontaneous). The mother and son can each be asked to predict, separately and secretly, each evening, whether an exception will happen that night. Then the next morning they share their predictions and keep track of their successful predictions. This process seems to encourage more and more exceptions to happen.

In all this, what the patient wants is the focus. For example, consider the following case.

Case Example: In Which the Therapist Almost Jumps the Gun

A woman presented with complaints about her 35-year-old son who was living with her. John did not hold a full-time job and was not particularly helpful around the house. He was somewhat sullen and uncommunicative. Her other children often criticized her for not kicking him out of her home.

I was busy thinking of useful interventions to help her encourage independence in John, and was about to begin to deliver them (it being about 30 minutes into the first session), when in a rare moment of thoughtfulness, I asked her, "And what would you like me to do to help you?"

To my shock, she immediately said, "I want you to tell me how to improve the unity in my family." She told of her great pain because her family was argumentative and divided, criticizing one another. And while the stay-at-home son was some concern to her, it was clear she had been telling me about him because that was what her family wanted her to talk about and not what she wanted.

Accordingly, I suggested she go slowly on the matter of John living independently, and we explored family reconciliation strategies, which seemed to be much more interesting to her. I proposed that we could not know whether the son's remaining at home in the role of a teenager was a cause of the family dissension or if it was a result. I did not know whether her setting limits and encouraging John to assume a more adult role would improve the unity in the family or whether it would decrease it. I suggested she mostly concentrate on discovering when were the times of the best family unity and what might be done to promote more of those.

In the second session she reported that she had done as I had suggested and had noticed a family gathering in which there was a good deal of unity. She was gratified by that and wondered whether she might be focusing on the wrong thing. Perhaps she should do as her other children suggested and focus her efforts in treatment on helping John. We explored ways in which she was already promoting John's independence and talked at length about how having him at home with her helped in many ways. She thought of herself as having been a poor mother, and having him at home allowed for another attempt at improving her mothering. John had benefited because he was much less sullen after living there for a year. He would occasionally converse, and if she asked, he would help around the house.

I expect that if I had insisted in the first session that we focus on John, I would have alienated this woman and simply become another person dividing the family. When I accepted her notion, suggested she go slowly on changing John, and did not push her, that allowed her the space to become more committed to the focus her children had been suggesting.

At the End of the First Session

Time-sensitive therapists do not automatically plan to see patients in one week. The main benefit of scheduling people at one-week intervals is to simplify the therapist's schedule, which is then more predictable.

If we reverse our priorities, we will schedule the next session based on the patient's status. Suppose a patient has a strong commitment to work hard ("customer") and there is a clear and potentially useful homework assignment at the end of that session. It makes no sense to have the patient return in one week. Since the therapy has a homework slant, it makes more sense to schedule a return in two or three weeks.

Suppose another patient is a customer, but the therapist has little or no confidence that he will benefit from homework. Perhaps the patient is so despondent that he probably will not carry out the homework effectively. Or perhaps the therapist has not been able to think of a good homework assignment. Or perhaps the treatment approach chosen is complicated and requires more time with the therapist, at least at the outset. In these cases, it makes more sense for the patient to return in a few days, and for the treatment to proceed more intensely. So we recommend that people not be generally seen on a weekly basis. The decision about frequency must be made in accordance with patient needs.

Subsequent sessions should be scheduled so as to communicate values and processes to the therapy relationship, not as a default process to fill the therapist's schedule. The therapist must even decide what the meaning is if the patient is given the same time every week, as opposed to being seen weekly but at different times in the day. The patient who is seen the same day every week is invited to think of the relationship with the therapist as a regular part of his life, to which he is to become accustomed. Conversely, a patient seen at different hours during the day, but still on a weekly basis, might be invited to think of the therapy as a temporary state, to which she will not become accustomed. The first patient may see the therapy hour as crucial, whereas the second patient sees the time between sessions as crucial. So our first patient is invited into a dependent relationship and the second into a relationship of independence and cooperation.

Consider a patient who agrees to do homework but by the next visit has not done anything. A possible response to that would be to talk a great deal about why the homework is not done. Perhaps further talk about the problems facing the client should be postponed while the issue of homework is minutely examined. This process invites the client to see herself as powerful and her own behavior as crucial to making improvements in the problem. The therapist can explore whether he or she has misunderstood the actual goal of the patient (as in my example above) and therefore whether the failure to complete the homework is actually a very helpful message to the therapist to pay more attention to the patient's goals. This would not necessarily affect the scheduling of the next appointment.

Another possibility when the patient does not do homework is that the therapist has not been sensitive to the patient's use of time. A therapist recently told me about a patient she saw for the first time. She wanted to be a time-sensitive therapist. She thought she had done a beautiful job of brief therapy (there was a clear focus and a definite homework assignment) and scheduled the patient for two weeks. He did not show up, and she felt disheartened, thinking she had failed. But he did show up on her schedule two months from the first session. In fact, by the time of the missed appointment he had not done the homework and thus had not wanted to return, since he had yet to carry out the agreed-upon experiment. He did begin to work on the homework, and then made a new appointment. He came in feeling proud of the fact that he had completed all the homework and was ready for the next session. Now they are working at therapy every two months, and he is making satisfactory progress.

When the patient hasn't done the homework, but has no real explanation, consider changing the schedule of appointments. The next session can be postponed indefinitely, with the statement that the client needs to think about whether this is a good time for him to be in therapy. Perhaps the therapist is pushing too hard and needs to back off. Perhaps outside distractions are keeping the patient from concentrating on treatment.

Such a move is likely to surprise the client, since the expectation from childhood is, when I resist something, a parental figure will try to motivate me. When the therapist backs off rapidly and encourages more caution and less involvement, it has had a remarkable effect. The patient generally finds his motivation increasing as a result of the therapist's backing off. It is really quite possible that the patient is not ready for therapy at that time. The paradoxical message contains a powerful truth: Therapy takes energy and resources, and so one should not enter therapy without first counting the costs to determine whether one has the resources to complete the tasks.

THE LENGTH-OF-SESSION QUESTION

Sessions last 45 or 50 minutes strictly for the convenience of the therapist and the reimbursement systems. In a rational world, some sessions might last an hour, others two hours, and others ten minutes. In fact, it might be that hypnosis-oriented treatment and exposure-based treatment of PTSD ought to last at least 90 minutes to two hours. Conversely, many problems can be dealt with in much less time than 50 minutes. There is certainly no rational reason to rigidly cling to a 50-minute hour. Some therapists may be quite capable of doing effective interventions in 20 or 40 minutes, and they should be encouraged to do so. Perhaps with skilled brief therapists, billing should be based on the procedure, namely understanding the goal and designing and delivering an intervention, and not based on whether it took 20 or 40 or 100 minutes.

Using Time within the Session

Some patients like to save revelations until right at the end of the session, hoping perhaps the therapist will do less damage that way. Whether the session is 30 minutes or 60, the revelation will come at the end. A patient wishing to test the therapist's love might schedule the new information for the last minute of the session, to see if the therapist will offer more time. Whether the session is an hour or 30 minutes, that is the length of the session, and generally the therapist should not extend the session because of a titillating secret.

The obvious exception is when the therapist discovers a suicide plan. Some patients may talk of suicidal intention as a ploy, but the therapist must assume the patient is deadly serious and spend whatever time is necessary for stabilization and safety.

Brief therapists must develop a sense of where they should be at the end of the first third of the session and at the end of the second third, so as to be able to end gracefully. If there is no clear idea of what the intervention will be by the end of the first third, or at least by the halfway point, then the session is in trouble. By about the two-thirds point the patient and therapist should be discussing homework, so as to leave some time for objections and problems regarding the homework that might be discovered.

At the Brief Therapy Center in Milwaukee, therapists use a 50-minute hour and take a break at 40 minutes. During this break, the therapist leaves the room, either to discuss the case with colleagues if he has observers watching through the mirror or simply to think about the case and formulate a homework if working alone. I have occasionally used this model, especially when colleagues are observing my work through the mirror. Sometimes I have taken a break even when I am not working with a team behind the mirror; it is a refreshing and helpful time. I think about the session and make some notes to myself about strengths and possible compliments I can offer the patient. I outline how I will present a homework assignment and think of any objections the patient may have. When I return, I offer a compliment, sum up my thinking, and suggest homework, based on my understanding of the patient's needs and therapeutic focus.

MISCELLANEOUS NOTES ON TIME

Whenever possible I arrive at the office early enough to pull all the charts for the day's work. I look over each chart and remind myself of what homework assignment I had suggested in the last session. I make a few notes on possible responses to the homework and predict the theme for the session. I try to think of possible homework modifications if the assignment I gave did not work as I would like. This meditation about the day's work has a wonderfully refreshing effect on my efforts. I recommend it.

I often meet therapists who do not enjoy full-time practice and hope to move into other areas of work — administration, writing, or seminars. I wonder if their use of career time (moving out of direct service into other areas) is a result of either having unrealistic expectations of what therapy can do (or how important it can make them feel) or perhaps having less than optimal skills. I challenge those therapists to rethink their positions. I believe it takes about ten years of focused and supervised work to become a competent therapist, capable of working with a wide range of patients and problems. In a meta-analysis, Stein and Lambert (1995) found that experienced therapists have better outcomes and fewer dropouts. It seems to me a terrible shame to spend ten years becoming skilled and then move out of one's area of expertise. And since we now know that psychotherapy can be a very helpful and powerful intervention into people's lives, failure to continue in the profession is a dreadful waste. Perhaps it should be expected that everyone in a mental health organization, whether a public or a private agency, would continue to see at least a few patients. It would not be unreasonable to suggest that those in managed care, from the psychiatric review specialists up to the department heads, have a moral obligation to continue to work with flesh-and-blood clients. A manager or a director who cannot make time to see clients is simply too busy and is in danger of losing touch with the realities of the profession. And wouldn't managed care reviewers be much more understanding if they carried a few challenging or even "interminable" patients?

Successful therapists seem to have an orientation toward present and future aspects of time, as opposed to past events. The therapist who is curious about how her plans and hopes will become tangible is a therapist who can convey that same sense of hope and faith in the future to her patients. While seldom miraculous, therapy is a deeply satisfying activity and deserves our best and most optimistic dedication.

CHAPTER 8

Increasing Motivation and Compliance

We went willingly because we had to.

—*Brigham Young, commenting on the Mormons being driven out of Illinois*

In graduate school, Doug was finishing his course work but was stuck on his dissertation. He needed to do a good deal of writing (five chapters, actually), and didn't seem to be able to get to it. Finally, in desperation, he gave a peer $100 in $20 checks (recall that 25 years ago, $100 was a lot of money to a graduate student), made out to the American Nazi Party. Doug and his friend set up a schedule for him to finish his dissertation. If he failed to produce the required chapter by a certain day, a check would be sent to the Nazi party. If he did make his goal, the friend would return one of his checks. He could then gleefully destroy that check. Doug graduated on schedule, and the Nazi party got none of his money.

Cloé Madanes once said that 90% of her effort in psychotherapy was motivating the patient. At the time I wondered why I had never heard anyone else talk about motivation. The answer is that brief therapists like Madanes attempt to create significant change in a short time, so the issue of motivation is much greater than for therapists practicing a long-term model. For this reason, the practice of brief psychotherapy is more difficult than that of long-term therapy, since every session should be a planned, well-executed step forward. The session should end with an understanding of how the patient will experiment between now and the next session, and the patient should leave the session with a strong desire to carry out that experiment.

An operational definition of motivation is in order. A patient has high motivation when he or she will carry out behavioral changes and homework assignments the therapist suggests, or when, between sessions, the patient actively experiments with her behavior, thoughts, and relationships and observes what difference those experiments make. The more motivated the patient, the more we can ask in terms of change of behavior. Motivation is another way of looking at whether the patient adheres to what the therapist asks, as well as whether the patient creates his or her own experiments.

Some models of brief therapy emphasize assessing patient motivation. The notion seems to be the patient either has motivation or does not, and if not, brief treatment is not appropriate. And there is certainly significant evidence that patients who are strongly motivated to change are the best candidates for briefer forms of treatment (McConnaughy et al., 1989; Prochaska & DiClemente, 1986).

In the real world, it is difficult to refuse treatment to those judged unmotivated. The "in the trench" counselor doing an initial interview at a mental health facility is ethically obligated to offer the best treatment possible, and not to simply rule out a client because of a "lack of motivation." An integrative model must go further and emphasize the impact the therapist can have on motivation. In short, the counselor should work to create and increase patient motivation rather than to simply assess it. As Alexander and Parsons (1982, p. 2) point out in their discussion of family therapy, "motivation is to a great extent the responsibility of the therapist not just the family." Furthermore, in view of the fact that most therapy techniques seem to produce roughly equivalent outcomes, it may well be that increasing motivation is one of the therapeutic activities which make a real difference.

Components of the integrative brief therapy model are recursive: Motivation influences how much the counselor can accomplish, and other aspects of this model influence motivation. Take the use of time, for example. Brief therapists are likely to use time in flexible and innovative ways, such as setting time limits on therapy or delaying sessions until homework is completed. Such limits create a powerful motivation for the client to do something *now* about the problem, even though change is uncomfortable and difficult. There is even some evidence that patients who are given a relatively long time limit (12 sessions) have half the dropout rates of patients offered either long-term or brief treatment without time limits (Sledge, Moras, Hartley, & Levine 1990). Ironically, time limits may influence patients to stay in treatment longer! Sledge et al. speculate that the patients remain with therapy because they are given a target and are willing to persist in treatment beyond the time that might typically be expected. Of course, it is also possible that patients felt entitled to 12 sessions because they were told that was all they could have (although perhaps they would have expected and wanted six if the limit had not been mentioned) and would have felt deprived if they had received less. This follows the principle of "scarcity" explained by Cialdini (1984) in his social psychological analysis of influence. He found that salespersons frequently create an impression of limited supply or scarcity, which serves to motivate persons to buy or commit to things they wouldn't ordinarily pay for. So if I tell you that you may only have 12 sessions, you are more likely to keep coming, just like the customer who is told that the last expensive model of a stereo was just sold. Though he wanted to spend less, the customer immediately wants the expensive model, because it cannot be had. Then, strangely enough, one more expensive model is discovered in the back room.

In brief work a clear, well-defined and contracted-for focus motivates both the therapist and the client. If the therapist is accountable for achieving some changes in a specific area, within a specific time, the efforts are likely to be carefully thought-through and likely to succeed. Likewise, the patient is motivated by the crystallizing of the vague problems which beset him.

Of course, sometimes a patient should not adhere to therapist instructions. Our homework may be impractical, poorly thought-out, or even destructive. After all, it is useful for us to bear in mind the long history of medicine and the absurd cures and treatments that have been prescribed. When I remember foolish homework assignments I have tried to get people to follow, I am grateful for their noncompliance.

Therapists who are interested in a more thorough treatment of motivation should consult Meichenbaum and Turk (1987), for more than one could possibly adhere to about treatment adherence. O'Hanlon (1987) reviews some of the unique ways Milton Erickson motivated patients, and is well worth consulting.

USING TIME IN MOTIVATION

Ask, why now? Be sure you completely understand what has brought the patient into treatment at this particular time. Often the patient will express general reasons for being in treatment but skip over the particular issue that made treatment something she wanted to do *now*. It may have been an uncomfortable confrontation or consequence that evokes embarrassment in the patient. It may be a painful memory or a loss that the patient doesn't like to discuss. There may be good reasons the patient doesn't wish to discuss the "why now?" question, and these should be recognized. But understanding that motivation is vital. When it is time to ask the patient to make some significant change which takes effort and courage, the therapist can refer back to the "why now" issue and help the patient recall the level of motivation that brought him/her into treatment.

Assess pre-session change as a springboard to further therapeutic change. While Howard et al. (1986) extrapolated from their data that only 15 % of patients had improved prior to the first session, Weiner-Davis, de Shazer, and Gingerich (1987) and Talmon (1990) found that actually well over half of patients have noticed (or will notice, when asked) some positive change *between the time they call for an appointment and the time they actually come in for the appointment.* This finding can form the basis for increasing motivation through giving compliments and asking the patient to continue the good work. Talmon (1990) gives the assignment of noticing what things the patient approves of and wants to continue in the initial telephone contact. He suggests that it might be unwise for the therapist to schedule the appointment too quickly, so as to allow time for the pre-session positive change phenomenon to develop. On the other hand, some patients want to come in quickly, and it may well be that seeing them in a day or two of their call is helpful and motivational. This implies that the therapist and not a secretary should talk to the patients on their first telephone call, so as to assess who should be seen quickly and who should be allowed to develop some resources before the first session.

Set formal or informal time limits in therapy, and communicate them to the client as an opportunity to make treatment work effectively. The attitude of the therapist is crucial in creating motivation (as opposed to resentment about the brief time allotted). If the therapist expects rapid change, the patient is empowered; alternatively, if the therapist resents the time limits, the patient is disempowered and harmed. So it is important for the therapist to view the limits as helpful. For example,

> After ten sessions a report is required by your insurance. This is a good time to assess our progress. We will examine what we have achieved. If we haven't accomplished some of the things you are here to achieve by that time, you should consider replacing me as your therapist, since if I can't help you at all in that time, I probably can't help in 50 or 100 sessions.

> Our agency policy is that 12 sessions of individual therapy is the limit, and all patients going beyond 12 individual sessions will become involved in group therapy. You might not feel comfortable with group therapy. But if we can't make enough of a dent in your problem to terminate or break from therapy after 12 sessions, you will be able to experience group treatment firsthand. So this is an opportunity to get help in a way you wouldn't have expected. Since the whole purpose of therapy is to do things to help ourselves that we haven't done before, this policy has been very helpful to people who wouldn't have taken to group treatment.

It is important to emphasize the positive aspects of such a policy, since the patient may think being assigned to a group means failure as a patient.

The therapist might bear in mind that it appears most of the benefit of therapy comes in the early sessions; after about 20 sessions, actual progress seems to diminish (Howard et al., 1986). Steenbarger (1994), in a fine-grained analysis, finds that some patients (such as those with borderline or other personality disorders) do take much longer to reach a therapeutic plateau. Nevertheless, the therapist should expect a great amount of change, Steenbarger argues, in the very early sessions, when motivation and openness to change are at their peak.

Schedule sessions on the basis of completion of homework and other therapy-related issues, not to make your schedule more predictable. The patient should return for a second visit when the homework is accomplished, not when a week has passed. When scheduling appointments, the therapist can ask the patient how long it will take him or her to accomplish the homework in a satisfactory way.

With some patients, you may want to take a stricter approach. You can assign the homework, troubleshoot, and assure that the assignment is understood and accepted and that the patient believes it relates to the focus. Then ask the patient to *call for an appointment when the homework is accomplished.* When would you take such a direct and one-up approach? Not every time, obviously. However, some patients have a good deal of avoidant behavior but enjoy the therapeutic relationship and want therapy to continue. They may put off doing the homework as another avoidance, unless you are able to help them see how doing that homework will be necessary before another session happens. I have actually had very good results with this technique, with the patients feeling more empowered by the emphasis on their own activity.

Consider another patient who needs more frequent treatment, such as a PTSD patient with severe, disabling symptoms (see Chapter 9) or a patient with agoraphobia. Such patients may not comply with homework because of the avoidance behavior which tends to perpetuate their symptoms. They may need daily or at least more frequent treatment (as I discuss in the next chapter) for some period until they begin to assert themselves against the symptoms. With the time created by seeing some patients every two or three weeks, there will be openings in your schedule to meet their needs for more frequent contacts.

Consider a decreasing frequency in treatment. This guideline is especially useful for insight-oriented therapists. Suppose that 12 sessions have been authorized by an insurance company. Imagine that further sessions are unlikely to be authorized. Obviously, that does not mean you must end treatment after 12 sessions, since the patient can always pay. But it means you ought to consider ending treatment at that point. So you might schedule the sessions twice a week for two weeks, then once a week for four weeks, then once every two weeks for two sessions (four weeks), and then once a month for two sessions. You have made 12 sessions last 18 weeks, and the last sessions may be as useful and powerful as any you have had. Interestingly, Frank (1991) demonstrated that monthly interpersonal psychotherapy sessions had a very powerful impact on preventing depression relapses; the patients and therapists maintained very good working relationships and weekly sessions were not at all necessary. However, when organizing her study, she encountered a good deal of skepticism in therapists as well as patients that the monthly sessions would do any good. Since the results were dramatically the reverse, this study tells us something about therapists and their inability to make accurate predictions about intensity of treatment.

Mention the passage of time at each session, and ask the patient for thoughts about that. For example, a therapist might say, "This is our fourth session. How much progress do you think you have made on this problem over the past four sessions (or eight weeks)? What seems to have worked the best? What didn't work? How comfortable are you with my approach? What would you think I should have done more of during those session? What should I do less of?"

Use "therapeutic vacations" to assess progress and stimulate motivation. Since, as Howard et al. (1986) and Steenbarger (1994) point out, the patient's acceptance of change is at a high point early in treatment, it seems likely that periodic vacations from treatment, in treating long-term patients, would be a wise idea. I have used this notion from time to time and find that it is helpful. A patient may leave treatment when things are somewhat stable, but the goals are not yet met. I suggest this vacation with the idea of asking the patient to consolidate the gains for a period of time, before pushing on. I may use the analogy of a party of mountain climbers who establish a base camp high up on the side of the mountain, and who then rest at that spot for some time before mounting the assault to the summit. The period of rest allows their bodies to be accustomed to the new altitude and to gain strength for the big push.

RELATIONSHIP-ORIENTED FACTORS

The way the patient feels about the therapist is the most important element in predicting general therapeutic benefit (Luborsky et al., 1988), as well as the specific factor of whether a patient will comply with homework (Burns & Nolen-Hoeksema, 1992). If the therapist is seen as trustworthy, caring, honest, and competent, the patient is more likely to follow the instructions and suggestions. Careful monitoring of the therapy relationship (such as by using the empathy rating scales mentioned in Chapter 3) will help a therapist understand how much can be expected.

At the same time, therapist status has some impact on patient motivation. Obviously, Milton Erickson was probably able to get better compliance from people who had to travel hundreds or thousands of miles to see him than from those who traveled across town.

Below are some suggestions, in addition to the basic one of creating a very positive relationship, which may help increase motivation.

Reach out energetically to the patient. The Miami School of Medicine group (Jose Szapocznik, William Kurtines, and others, 1989) advocates an energetic outreach to patients, especially to the drug-abusing hispanic youth who are the focus of many of their research projects. Rather than following business as usual, the therapists will go to unusual lengths to involve the identified patient in family therapy. Dr. Angel Perez-Vidal (personal communication, September 19, 1994) told of a case in which he met with the family several times, but the drug-using teen would not meet with him. Finally he learned that the youth was in the habit of spending his late evenings on a particular street corner with friends. At 11 p.m., Perez-Vidal went to that corner, talked with the teenager, and was able to convince him to participate in the family therapy.

At a more practical level, outreach might involve simply calling patients before the first visit, talking with them about their concerns and goals for therapy, and perhaps offering some simple observational task to do between that talk and the first visit. It might involve making an effort to help the patient solve practical logistical problems. Especially with minority or immigrant populations, the cultural complexities can be daunting, so the therapist may need to do what is often scoffed at as "case management." Yet the willingness of the case manager to call a school and set up a conference with a teacher and counselor, and perhaps even go to that school with the client, may make the difference between success or failure in a case. And certainly the Miami group has the evidence from their research (see Chapter 11) to suggest that such energetic outreach greatly improves retention rates in therapy and results in excellent outcomes.

Ask the patient how hard she is willing to work on the problem. A patient who will make a strong commitment will tend to live up to it, so asking for commitment can help the patient feel more involved in treatment. I once saw a woman who had been in psychotherapy off and on much of her life. She had made several suicide attempts, but felt those attempts were quite ego-alien and wondered why she felt such strong compulsions to kill herself.

She was on state disability and had exhausted her insurance benefits on psychotherapy. She was allowed eight visits with me as some kind of "last resort."

In her first session it was quite difficult to create a specific focus for treatment, not because she was not cooperative, but because the idea of focusing on small achievable changes was a new idea for her. We finally negotiated something I hoped would be workable, and I asked her, "Are you willing to work very hard to achieve these things?"

She looked stunned, sat in silence, and then said, "I've never been asked that before. . . . Well, I suppose I am." And she was, and after negotiating some helpful changes in her life, made no more suicide attempts. She didn't actually use all her sessions, but has kept them "in the bank" with me for possible future crises. She returned to work, fought off an episode of breast cancer, and still contacts me from time to time to refer friends and colleagues. After two years she recently told me suicide is no longer an option, although she still thinks about it when under stress.

David Burns says he tells his patients he is a mediocre therapist, so his patients must work very hard if they are to get well. He says he has a list of therapists in his desk who do not ask their patients to work hard, and will give that list to the patient if the patient doesn't want to work hard. Patients seem to be helped by this one-down approach, which correctly focuses on their role in treatment.

Use the customer status paradigm and follow the protocols for each relationship category. Therapists often resist my suggestions about how to work with visitors and complainants, feeling that they should confront them in order to somehow make them work on their problems. But those who follow those suggestions have reported that the patients work harder and they themselves are happier and less stressed. Certainly, in spite of the general finding that patients are most open to change early in treatment, there are some patients who are not at all ready for treatment (McConnaughy et al., 1989; Prochaska & DiClemente, 1986, 1992). Studies using the Prochaska model (precontemplation, contemplation, action, and maintenance) have demonstrated that these phases seem to carry over into all human change processes. It seems likely that patients who are "visitors" or at the "precontemplation" level are best helped by environmental manipulation, such as family and network therapy.

To make this memorable, take the example of Willie Sutton, a 1930s bank robber who was supposed to have said, when asked why he robbed banks, "Why, that's where they keep the money." In a social network, when one member is creating problems or exhibiting difficult behavior, if that member is not motivated to change (e.g., has no "money"), it is likely *someone* is motivated to see that person change. If that person can change how he or she responds to the family member who is causing trouble, it is quite likely that he will also change (Szapocznik, Kurtines, Foote, Perez-Vidal, & Hervis 1986).

Use nonverbal pacing. Match the patient's style of speech (rapid or slow, loud or soft). Speak when the patient is breathing out, and synchronize your breathing when the patient is speaking. Listen carefully for unique tonal or rhythmic speech qualities and match those. I once had a patient who would start each sentence with an elevated tone that would decline through the sentence and end on a low note. As an experiment I tried to match the tone but disagree with the content of each sentence. At the end of the session, he said he had seen several counselors but I was the only one who had ever understood him!

The Miami group calls this *mimesis* and recommends it as both a relationship-enhancing technique and as a change technique in family therapy, suggesting, "The therapist wants to be the family's leader and lead them out of their dysfunctionality. However, a leader first becomes a leader by knowing when to follow. First, the therapist follows the family through mimesis and by tracking the family's interactional patterns. Then once the family is secure with the therapist and trusts him or her, the therapist can become the family's leader" (Szapocznik, Foote, Perez-Vidal, Hervis, & Kurtines, 1985, p. 7).

Positively reframe complaints. Especially when a patient is being "resistant," try to take the patient's side and find good reasons why she should not change. Encourage the patient to go slow and be cautious about trying new changes out. For example, a patient with recurrent depression complained that he was feeling down again and felt ashamed of it since in therapy he should be getting better, not worse. I pointed out that the fact that he was honest about his depression was actually a demonstration of his integrity, since he wanted my approval and might have been tempted, if he were less honest, to pretend he was doing better than he was. He had a moment of surprise and said he realized that was true.

Reframe complaints as being as normal whenever possible. Patients who feel they are like other people or who understand others have struggled with similar issues are more likely to work hard and comply with suggestions. For example, a patient says, "I feel so very depressed." If the therapist replies, "Of course! Of course you do! Given what you have gone through, it is very natural to feel discouraged and saddened," the patient often feels encouraged to tackle some homework to change the feelings.

Go slow; advocate the problem. With some patients who have low motivation, there is considerably more power in opposing change than in advocating it. When the therapist advocates change, there is seldom a useful outcome; if the therapist advocates going slow, asks the client about the advantages of the problem, and suggests that there are some good reasons for the problem behavior to continue, the patient is left completely responsible for the behavior. The patient will either respond with more motivation and take the position opposite to the therapist, advocating change, or agree with the therapist but at least view the therapist in a much more positive light and see therapy as a more empowering experience. Then, when conditions change and the patient is ready to change, therapy will be a strong possibility.

Experiment with being one-up and one-down. Therapists usually like to be in a position of benign superiority, or one-up on the patient. However, I often have better results when I resist that temptation and go one-down, emphasizing my own limits and the patient's power and ability to act.

A patient once had seen me over 12 times for chronic headache, and she said the pain was no better. I took responsibility for that, saying somehow I had failed to understand or treat the headache appropriately. She seemed frightened and asked whether that meant I was not going to see her anymore. I replied that she was welcome to see me as long as she wanted, but with the way I had failed her in the treatment, I couldn't offer anything more than reasonably pleasant conversation. She looked thoughtful and then said with visible relief, "Well, I have been getting better, I just hadn't told you." It turned out she greatly enjoyed the psychotherapy and didn't want it to end.

Involve family or members of the social network whenever possible. Simon Budman has encouraged therapists to invite significant persons, such as family members, into the therapy hour. Budman even encourages roommates or peers to attend with the patient. Often when a patient makes some explicit or implicit commitment in the presence of significant others, that commitment has more potency and power.

The family and network members can be useful in several ways. Here are some questions to keep in mind:

- How does each person see the problem?
- Are the others aware of any exceptions to the problem the patient has overlooked?
- Are they aware of strengths in other areas the patient may have overlooked?

- How important does each person believe it will be for the patient to achieve the goal?
- If the patient is not a "customer" at that time, is here anyone in the network who is willing to work hard to make the goals turn into actualities? Recall the story of the excessively optimistic little boy who was given a pile of horse manure for a birthday present. He was thrilled, and when asked why, replied, "With all this manure, there's got to be a pony around here somewhere." Look for the pony in the pile.

Since working with court-referred patients is generally quite difficult, it is vital that the probation officer accompany the patient in the first session. Every effort should be made to get other persons who may be involved with the problem to attend. This can save much time and effort, and prevent your chasing down blind alleys.

Manage contingencies. Encourage patients to create various contingencies for their own benefit, either involving relationships with others or with themselves. As my friend Doug with the checks to the Nazis demonstrated, it is possible to use many positive and negative consequences to achieve new behaviors. For example, some smoking and weight loss programs ask for a deposit, which will be returned if the patient is successful in changing his or her behavior. Milton Erickson once took a couple into therapy who had very little money. He told them he would use experimental therapy on them, and if it worked, he would learn from them and they would not owe him any money. However, if it didn't work, he would not learn anything so they would owe him his standard fee. The couple improved.

Check up. At the risk of stating the obvious, when a therapist assigns homework, it is vital that he ask about it. The therapist should emphasize the importance of the homework both verbally and nonverbally. Talk about whether it is a feasible project, ask about whether there are any reasons it cannot be done, and ask the client to critique or change it.

I consulted to a therapist who asked for advice about creating homework for a patient. After she described the problem, I asked what homework had been assigned. She thought a bit and then explained what she had proposed. When I asked her what the patient said in the next session, she looked confused and finally said, "Well, he didn't mention whether he had done it." The session had then drifted off into intellectualizing and failed to accomplish anything.

Be cautious about what you ask the client to reveal; reveal a moderate amount of relevant information about yourself. Meichenbaum and Turk (1987) demonstrate that patients asked to reveal a great deal of very personal information actually feel less motivated and empowered, whereas a moderate level of self-disclosure enhances motivation and compliance with therapeutic regimens (pp. 79–80). In consulting with therapists, I have often noticed that they ask for too much disclosure early on, and are then surprised by the patient's lack of cooperation or early dropout. On the other hand, Hill (1989) demonstrated that patients whose therapists disclosed a moderate amount of relevant information about themselves were more motivated and benefited more from therapy than those whose therapists maintained complete anonymity. Therapist self-disclosure was most positive and motivational when a therapist revealed personal conflicts or problems that were not resolved. The patient felt paradoxically motivated by knowing that the therapist could live well without solving all problems.

COGNITIVE TECHNIQUES

The way a patient thinks about the problem obviously greatly influences motivation and compliance. This section emphasizes using or influencing the thinking style.

Match the client style with the homework style. Some patients are random and impulsive in their style, while others have systematic and effortful styles. A typical therapist can easily cooperate with the systematic and effortful style; she recognizes it from her own graduate school days. But how do you cooperate with a random style? You might consider giving the patient a coin to flip or asking him to draw from a deck of cards. The homework is either done or not done, depending on the luck of the coin flip. For example, if the coin is heads, the patient will do the homework, and if the coin is tails, the patient will do the problem behavior.

Another style variable is vague versus specific. Vague patients seem to respond well to homework that includes doing one of several tasks and noticing which of those has the most appeal. Often the vague patient does something that is quite unrelated to the homework assignments, but nevertheless shows an attempt to solve the problem.

Yet another style is symbolic versus pragmatic. I seem to have no response at all to symbolic activities; they just mean nothing to me. My wife believes if she painted our home red or black, I would not notice. She is probably correct. That is a serious lack in my life, and when I go through symbolic actions, there is just no emotional response. However, many of my patients are much more responsive to symbolic homework than, for example, to pragmatic cognitive-behavioral homework. I believe I can recognize symbolic patients from the numerous analogies and metaphors in their speech. Patients who speak less poetically seem to respond better to behavioral assignments.

Discuss in great detail the efforts the client has made to solve the problem. Look for what worked and what did not. Emphasize how the failed efforts did not work, and ask how ready the patient is to try new things that may work better. Emphasize the exceptions, and ask the patient how the relief from the symptoms helped. How willing is the patient to enjoy more of those exceptions, even if it is hard work? Point out that, although some of the efforts to solve the problem failed, the intention behind the effort was a success, since it proved the patient really wants to solve the problem.

*Use the crystal ball technique.** Ask the patient to imagine he can see the future in a crystal ball. How will life be when the problem is solved? Who will be first to notice the problem is solved? What will his reaction be when he notices? How will the patient let others know the problem is solved? How will they react?

Another crystal ball can demonstrate the future if there are fewer changes, and yet another ball will predict the future if no change at all occurs. For people who do not relate to the specific image of a crystal ball, a television with a videotape from the future will do just as well. Various videotapes represent the various trajectories the future might take, depending on the patient's efforts. As Yoda says, "Always in motion, the future is."

Do a cost-benefit analysis. Help the client make a list of pros and cons for change, the costs and benefits of an intense change effort versus staying as he is. Efforts to change the problem behavior are going to create their own problems, and these should be anticipated and thought through. Paradoxically, it has been the experience of therapists using this approach that taking the "devil's advocate" position results in the patient's feeling more motivation to change.

Conversely, if you don't want the patient to change, it might help to strongly confront the patient with the need to change. It appears that the more strongly I feel about the need for someone to change, the less strongly he feels about it.

---

*Is this a cognitive technique? I think so, since it focuses on a change in the style of thinking (from past to future) and a restructuring of that style. It suggests an attention to what in the patient can be immediately changed to produce a concrete change in feeling and behavior. Creating an image of a future without the problem (or with the problem even worse) certainly changes the thinking a person does about the problem.

Discuss the task. As the therapist gives the homework, there should be extensive give-and-take about the task:

- "Please rate, on a scale of 1–10, how important to you it will be to accomplish the goal we are working on?"
- "Do you understand the need for doing this homework? Is it clear to you why I want you do to it? What do you think is behind my asking you to do this?"
- "How likely are you, on a 1–10 scale, to do this homework? What could make it slightly more likely?"
- "What things might make it more difficult for you to do this experiment? What could make you forget about it? How can we solve those problems?"
- "How much do you expect this homework to help? If you notice it helps less than that, but still helps a bit, would that be enough to make you continue the work?"
- "How will you remember to do it? How do you usually remember things that are important?"

Ask the patient to feed back to you what she thinks the assignment is. Patients who accurately recollect their instructions are three times more likely to comply than those whose recollections are blurred or inaccurate; two items in doctor instructions are likely to be remembered perfectly; with four, one will be forgotten; with eight items, half will be forgotten (Meichenbaum & Turk, 1987, p. 138). Remind yourself to keep the experiments quite simple and to stick to one homework assignment per session. Homework should have very few steps; if the patient cannot feed back the steps and essential elements of the assignment, it is too complicated.

Tape record sessions and give the tape to the client. As the client listens to the tape during the week, the session's learnings and reframing are reinforced. Patients will sometimes think of the problem from a different perspective when they hear the problem described on the tape.

Use language that presupposes the problem will be solved, the patient will do the homework, and life will improve. "When you have solved this problem, what difference will it make in your life?" "How will you remember to do this homework?" Rather than use conditional language ("if you improve"), use language that conveys your absolute conviction that the patient will get better. The only uncertainty is how, when, and how to adjust when that happens.

Milton Erickson told me a story about one of his daughters who served as a demonstration subject for a group of doctors who were learning hypnosis. They tried to induce a "glove anesthesia," which means the patient feels very numb in the hand. She was not demonstrating glove anesthesia no matter what they did, so Erickson called a colleague in. He quickly worked with her and produced the desired result. While she was still in hypnosis, the neophytes asked her, "Why could Dr. X induce glove anesthesia in you, and we couldn't?"

"Oh," she replied, "when he asked me to have glove anesthesia, *he really meant it.*"

Erickson then commented on the exquisite sensitivity in patients to our very subtle emotional states. If we have doubts about the patient, the patient will percieve it, no matter how we try to hide it. In hypnosis, that perception is simply more accessible and can be reported on. But it is always there. As Beier says, "The unconscious is always showing."

As you, the therapist, become used to using definite, presuppositional language, this has a therapeutic effect on you, and eventually it will also affect your patients. It is more important for you to change than your patients, since they can then follow your lead.

Use charting and contracting. When the patient writes down behaviors, that act in itself has an impact on their occurrence. Behavioral techniques of rewards and response-cost are useful here. Contracting is especially helpful with teenagers, if you can create a menu of rewards. For each positive behavior, the parents give the teen points on a chart. Then the points can be spent, like money, for various activities, such as roller-skating, time away from the family, CDs, and so on.

ORDEALS AND BINDS

Milton Erickson was a great believer in putting people through ordeals to motivate them. He would ask them to do very difficult, embarrassing things; he found that subsequently they would do easier things with great relief. Therapists seldom use ordeals because of the difficulty in gaining compliance. Erickson would often accompany patients who had social phobias into various extremely embarrassing situations, doing everything he could to make the situation even worse. He asserted that the patients would then do a good deal more than they had prior to the ordeal. How he kept the ordeal from becoming traumatizing to patients was never clear to me. Perhaps it was his presence in some situations; however, in others the patient was alone. I recommend that therapists never use ordeals unless they have received skilled and competent supervision in their use, since if done unskillfully they could become traumatic rather than empowering.

The most likely outcome in such a case is that the patient leaves, unhappy with therapists and missing an opportunity to change.

Converting Ordeals to Binds

A variation on an ordeal is to ask the patient to do a very difficult task, and then allow the patient to turn it down. Afterwards the patient can be asked to do something rather less difficult. The patient often feels compelled to accept the second task, since it is a compromise. Cialdini (1984) discusses this sales ploy, illustrating it with the Boy Scout who tried to sell him tickets to a Scout-O-Rama for $5.00. He refused. The scout then offered a $1.00 candy bar, and Cialdini felt compelled to buy two of them. He refers to this as "reciprocity," meaning the Boy Scout had done something for Cialdini (letting him off the hook for the Scout-O-Rama tickets) so Cialdini had to reciprocate by buying two candy bars.

Another bind is to start with a small commitment (ask the patient to sign a statement in the session of some positive intent, such as, "I think I should not yell at my wife"). Having done that, the patient is more likely to agree to doing a difficult task, such as perform some unpleasant activity if he does yell at his wife (such as spending a good deal of money on his mother-in-law whom he dislikes). In either variation, there is some advantage in having a step-by-step strategy for helping the patient carry out homework assignments.

SOCIAL AGREEMENT

Cialdini (1984) has illustrated the powerful influence other people have on our behavior. (Anyone who lived through the late '60s can testify to some of the foolish and cruel things people did as part of group think, such as spitting on soldiers returning from Vietnam.) Group therapy takes advantage of this phenomenon. In particular, patients can benefit from seeing other people try out assertiveness or nondefensive communication, and are more likely to try it themselves as they see others doing it.

Use anecdotes to decrease resistance. If the patient is likely to resist a homework assignment, I can tell a brief example of someone who had a similar problem early in the session. Stories are an excellent way of reducing doubt about an assignment, and they take advantage of the human tendency to structure our behavior based on our understanding of what other people would do in the same situation. Stories are perhaps one of the most ubiquitous forms of human thought. As Gregory Bateson's story has it, a man programmed all knowledge possible into a large computer, and then asked the computer, in his best Fortran language, "Do you compute that a computer will ever be able to think like a human?" After a pause, he read the answer, "That question reminds me of a story. . . . "

Use the group. One advantage of doing therapy in family, network, or group settings is that the therapist can carefully attend to the person who seems to be most agreeable to a task or experiment. Then, as the homework is presented, he can talk to that person first, to the next most agreeable person next, and so on, ending with the most resistant person last. In family therapy, ask for compliance in a homework assignment with the most motivated family member. Invite roommates and friends of the client to attend the session and ask them for some very small act to help the client achieve his goals. Then ask the client himself for a bigger commitment.

RELAPSE PREVENTION

When a patient begins to make any sort of progress, I immediately begin to ask myself and the patient about relapse. Since variations in behavior are natural and normal, it is also natural for patients to have lapses back to previous forms of behavior. If the therapist can predict and discuss this ahead of time, it motivates the patient to continue in the good behavior despite relapses. By discussing the relapse, the therapist normalizes it as variation which is to be expected, even learned from. But if the therapist were to avoid discussing relapse, the patient might interpret a slip as a catastrophe and give up any effective coping.

So whenever the patient reports some improvement, I do one or some of the following:

- *Predict the relapse.* Point out the variability in human nature and how the problem behavior may feel quite lonely and want to return. By discussing this, the patient is being prepared for such a possibility.
- *Advocate the relapse.* I sometimes advocate relapse as a learning device. "What do you think you can learn if you were to relapse? How could a relapse actually strengthen you?" When I have a relationship where I can gently tease the patient, I may point out that with such rapid progress I won't make very much money and won't be able to live quite so well. It would be very nice to have a relapse occur so as to improve my income.
- *Rehearse relapse and recovery in fantasy.* Ask the patient to imagine the first part of a lapse. How will she react to that? There are obviously choice points early on that determine whether a full-blown relapse results or merely a small stumble will follow. For example, I might say to the patient, "Suppose you could win ten million dollars by having a genuine relapse. If that were the case, how would you go about it? How far into

a lapse would that take you? What would you have to do then to go even further into a relapse? What would undermine your relapse at that point?"

In general, there is a good deal of research suggesting that relapse prevention is powerful and useful. There are no actual studies of my particular techniques. However, my results are good, so I would ask the reader to keep an open mind and try them out. I find that the patients gain a certain amount of motivation to continue with their work on an issue when some effort is made to prevent relapse.

Kurtines, Hervis, and Szapocznik (1989) discuss a successful family therapy in which a relapse occurred. They comment, "*This was the family system's effort to return to its previous pathologic homeostasis, and it is in this situation that experienced therapists' skills distinguish them from naive therapists*; they have to help the family overcome the crisis while maintaining the gains made in therapy" (italic in original). While there are those who suggest that relapse is a construction of the therapist and is not likely to occur unless the therapist expects it, the preponderance of evidence contradicts this, and so the wise therapist will be prepared for setbacks and prepares the patient or family for them.

SECTION III

*Specific
Applications*

CHAPTER 9

Time-Sensitive Treatment and the Traumatized Patient

A psychiatric consultant to a large managed care program privately considers certain patients to be almost untreatable, namely those with the constellation of symptoms arising from early and sustained trauma. These include post-traumatic stress disorder, dissociative identity disorder, and some of the character disorder spectrum, especially borderline personality. He calls these the psychological equivalent of serious, chronic, untreatable physical diseases. He made this judgment after reviewing cases where the patient had a long treatment history punctuated by many crises and little or no substantial progress.

In mental health centers around the country, I have heard this same belief frequently expressed. Therapists find treating the trauma group to be slow, frustrating, and unrewarding work. The trauma survivor may even be seen as a troublemaker, someone who seems to take perverse delight in stymieing the good intentions of the counselor.

COMMON TREATMENT TRAPS

In reviewing cases from around the country for managed care, I have seen definite patterns in the ineffective treatment of these patients. The therapist typically perceives quite correctly that the patient's defenses serve to avoid remembering and working through a traumatic event or series of events. The therapist assures the patient that she will be well once the trauma is uncovered. The patient valiantly tries to remember the trauma and in fact does recover painful and frightening memories. As that happens, the patient begins to experience dramatic worsening of symptoms, often including self-injury (the "parasuicides" of Linehan, 1987) and a variety of panic symptoms. The patient is fearful and reaches out to the therapist, who tries to be available. The therapist may give a home number and encourage the patient to call if things get suicidally bad.

The sessions become more frequent, several times a week. There are frequent desperate telephone calls. However, not infrequently the heroic efforts aren't enough, the patient's coping deteriorates, and the patient requires hospitalization. The symptoms are usually assumed to hide more and more trauma. Hypnosis may be utilized to uncover those wounds. Repeated "abreactive" events may take place. The patient becomes less functional and declares that if she is released from the hospital she will certainly kill herself.

Eventually a stabilization of sorts occurs, and the patient is released from the inpatient acute treatment setting. There follows a long period of intensive therapy, again marked by uncovering of more trauma, more exacerbations of symptoms, and increasing intensity of treatment. Day treatment or repeated visits to the acute care facility may occur. This type of pattern following the valiant and sincere efforts of the therapist leads to a general pessimism. The patient believes she will never recover, and privately the therapist may be inclined to agree.

THE EXPERT VIEWS

Experienced therapists specializing in this area take a different view. They propose dramatically divergent models of treatment but all agree that the trauma group is quite treatable (Beahrs, 1982; Beahrs, Butler, Sturges, Drummond, & Beahrs, 1992; Dolan, 1991; Herman, 1992; Horowitz et al., 1984; Kernberg, 1975; Kluft, 1982; Kohut, 1971; Linehan, 1987; Masterson, 1981; van der Kolk, 1987). There is a split, even a gulf, between the experts in the field and the frontline therapists.

It may be that common thinking and expert views differ about treatability of these patients because the typical therapist does not follow the same treatment patterns and plans the experts do. It is most important, therefore, for psychotherapists to begin a dialogue with the goal of creating a reasonably common set of treatment protocols for the trauma group. The dialogue should be characterized by a considerate clash of ideas and may result in the development of technical improvements that will make this group treatable by the average therapist.

Certainly it is not necessary to engage in intensive, weekly, or even insight-oriented psychotherapy in order to help this group of patients, as the following case suggests:

Case Example: Life Without Hope

A 30-year-old woman complained of devastating levels of depression. She could hardly get out of bed. Life felt empty and flat. In therapy she exhibited unusual shifts. At times she would tell about a trauma during her teenage years, while at other times she would deny that any such thing had happened to her. She alluded to a rape that happened when she was 13, but then suggested it was not what was really bothering her. Slowly the picture emerged of a woman who had been victimized by a predatory pedophile, a man who carefully groomed her to become his sex object when she was only 11 years old. This relationship persisted for a year and a half. She remembered the experience only slowly and with great pain. During that time, she abused alcohol and drugs and cut on herself as a way of alleviating the emotional pain.

Her treatment was different from what might be considered usual in two aspects: First, a strong emphasis was placed on developing feelings of confidence and comfort (Dolan, 1991), something she claimed she never experienced. Before any attempts at helping her remember or work through trauma, she practiced again and again creating feelings of safety and security. And second, in place of weekly sessions, she often came only once or twice per month. This was mostly because of financial limitations and insurance difficulties. Because of her difficulty in attending weekly sessions, the therapist had to put much more emphasis on homework assignments designed to help her desensitize herself outside of the sessions.

In spite of a less intensive treatment regimen, she did make good progress, although complaining bitterly about anhedonia (lack of pleasure). She went through a bout of cutting on herself, but responded well to an hypnotic intervention. This intervention was based on the observation that exposure and response prevention were the treatment of choice for obsessive-compulsive disorders, and her cutting seemed to fit that paradigm. She would feel increasing tension when she happened to see a knife, which was only relieved by making small cuts on herself. While the knife had significance in her abuse history, insight about the origin of the feeling made no difference.

The intervention was based on her high degree of hypnotizability. She was encouraged to experience two simultaneous phenomena: time distortion and catalepsy (inability to move). When she felt each minute seeming like a long time (as much as an hour), she was asked to see a knife in front of her, which would divide into two, the two becoming four, the four becoming eight, and so forth. Over a period of an hour of "real" time, many hours subjectively, she saw knives without being able to act on her desire to cut on herself. Suddenly, she relaxed and said, "They are just knives." From that day on she had no cutting episodes.

She did not respond to several antidepressants, fell into and climbed out of drug and alcohol abuse, but over several years of therapy obtained a college education and professional level employment, identified and worked through a number of early stressors, including the prolonged sexual abuse, and improved her marriage, avoiding at least once a threatened divorce. She did a good deal of reading, learned the meaning of "borderline personality disorder," which she decided fit her quite well, and was quite dismayed at the grim prognosis given her condition by commentators.

As the therapist, I was pleased and surprised at the progress the patient made, in spite of not attending therapy every week. Is it possible the intensive (weekly or more often) model of treatment is not necessary? Could it be that in some cases intensive treatment may cause deterioration? Therapists need to determine the most effective and efficient way of treating patients with traumatic childhoods. If weekly therapy is not necessary, this fact must be discovered and communicated.

In this process, it is wise to continue to listen to William of Occam, whose voice echoing down through time tells us the simplest explanation is the best. With his "razor" we cut away approaches involving intensive individual therapy, unless it can be demonstrated that those approaches are superior to less intensive approaches. And that cannot be demonstrated, partly because these are difficult questions to answer, and partly because at least one investigation has indicated that a less intensive alternative produces equivalent outcomes (Beahrs et al., 1992). Beahrs and his group have found that monthly individual therapy and optional weekly group therapy seem to be as useful as more intensive therapy; we can learn from studying their results.

DANGERS OF INTENSIVE TREATMENT

It may even be that much intensive treatment is dangerous. As Beahrs (Beahrs & Torem, 1990) points out, regression is the most common iatrogenic factor in treatment of dissociative identity disorder patients. He points out that this regression results from an "overly nurturant" therapeutic stance. He offers the example of a patient who shows both enormous dependency needs and excessive demands for autonomy. When the therapist tries to meet the dependency needs, the autonomy demands are threatened, leading to difficulties and distancing in the therapy. This promotes fear of abandonment, which leads to more dependency needs, and so on.

Beahrs (personal communication) has documented cases in which the patients are more disturbed after such treatment than before. He believes this deterioration is likely to be caused by treating the patients as special or unique. The dissociative patient may be offered abundant nurturing, with a good deal of attention being given to her distress and incapacity. Therapists may believe it is unrealistic or even cruel to require responsible behavior from the patient or to fail to meet her needs for being taken care of. They may see themselves as likewise special, with unique depth of understanding that will allow them to help the patient where others would fail (Beahrs & Torem, 1990, p.4).

DEVELOPING ALTERNATIVES FOR TREATMENT

Linehan also proposes an alternative to the traditional individual treatment, based on cognitive-behavioral therapy, and we can learn by comparing her approach (Linehan, 1981, 1987; Shearin & Linehan, 1989) to Beahrs'. While Linehan's techniques are helpful, hers is still a fairly intensive approach. Also, specific strategies for treatment can be derived from Dolan (1991), who is not specifically "brief" but whose style may encourage briefer treatment by not adhering to the requirement that therapy take place weekly and only in the therapist's office. Instead, she links therapeutic progress with homework assignments and building internal resources, consistent with Beahrs. Because Dolan is often unavailable because of her teaching schedule, her patients necessarily go more than a week without contact with the therapist. However, they do not go two or three weeks without treatment, since they are carrying out treatment on themselves constantly. It should be noted that there is a backup therapist available by telephone or in person, but this has seldom been necessary. In fact, Dolan reports (personal communication, June 17, 1994) that many of her patients experiencing intensive recall of memories choose to schedule their session every three weeks. This helps them feel in control of the rate at which they are working on the memories. She recommends that the therapist respectfully ask how often the patient needs to come; in addition, she gives patients the option of canceling sessions when they feel strong enough to go without the contact. They know they can keep the session if they need it, but they can and often do cancel it. This is a dramatic departure from the common practice of wanting weekly or more frequent treatment.

She also finds that patients often take breaks from treatment of two or three months when they need to do so. Since the healing is not linked to working with the therapist, those patients are continuing to improve. Dolan believes intensive therapy can exacerbate the patient's symptoms in some cases, although other patients may benefit from intensive treatment.

REVIEW OF THE BEAHRS MODEL

The Beahrs et al. (1992) study proposed a comparison between intensive individual psychotherapy and "strategic self-therapy" for a range of challenging patients, including diagnoses of multiple personality disorder (now called dissociative identity disorder), dissociative disorder, PTSD, and borderline personality disorder. The results are very encouraging. His group found that intensive individual therapy and self-therapy produced equivalent outcomes, with the advantage going to self-therapy, since the patients were seen much less often individually (once per month, generally), with the emphasis being on group treatment and individually designed and implemented homework assignments.

Strategic self-therapy (SST) is derived from hypnosis and strategic therapy, which view personality as capable of significant change without the extensive "working-through" of individual psychodynamic therapy. Beahrs et al. (1992) describe the features as follows: Individual therapy is limited to one regular and one optional, additional hour of individual therapy per month. Patients may substitute the second individual hour of therapy for a weekly therapy group. The goal of the therapist is to help the patient define activities that can be done *outside* of the therapy hour which will result in a change in the character structure. Linehan's model (Shearin & Linehan, 1989) also emphasizes both group and individual therapy, with distinct tasks for each treatment.

SST emphasizes the healing nature of explicit definitions of roles, responsibilities, and therapeutic boundaries. The very act of defining those creates safety and a focus on achievable goals, something the traumatized person often has never had.

The patient has two responsibilities, work and safety. The patient must agree to work on therapeutic tasks for identifying and resolving conflicts, learning new perceptual patterns, and changing behaviors. The patient's responsibility for safety means guaranteeing no destructive actions to self or others. The therapist is not a protector; if the patient cannot remain safe, she must reach out to crisis agencies or emergency rooms. Hospitalization to ensure safety is a valid option, but inpatient stays are protection, not treatment. The patient remains in the hospital until ready to resume treatment. The therapist does not try to treat the patient while she is hospitalized.

SST explicitly requires a variety of social supports. The therapists do not protect the patient, so other agencies must be available for this task. As stated, emergency rooms and crisis hotlines are resources; even the police can be useful supports. The therapist must be well acquainted with emergency resources in the community. The boundaries of the therapist are emphasized here. It is simply impossible for the therapist to be a safety source for the patient. Patients are expected to learn and to use the emergency resources in the community, and the therapist maintains clear communication with those resources.

Beahrs' view of the therapist is essentially that of a coach or a consultant.

The therapist reframes negative behaviors as having positive functions or intentions, suggests homework assignments, and engages in teaching and explaining. The relationship with the client is marked by delineating what the therapist can and cannot do. There is little emphasis on working through historical trauma in this model, and a stronger emphasis on (a) changing the viewing of the problems, (b) changing the doing of the problems, and (c) enhancing the general sense of competency and mastery.

(a) *Changing the viewing.* Both Beahrs and Linehan (Shearin & Linehan, 1989) emphasize the paradoxical acceptance and positive reframing of negative symptoms. In my own experience in consulting and supervising therapists, this is one of the most difficult aspects for the therapist, although not for the patient. Therapists tend to be too judgmental and rigid and fail to see the positive aspects of negative behaviors. For example, flashbacks can be seen as a signal that a memory is lonely and isolated and wants to get in and be with all the other (positive and neutral) memories. If a patient is resistant to therapy, this is congratulated, since it shows a great deal of independence of thought and action. Depressive symptoms are seen as attempts to grieve the loss of childhood trust or safety. Panic symptoms are a warning to go slower in treatment, perhaps as communicating a need to see the therapist less often. Missed appointments are seen as a strength, denoting that the patient secretly (unconsciously) feels strong and needs less frequent appointments. I follow through with that by encouraging the patient to take a break from another two scheduled appointments when one is missed. Patients who see themselves as "wishy-washy" can come to see that as flexible and open-minded. The essential element, Beahrs et al. (1992) argue, is to approach and even accept what was formerly avoided. This creates a change in psychological structure and alters the entire pattern of drives and defenses. In addition, the reframing is a metalearning about accepting ambiguity and a multiplicity of viewpoints as intrinsic in life.

Beahrs also emphasizes the ambiguous nature of many symptoms of multiple personality disorder (dissociative identity disorder). He views the patient as being both multiple and unitary at the same time (Beahrs, 1982); since there is a choice about how to see the disorder, he chooses to view it with emphasis on the unitary nature. This view enables the therapist to accept but deemphasize the discrete personalities, with observations that a personality state can alert the therapist to unmet needs with simply a grimace or a grunt, without "coming out." The assumption is also that vital information will somehow permeate the other personalities and that amnestic barriers, while valid, are also more flexible and permeable than might be first thought. Since suggestibility is part of this syndrome, by assuming it is true it becomes so. The experience of a dissociation can be seen as an opportunity to appreciate one's own flexibility and to increase one's leadership skills. Dealing with the multiple aspects of one's personality is very much like trying to get a work group to cooperate and work together.

(b) *Changing the doing of the problem.* Each month, as the therapist and patient meet, there is a review of the previous homework assignments and how they are going. The patient is not criticized if the tasks have not been done, but a good deal of interest is shown when they do get done. Beahrs emphasizes the patient's "self-therapy" projects of defining one's personal identity. This can be done by asking the patient to write a description of (1) the current self-description, (2) a statement of moral priorities, i.e., what the patient stands for, and (3) the direction the patient will follow, roadblocks and challenges, and plans for overcoming them. Beahrs emphasizes the process of positively reframing discordant statements in such a project; patients and therapists look for contradictions and positively connote them. It would seem likely the notion of externalizing the problem and internalizing resistance to the problem would be useful here. In other words, following White (White & Epston, 1990), one would inquire about how the problem had influenced the patient as opposed to how the patient had influenced her/his own life.

(c) *Increasing patient experience of competence and mastery.* This involves meditation or relaxation skills, improving personal habits such as exercise, eating, and sleeping, vocational projects such as job training or classes, and so on. These stress management techniques seem to have a generally useful effect.

OTHER TREATMENT APPROACHES

In addition to Beahrs' techniques, cognitive and behavioral approaches provide useful tools for the therapist treating trauma. Protocols focusing on acute trauma (e.g., rape) have emphasized two general strategies that can be applied to the more chronic patients. These are stress management (general coping skills) and intensive working-through of the traumatic memories, that is, a strong exposure-based treatment, as demonstrated in the earlier case.

Stress Inoculation Training

Based on the concept that trauma leaves one feeling out of control and helpless, the goal of stress inoculation training (SIT) is to teach skills that give a sense of mastery (Kilpatrick, Veronen, & Resick, 1982; Kilpatrick & Amick, 1985). The argument is that a feeling is mastery is directly helpful and healing in combatting the helplessness of rape. Specific components of the treatment are:

1. Cognitive understanding of PTSD symptoms; symptoms are reframed as attempts to help master the trauma. Symptoms are broken down into three categories, and the patient thinks of examples of each:

   (a) Physical symptoms and autonomic arousal (shaking, heart racing, etc)
   (b) Behavioral symptoms and responses (e.g., avoidance, non-assertiveness)
   (c) Cognitive processes: thoughts, beliefs, memories (e.g., flashbacks, catastrophic fears, self-doubt and self-criticism)

2. Two coping skills for each channel are taught: a primary and a backup skill. The patient selects three target fears she would like to reduce and keeps a scale diary of fear and happiness three times a day. The patient also keeps a diary of thoughts about the fear three times a day.
3. Skill package:

   (a) Muscle relaxation (usually progressive relaxation)
   (b) Breath control (diaphragmatic controlled breathing)
   (c) Covert modeling and mental rehearsal of responses to anxiety-provoking situations
   (d) Role playing of assertive and coping behaviors
   (e) Thought stopping
   (f) Assertive cognitive therapy: practice in adaptive self-talk

Foa, Rothbaum, Riggs, and Murdock (1991) found SIT effective in treatment of rape, compared with supportive counseling or with the waiting list group. It was more effective immediately after treatment, when compared with prolonged exposure and supportive counseling. Prolonged exposure, however, was more effective at follow-up (approximately 3.5 months after treatment).

Prolonged Exposure

The purpose and rationale of prolonged exposure (PE; Foa et al., 1991) are to promote adequate cognitive processing of the memory and a change in response to the memory through cognitive restructuring. The notion is that when the victim recalls in detail the trauma in the presence of a safe party, the therapist, the desensitization effect will occur. There is a reciprocal inhibition effect from the contrast between the safety of the office and the horror of the event. The treatment protocol is: The victim is asked to recall the memory in detail, and to talk about it with the therapist. Then:

1. A hierarchy of components of the memory is constructed, with emphasis on aspects of memory and environment that are feared/avoided. Note some items are memory, and some may be actual stimuli, such as certain locations.
2. Sessions last 90 minutes or more. The client is encouraged to repeatedly describe items from the hierarchy. By the third session, the patient is encouraged to be very specific and detailed in her descriptions.
3. The patient's descriptions last at least 60 minutes of the session. These are tape recorded, and the patient is assigned the task of listening to the tape in between sessions.
4. Patients rate their level of distress throughout the session, and are helped to reduce their distress before the end of the session.
5. Homework is constructed by identifying safe but feared activities. The patient is assigned to expose herself to some of those activities and to prolong the exposure until some reduction in fear is noted. The patient keeps a diary of her reactions to the homework; that is reviewed with the therapist. Additional training, such as for assertiveness, is offered on an individual basis, depending on needs of the patient.

Cognitive Processing Therapy

Since both stress inoculation therapy and prolonged exposure have been demonstrated to have clinical value in treating rape victims, Resick and Schnicke (1992; Calhoun & Resick, 1993) propose a combination. Their protocol is as follows:

1. Before first session: Since clients are marked by avoidance and often do not show, the therapist contacts the patient prior to first session and discusses resistances, normalizing desire to avoid, encouraging a new approach rather than same old coping. Usually therapists and patients are matched by gender. Resick's studies focus on rape and her therapists are female. It is not clear whether this is necessary.
2. Patient assessment includes the Symptom Check List (SLC-90, Derogatis, 1977), PTSD Symptom Scale (Foa, Riggs, Dancu, & Rothbaum 1993), and Impact of Events Scale (IES, Horowitz ,Wilner, & Alvarez, 1979). Therapists who regularly treat PTSD can benefit from Resick's emphasis on measurement. The use of such standard inventories can help the therapist and patient track progress. Dolan (1991) has created

a Solution-Focused Recovery Scale (a version of which is found at the end of this chapter), which is well suited to tracking progress. The main difference between the package Resick uses and Dolan's scale is the emphasis on positive coping in Dolan's work, as opposed to the more typical emphasis on "what is wrong" in the other assessment tools.

3. Patient discusses the memory in detail. Memories discussed in therapy are taped and listened to in between sessions. However, more emphasis is put on confronting misattributions, self-blame, unrealistic expectations, and so on than might be done in prolonged exposure (PE). This reminds one of Dolan's emphasis on titrating the recall of trauma. However, Dolan focuses on associative cues for safety, instead of the cognitive interpretations. Resick's steps for confronting misattributions are:

(a) It is assumed that prior schema and conflicting information produce maladaptive symptoms (see Horowitz, 1986, for a more extensive discussion of this). The patient is educated about the nature of the conflict between her beliefs and her experiences. The symptoms of PTSD can be normalized in this process.

(b) Memory is dealt with by asking patient to *write* the memory of the event, in a safe, private place. She is to emphasize her emotions and to read that description to herself daily. (This reminds one of the PE homework of listening to the audiotape account recorded during therapy, as well as the write-read-burn assignment of de Shazer, 1985.)

(c) In session the therapist and the patient read the account. The therapist helps label feelings and identify stuck points. The cooperative nature of this task supports desensitization to the memory, since there should be some reciprocal inhibition of the stress response syndrome resulting from the sharing of the memory with a sensitive and sympathetic counselor.

(d) Treatment emphasizes cognitive therapy. An A-B-C-D-E homework is assigned (At first, the assignment is only A-B-C; the D-E part is added when the client has understood the first part.) The patient writes thought diaries and the therapist helps her walk through the steps. A = Action or adverse experience, which triggers B = Beliefs about self, other, the future, the world generally, and so on, which cause C = Consequent emotions and behaviors (e.g., avoidance, depression, etc.). D = I can Develop new beliefs and Dispute the old ones. This is done through analysis of the thoughts and labeling/reframing them with typical cognitive categories, such as mental filter, catastrophic thinking, allnone, mind reading, fortune telling, and so on. E = I can notice the Effect of reframing my own thinking patterns, which lets me plan new behaviors for the future. This and similar cognitive assignments give a patient some sense of control over her thoughts and feelings.

EYE MOVEMENT DESENSITIZATION

Shapiro (1989a, 1989b, 1991a, 1991b) has proposed a procedure for treating stressful memories and unpleasant emotions. The procedure involves creating a hierarchy of memories or unpleasant emotions, self-talk, or images, and asking the patient to vividly imagine a particular scene while moving the eyes. Somehow the movement of the eyes seems to desensitize the patient to the painful memories.

The technique itself is fairly straightforward. Creating a hierarchy results in specific scenes in the traumatic memory being scaled as to their current upsetting quality. For example, the patient may describe a memory where she was beaten by a gang. When she remembers it now, she rates her level of fear and upset at "7" on a 1–10 scale.

The patient is asked whether some kind of self-talk goes with that memory, such as "I was stupid to go there." If she does that kind of self-talk, the cognitions are assumed to help maintain the upset, fearful feelings. She is then asked to identify a goal, something she would like to believe. Perhaps she would like to believe "I was innocent." The patient then creates a rating of how much she believes the goal statement. For example, on a scale of 1–10, with 1 equal to "I don't believe it at all," and 10 equal to "I totally believe it," the patient may rate her belief in the idea, "I was innocent" at a 3.

It is essential to phrase the goal statements in positive language, such as "I was innocent," as opposed to "I was not guilty," since negative language is well-known to be more confusing to patients. To illustrate this, consider the difference between saying "I want to stop drinking" and "I want to live fully and enthusiastically in a sober lifestyle." The second, while more cumbersome, actually provides a goal; the first merely emphasizes avoidance. And as long as a patient avoids something, her mind remains on that something.

The patient is also asked to isolate the physical component of her feelings within her. For instance, she might describe a "knot" in the stomach. These components—the emotional reaction, the self-talk component, and the physical reaction—are all appropriate targets for change. In other words, each component might form the basis for attention during eye movements.

The patient is asked to keep the memory continuously in mind while at the same time following the movements of the therapist's hand in front of her face. The therapist moves his/her hand horizontally 12 inches in front of the patient's face, back and forth approximately 12 inches. The rate is two back-and-forth movements per second, and a complete set consists of 12 to 24 movements (Lipke & Botkin, 1992).

After that the patient is asked to again rate her level of discomfort. The patient also focuses specifically on the dysfunctional cognition and replaces it with the positive cognition while tracking the therapist's hand with her eyes. Validity scaling of the new cognition, how believable and valid it seems, is obtained before and after each trial.

Shapiro has reported some remarkable results from EMD (Shapiro, 1989a). While the procedure appears clinically quite helpful, unfortunately no comparative studies have demonstrated any therapeutic effect beyond placebo. Shapiro's research has failed to compare the treatment with an active ("attention placebo") condition, to measure the effect of the trauma using objective or physiological measures, and to "blind" the procedure (e.g., Shapiro both performed the therapy and measured the outcome, so "demand" and experimenter bias are present). Lytle's (1993) doctoral dissertation compared eye movement desensitization to an attention placebo, using a more exacting experimental design, and found no difference between them. At this time it is unclear whether the technique will prove more than placebo. However, therapists frequently experience amazing results with this process, the author being one of them, so it is wise to experiment with the technique clinically.

TUNING UP TREATMENT: CREATING A PROTOCOL

By now it seems clear that, while the trauma patient must be helped by some kind of desensitization procedure, to do so too early may expose the patient to relapse risks. It is also clear that elements beyond exposure are quite helpful. In any case, therapists must have some clear protocols to serve as a map, since the experience one often has with these patients is to be surrounded by endless trauma with no map for extricating oneself. It is not possible at this time to choose one protocol that is the best, based on research and clinical experience. But clearly, the protocol must include those elements that have been objectively shown to produce good treatment response with this population. I propose the following integrative treatment protocol, pointing out how the protocol follows the meta-model of effective psychotherapy previously reviewed. In other words, following a protocol and the integrative brief therapy model, the traumatized patient is not seen as unique or needing arcane, obscure therapist skills, but as someone who responds to the same basic principles of good treatment.

THE THERAPY RELATIONSHIP

There is clearly a fine line between being too helpful and not helpful enough, with the relationship suffering either way (Beahrs et al., 1992). The initial negotiation of a focus and delineating therapist and patient responsibilities appear to be vital. Using some kind of post-session relationship scale may be essential to avoid a deterioration of relationship with this population. The Burns Empathy Scale has been validated with persons with a borderline personality diagnosis (Burns & Nolen-Hoeksema, 1992).

It would be unwise for the therapist to promote or agree to a focus that includes goals of remembering all of the trauma, understanding all that has happened and so on. These are techniques, not goals (since goals tell us where we are going, not where we have been), and bear a questionable relationship to the outcome. Rather, the technique should be to remember only what is necessary for the patient to put her life back in order (Dolan, 1991). The therapist should emphasize the limitations of therapy and not encourage unrealistic dependency or hold out exorbitant hopes (Beahrs et al., 1992). If the therapist cannot actually do something, that fact should be made quite plain.

Many therapists resist this formulation, pointing out that the therapist knows what a healthy life is, and often the patient does not, so the therapist should take the lead in defining goals and appropriate behavior. There is much to be said for this position, but it also has some potential costs. With such patients one can argue that avoidance of unrealistic dependency is crucial, as is empowerment of the patient. These can be accomplished indirectly by accepting patient goals at face value or by negotiating achievable goals based mostly on patient goals. Emphasis with the patient on the aspects of her life that are going well is certainly not compatible with a dominant position on the therapist's part suggesting, "You have not dealt with this, and you need to." While each therapist must make an individual decision, it must be pointed out that many therapists find the costs of a dominant, one-up position to be rather high, and the results to be rather moderate. For therapists who appreciate high costs and moderate results, this position can be recommended.

Boundaries and Limits in the Therapy Relationship

It must be very clear that the patient's personality can be seen as weak or strong, depending on how the therapist chooses. The traumatized patient is often suggestible, so when the therapist chooses to see the patient as weak, the patient will behave consistently with that formulation. I have treated my patients as strong, especially in light of the terrible trauma they have suffered.

I am always impressed with how well they manage to do. And I do not see the iatrogenic regression Beahrs (Beahrs & Torem, 1990) warns of.

The therapist is not the ultimate resource. It must be agreed that the therapist is not particularly available and is not responsible for keeping the patient alive during times of crisis. Since the therapist cannot reasonably be expected to be a safety net for the patient, there must be a clear understanding that the patient is responsible for doing whatever is necessary to keep herself alive and safe, including using outside resources such as crisis lines and emergency rooms when her own coping skills collapse.

Flashbacks, regression, and crises all occur; the patient must be given specific skills for dealing with them (Dolan, 1991; Kilpatrick et al., 1982; Kilpatrick & Amick, 1985). The patient must develop a series of skills and concrete, actual symbols of safety and security that can be held or otherwise serve to ground her in a feeling of self-care and self respect during difficult times.

At the end of the time limit, the patient may be ready to break from treatment. This is not termination, merely a break from therapy and a time to experiment with the gains and skills mastered thus far. Accountability extends to the patient, and she is expected to actively practice her coping skills outside of the regular therapeutic contact. In this way, the therapist may discover the patient is more robust and less needy that might be thought.

Relationship Plus Therapist and Patient Activity

Recalling that the relationship is influenced by agreement on tasks and goals, the first order of business is to identify and promote times when the patient feels safe, secure, and competent. Those feelings can be generated by carefully examining the situations, probably overlooked, in which there is some sense of those emotional resources (Dolan, 1991). The patient may be helped to feel safe by:

(a) Encouraging her to express and talk about those things she feels safe expressing.
(b) Identifying times and places of safety, and asking her to fantasize being in those situations. Scale the feeling of safety before and after practicing the imagery associated with safety.
(c) Teaching the patient meditation, progressive relaxation, or self-hypnosis to soothe and calm herself. As she routinely practices these skills, a feeling of competency is enhanced.
(d) Using the cognitive-behavioral techniques to undermine thinking patterns that promote feelings of vulnerability and fear.

When the patient is able to demonstrate to herself that she has achieved some skill at self-quieting, she may benefit from desensitizing to her trauma. The success of SIT treatment suggests the importance of enhancing the patient's sense of competence and capability and restoring a feeling of control. This may be juncture where many therapists get into difficulty with the traumatized patient, hurrying toward expression of the trauma without making sure a firm foundation of control and strength is developed.

Of course, there could be some abuse of this principle as well, with therapists not letting people talk out their immediate memories (cf. Nylund & Corsiglia, 1994). But this is the same problem which occurs with any model, namely the therapist tends to forget at times that the map is not the territory, and that the model must always be subservient to the live patient. Thus, clinical skill and judgment must temper the principle of developing inner resources first, and if the patient wishes to first discuss the trauma, she should not be prevented from that.

Creating the Clinical Focus

Nylund and Corsiglia (1994) have illustrated how rigid application of a solution-focused/forced approach (i.e., the therapist insisted the patient talk not about the trauma but only about the goals and outcomes desired) can destroy a therapy relationship. The patient felt invalidated and refused to return for a second visit. Later she called and asked for a different therapist.

The patient's views and the therapist's ideas about how to proceed must be reconciled. The patient's goals may be understanding or being able to recall completely what happened or to prove that something did happen. These may be difficult goals for the therapist to accept; he may suggest that they will be more easily achieved if the patient practices some resource skills, such as meditation, assertiveness, cognitive restructuring, and so on. In other words, the therapist must find a winning combination of what he can do well and what the client wants.

Using Time Limits

A time limit on therapy should generally be instituted at the beginning of treatment. Twelve individual sessions beginning at once or twice per week should be offered, with a shift at the end of that time to less frequent treatment. For example, it would seem reasonable to shift at the end of 12 sessions to group therapy, which is only occasionally supplemented by individual therapy. Beahrs et al. (1992) found a high dropout rate in the strategic self-therapy condition, as patients resisted the proposed treatment of monthly sessions. This may have been because those patients believed a more intense style of therapy would be necessary to help them, and thus rejected the requirements of safety and work the approach required. Beahrs (personal communication, May 1994) has since reduced the dropout rate by careful attention to initial relationship-building. A simple way of avoiding dropouts would be to offer brief intensive therapy at first with the self-therapy segment later. The integrative therapy model emphasizes the flexible use of time, instead of the rigid and sometimes unthinking use of weekly treatment.

Some patients may be able to complete 12 sessions of planned brief therapy focusing on the trauma and achieve a reasonable level of integration and functioning from that. Horowitz et al. (1984) have described a treatment stress response syndrome treatment of 12 sessions, with referral of patients with borderline style for further treatment at the end of the course of time-limited treatment. The Kilpatrick, Foa, and Resick models typically use 9–12 sessions to achieve a reasonable outcome, so it would seem a 12-session limit would be reasonable and helpful.

Combining Patient Involvement and Therapist Activity

The patient should actively desensitize herself to trauma. Remembering trauma should be secondary to gaining mastery over the memories to which she already has access. This desensitization can be accomplished by:

(a) Tape recording a session in which the patient describes a segment of trauma, and then encouraging her to listen to that tape repeatedly. Patients may overwhelm themselves if they listen without some sort of reciprocal inhibition procedure; I have had good success encouraging the patient to listen while jogging or exercising.

(b) Asking the patient to write a description of her trauma and then read it to herself once a day. I have had remarkable success the "write-read-burn" assignment described by de Shazer (1985). With this homework, the patient writes a letter of a page or more about a traumatic incident on one day. The next day, the patient reads the letter out loud, and then burns it. Some patients do better when reading the letter in the company of a witness. Often, one letter, written with the instruction to describe everything about the trauma, is sufficient. If needed, a new letter is generated. This continues until the patient is able to describe the trauma without undue emotional arousal.

(c) Following Dolan's (1991) treatment protocol: Intersperse memories of the abuse with recollections of "resource states" or feelings of safety, security, and comfort. The therapist encourages the patient to titrate the reexperiencing with positive experiences. Abreactive or cathartic experiences are discouraged, unless the patient desires such a procedure. As the patient is remembering and explaining the trauma, the therapist carefully monitors the patient for signs of distress. If the distress increases, the therapist respectfully asks whether the patient would like to take a brief break and remember the resource state. The therapist encourages the patient to discuss only those aspects of the trauma which will help the patient make a recovery from its effects. The patient is validated if she says she cannot discuss some aspects of the trauma by encouraging her to go slowly and not rush things.

(d) Asking the patient to vividly imagine what she would learn from the abuse if she were to relive it from her adult perspective. A child is completely overwhelmed by a trauma that would be understood if it happened to an adult. This helps the patient to realize the cruelty of early abuse partly in that very overwhelming quality. My own dentist, when I was a child, did not believe in using much pain killer, so I was highly apprehensive about dental work. Unfortunately, I required a good deal of dental work, and it was a horror to me to face those appointments. As an adult, I have had to undergo a variety of painful procedures, but I no longer dread them because I understand something that I didn't as a child: Pain is finite quantitatively and temporally; it always comes to an end, and I can look forward to the end of that pain. As a child, it seemed the pain would fill the universe and continue forever.

By the same token, children cannot benefit from the horrors of abuse, but oddly enough, adults can. Many men (not all, however!) who were prisoners of war in Vietnam felt that, while horrible, the experience was also one of the greatest learning episodes of their lives (Norman, 1990). Oddly enough, the average POW had a higher IQ after he was released from prison than before he was captured. While this notion that there could be some redeeming learning from abuse is offensive to some therapists, there is support for it from the POW accounts and others (for example, see "Vicki," 1994, describing her experience of being a victim of rape, beating, and attempted murder as an important learning experience).

The patient is encouraged to relive the experience from the point of view of an adult mind in the child's body, looking for information that the child could not have understood at the time. The new information comes from the patient; the therapist does not suggest anything except the undeniable fact that if such a reliving were possible, new perspectives would be inevitable. The new perspective can vary but frequently centers around the issue of responsibility. Whereas the child may have felt responsible for the abuse, the adult knows that the child is not responsible. Sometimes, although not often, patients will also see something that allows them to forgive the abuser. This new information is processed in therapy, with the patient discussing how the new viewpoint would change her thinking about the self, other, and world generally if she had been able to see it from that perspective when it happened. The patient is encouraged to think of how her future would be different if she were to come to believe her new views.

(e) Eye movement desensitization. When it helps, it often results in rapid progress.

Homework and Patient Involvement

Since the patient's daily life should demonstrate that healing is taking place, a menu of desired activities and behaviors that will symbolize healing is generated. The patient might wish to be able to go for walks by herself or to not fight with friends and associates. She might desire to be able to "trust others," in which case a variety of specific behaviors connoting trust in others (and in the self) are generated. Scaling her progress in those areas is very important, both to document progress and to keep the therapeutic focus. Scaling is also quite motivational for patients who tend to think in all-or-none terms, since it helps them see small therapeutic steps.

(a) Homework assignments should be a part of every session, and the patient should be asked about the homework in each session. The most successful treatments seem to involve high levels of effort on the patient's part outside of treatment.

(b) The patient should be helped to see the circular nature of homework. As she completes homework assignments, the therapist should investigate how the homework was helpful. There may be overlooked social reverberations, so the therapist should probe how others might be seeing the patient differently as a result of her doing that homework.

Keep the Focus on the Patient's Responsibility

The patient's focus should be on things that are her responsibility. Complaints about others must be tactfully but firmly deflected, even though those complaints may be justified. Beahrs et al. (1992) give many suggestions of appropriate treatment foci and homework assignments.

If a patient persists in complaints about others, the therapist can follow Weakland's suggestion (Weakland et al., in press). Before describing it, let me say that the reader should be warned and encouraged to keep expectations low. The technique may seem offensive to some. However, the writer has had some limited success with it, and as Senator Everett Dirksen once said, sometimes we have to rise above principle.

The therapist should thoughtfully agree that those problems are indeed difficult, and then apologize. The therapist has been looking for ways the patient can change her life, but is unable to see any. It appears the patient is not really involved in any of the problems she is complaining about, but is simply a victim of "damn bad luck." And while the therapist is sympathetic, there is nothing psychotherapy can do about bad luck. Therefore, the therapist encourages the patient to not expect any actual progress from the therapy. Thus, the therapist respectfully but firmly encourages the patient to talk only about those things for which the patient is a "customer," discouraging complainant talk.

Clearly, the therapist has spoken a painful but undeniable truth. There is little value to be gained from sharing with others the sense of misery over the way people and events treat us. There is a good deal of "damn bad luck" in life. Feeling enraged about bad luck has no appeal as a worthy strategy. And it is quite clear that psychotherapy does not change one's luck; otherwise, we would be in therapy during the week and casinos on the weekends. And though it is painful, one must occasionally confess to one's patients not only that one is not Santa Claus, but even worse, there is no such person. Often my patients will admit that they know these things are bad luck and then refocus their efforts onto more controllable aspects of their lives.

The therapist is also respectful of the patient's content and overt meaning. While therapists are often trained to confront and interpret, putting themselves in a "one-up" position vis-à-vis the patient, it can be argued that accepting the manifest content of the patient's complaints is much more considerate and promotes a cooperative relationship. In contrast, if the therapist insists he or she knows what the patient is *really* thinking, there is a considerable risk with these patients of triggering some unpleasant responses.

When the patient persists in discussing "complainant" issues, the therapist should accept that graciously but be mostly interested in how the patient copes or how she recovers when those negative experiences do happen.

Group Therapy Skills

Optimal group therapy with the traumatized patient may be somewhat different from typical group treatment (Beahrs et al., 1992). Patients are asked to complete homework assignments that may seem simplistic or trivial to the therapist. Nonetheless, these assignments seem to be quite helpful. They include discussing the necessity of abstaining from harmful activities* (e.g., cutting oneself) that interfere with the treatment and may be the equivalent of alcohol intoxication (van der Kolk, 1987), analyzing the effect of transference in their own lives and restraining the behaviors that arise from those transference feelings and discussing them in group. Other assignments for the group process would be to prepare reports on the proper role of anger in life, present reports on the patient's own values and conflicts, demonstrate proper self-care skills of eating and exercise, meditation or self-hypnosis, and so on.

The group leader should make extensive use of the solution-focused questions developed by the Brief Therapy Center of Milwaukee (de Shazer, 1985, 1988, 1991). These include (1) exception questions, (2) outcome questions, (3) scaling questions, (4) coping questions, and (5) questions to clarify issues, such as "How does that help?" and "How is that a problem?" As illustrated in Chapter 6, homework can often be derived parsimoniously through those questions.

Patients are instructed about the solution-focused questions and, as the therapist models them, begin to use them with each other. They often become quite skilled at asking about outcomes (What is the goal?) and exceptions (What are the characteristics of "better" times?). They must be cautioned to go slowly with those questions and be ready to respect a group member's right to complain about some "bad luck" situations and in that case to offer coping questions.

It is not clear whether this therapy group ought to be time-limited (Budman & Gurman, 1988) or ongoing, open-ended. In an open-ended group, a frequent topic of group discussion would be how one knows when it is time to break from therapy. The patient is not encouraged to think in terms of ending therapy, any more than a patient leaving a dentist's office is encouraged to "terminate" with the dentist. Therapy should be seen as a stabilizing force that one may need from time to time in one's life, and the patient should be free to return to the therapist or the group anytime therapy may be helpful. For this reason, doing "work" on termination feelings is probably not necessary with the vast majority of patients.

Having used individually constructed goals and scales, such as those suggested by Dolan's Solution-Focused Recovery Scale, the patient has some idea about when psychotherapy breaks can occur. This flexibility may be too disruptive for group therapy, though, since there might be no predictability about who is attending the group. Therefore, it may be wise to contract with the patient for 12 group sessions at a block. It may even be

---

*Often patients can find acceptable substitutes, such as soaking the arm in ice water instead of cutting. In other words, the intent is explored, understood, and a new behavior is substituted which may satisfy the underlying need.

useful to ask the patient to pay for all 12 sessions contracted for, whether she attends them or not. In this way, there is some predictability about who attends the group, as well as some "intermittent" quality to the therapy.

Budman and Gurman (1988) suggest that the group itself have a finite lifetime, perhaps 18 months. In this model, there would be a closed group (no new members) and an endpoint. The distinction between the time-unlimited group structure of Beahrs et al. (1992) and the Budman and Gurman model should be empirically investigated.

Thoughtful discussions about relapse should follow any reports about progress in the group (Dolan, 1991). After the patient is congratulated on her progress, she is asked to consider how a relapse may also be helpful. The therapist can suggest that a relapse might teach something instructive or enlightening about the old behavior. A relapse would make people around the patient who resent the progress feel better. It might help the patient be more convinced the old behavior really has nothing to offer.

The patient is encouraged to think of how a relapse might be arranged. If, instead of wanting the new behavior to continue, the patient wanted to relapse, how would she go about that? What sorts of situations could she concoct to promote a relapse?

And what if a relapse were to catch the patient unaware? How does she plan to respond to that? Positive thinking will not obviate the truth that bad things do happen in life, and we often feel more comfortable returning to previously learned behavior when under stress. There is a good reason to assume that the relapse will try to happen and may temporarily succeed, so a plan of action should be created.

In this way, a group norm about how to respond to a relapse is created. It is seen as a potentially instructive natural variation. The group ought to be curious, in the event of an actual relapse, about how the patient figures out it is time to end the relapse and get back to the business of recovering. Sometimes the patient will report a relapse but, when questioned, will actually already be in the recovery phase.

While much discussion of relapse prevention centers on triggers to re-lapse, I have found it more useful to discuss how the patient knows when it is time to end the relapse. What tells her that the relapse behavior is not delivering what it seems to promise? How did the patient know at *that particular time* that the relapse had run its course? Was it a relapse or just a momentary stumble? It may well be that the horrifying slide toward total regression is at least partly caused by the therapist's unwitting indirect suggestion in discussing relapse. Therapists who take the position that a relapse must never be allowed to occur may actually suggest it, as any well-trained hypnotist can testify. As the New Age cliché goes, "That which we resist, persists." When horror (on the part of the therapist) is replaced by active curiosity, the patient's relapses are actually minor experiences that create important learnings.

Finally, I find it is vital for the client to set herself goals which will indicate she is making progress. One helpful tool is Yvonne Dolan's Solution-Focused Recovery Scale. There are no published norms. High scores (up to 90) indicate good to excellent adjustment. She has generously allowed me to reproduce it in Table 9.1.

Table 9.1 Solution-Focused Recovery Scale for Abuse Survivors
Copyright © 1988, 1993 by Yvonne Dolan; 1995 by Yvonne Dolan and Lynn Johnson

Name _____ Date _____

Circle the number that applies to you today: 0 = Not at all, 1 = Just a little, 2 = Occasionally, 3 = Frequently or most of the time.

/ 0 / 1 / 2 / 3 / A. I am able to think/talk about the abuse or the sexual abuse when it is appropriate.

/ 0 / 1 / 2 / 3 / B. I am able to think/talk about things other than the abuse or sexual abuse.

/ 0 / 1 / 2 / 3 / C. I sleep adequately; I don't feel unusually sleepy in the daytime.

/ 0 / 1 / 2 / 3 / D. I feel part of supportive family.

/ 0 / 1 / 2 / 3 / E. I stand up for self (I am reasonably assertive).

/ 0 / 1 / 2 / 3 / F. I maintain physical appearance (weight, hair, nails etc.)

/ 0 / 1 / 2 / 3 / G. I go to work; I am on time, I am reasonably productive.

/ 0 / 1 / 2 / 3 / H. I am satisfied with my work.

/ 0 / 1 / 2 / 3 / I. I engage in social activities outside the home.

/ 0 / 1 / 2 / 3 / J. I have a healthy appetite.

/ 0 / 1 / 2 / 3 / K. I care for child, loved ones, pets. (I can take care of others.)

/ 0 / 1 / 2 / 3 / L. I adapt to new situations.

/ 0 / 1 / 2 / 3 / M. I initiate contact with friends, loved ones.

/ 0 / 1 / 2 / 3 / N. I show a sense of humor.

/ 0 / 1 / 2 / 3 / O. I am interested in future goals.

/ 0 / 1 / 2 / 3 / P. I pursue leisure activities, sports, hobbies.

/ 0 / 1 / 2 / 3 / Q. I exercise regularly.

/ 0 / 1 / 2 / 3 / R. I take sensible protective measures inside and outside house.

/ 0 / 1 / 2 / 3 / S. I choose supportive relationships over non-supportive ones.

/ 0 / 1 / 2 / 3 / T. I am able to relax without drugs or alcohol.

/ 0 / 1 / 2 / 3 / U. I seem to tolerate constructive criticism well.

/ 0 / 1 / 2 / 3 / V. I seem to accept praise well. I thank the person giving the praise.

/ 0 / 1 / 2 / 3 / W. I enjoy a healthy sexual relationship. I can give and accept intimacy.

/ 0 / 1 / 2 / 3 / X. I have long term friendships.

/ 0 / 1 / 2 / 3 / Y. I am satisfied with relationship with spouse or partner.

/ 0 / 1 / 2 / 3 / Z. My partner or spouse would say that our relationship is healthy and satisfying.

/ 0 / 1 / 2 / 3 / AA. My dreams are usually tolerable and not very upsetting.
/ 0 / 1 / 2 / 3 / BB. My attention span is fairly good and I can concentrate well.
/ 0 / 1 / 2 / 3 / CC. I experience a wide range of emotions, both pleasant and unpleasant.
/ 0 / 1 / 2 / 3 / DD. People would say I am more calm than jumpy.

OTHER SIGNS OF RECOVERY:
/ 0 / 1 / 2 / 3 / _____
/ 0 / 1 / 2 / 3 / _____
/ 0 / 1 / 2 / 3 / _____
/ 0 / 1 / 2 / 3 / _____
/ 0 / 1 / 2 / 3 / _____

CHAPTER 10

Accountable Treatment of Alcohol and Drug Problems

A woman drove me to drink, and I never even had the courtesy to thank her.

— *W.C. Fields*

The field of alcohol treatment has undergone dramatic changes since 1988 when I began to do reviews for managed care. Although one always hopes developments in the field will come because of increased knowledge, this one has come because of economic pressures. Just a few years ago, the standard treatment for alcoholics was a 28-day inpatient program. During those four weeks, the patient would be introduced to the 12-step philosophy and go through an orientation to that program. Either explicitly or implicitly the message was conveyed that any drinking would lead to a relapse into uncontrolled drunkenness, and so the only hope was to abstain.

However, at the same time, I had some reasons to believe there was more than one way to treat alcohol abuse. I had learned from my students. Scott Miller sought me out when he was a Ph.D. candidate at the University of Utah in 1984. He wanted to learn about strategic therapy, and we consulted for several years. When he first came to see me, he worked at a chemical dependency treatment center. He would present cases to me which would have typically received 12-step approaches, and we formulated strategic and utilization approaches, thinking together how John Weakland or even Milton Erickson would handle such a case. Until Scott challenged me with these cases, I had not really considered how one could apply anything other than a traditional AA approach with chemical dependency. I had simply thought of referring patients to the 12-step programs and having them return when they were sober. Scott forced me to think about other approaches. As we consulted, I began to formulate interventions that would surprise and challenge the chemically dependent patients and undermine their conviction that they couldn't live without drugs or alcohol. To my relief, Scott began getting some very solid and impressive responses. I had to stretch my own concepts to fit the results he was getting.

As I was going through this process, I returned to conversations I had had with Erickson, with Weakland, and with others I considered to have some ability to surprise and create change in difficult patients. I vaguely remembered a visit to Erickson at his home in Phoenix, where we had discussed chemical dependency. After some searching, I located the segment among my audiotapes.

Following is a transcript of an interview I had with Milton Erickson on the subject of alcohol and drug abuse on January 24, 1978. Marion Moore and Jay Wilimek were also present.

LYNN JOHNSON (LDJ): I haven't seen anything written in the hypnosis literature about working with people with addictions and alcohol problems.

MILTON H. ERICKSON (MHE): I've got a letter in the house, I think he was operated on a year ago for lung cancer. He's been undergoing an operation, he's been treated by psychiatrist, psychotherapist, lay hypnotist. Now he writes me because he can't get off his addiction of one pack a day. He has trouble breathing, he has emphysema. Now some people will tell you they want to quit smoking, and they don't. Now that man, I will answer his letter by telling him in essence, "In your letter you disclose no evidence you want to quit smoking. It does give good evidence that you are striving to achieve the dubious honor of being a martyr to a pack of cigarettes."

A man came in to me and told me he was very much an alcoholic and wanted to quit. In questioning him, I found out he owned a summer cabin in the desert ten miles from nowhere. No telephones, no electrical lights. The cabin was very plushly furnished. He could catch trout from his bedroom window. It was well stocked with food and liquor, and he and his wife always stayed there as much as two weeks at a time, living there in the nude. After he had told me his complete story about his intense desire to quit drinking, I told him, "It is very easy to have your wife drive you up to the cabin. She can take out all the liquor, and all of your clothes, and bring them back to Phoenix. She can have a friend drive her up, and take her clothes back. And neither one of you will want to walk ten miles over the desert, in the nude, to reach a telephone."

He sighed. "You know, I don't believe I want to quit drinking."

Some drug addicts were treated by a friend of mine. She found out what hypnosis could do. She quit trying to treat them in their way of treating drug addiction. Instead, they would come to her and say, "I want to go on a trip," and she would send them on a trip. And it was a much better trip than they could have on drugs.

LDJ: They could have all kinds of experiences.

MHE: And she had a great deal of success that way.

LDJ: That would fit with their personality. If they are looking for that special feeling, instead of forcing them into a mold where they are not going to have that anymore, just teach them a different way to have that.

MHE: Yes. A safe way. I have never been interested in treating alcoholics or drug addicts, even if they are socially misfits. I think that AA does a better job of treating alcoholics than most psychiatrists.

I did treat one alcoholic successfully, very simply. He had spent 20 of his 32 years in penal or correctional institutions.

LDJ: He went in when he was 12, then.

MHE: In some correctional institutions. He had been discharged from state prison after serving his full time. Now Pete was a very big man, well over six-feet, broad shoulders, well built. And a supervisor in a halfway house for ex-convicts sent him to me for psychotherapy. Pete listened to me for an hour, very politely, and when I was finished, he said, " You know where you can shove that." He walked out, and his girlfriend brought him back. He listened again, politely, and said, "You know where you can shove that," and walked out. For seven months he lived on his girlfriend. And he worked for drinks at the taverns. In seven months time, his girlfriend got tired of his parasitism and the tavernkeepers got tired of his brawling when he got drunk. And so they simultaneously threw him out. And Pete walked six miles from his girlfriend's house, in a temperature of 109 degrees. He had a horrible hangover. And Pete said, "What was that you tried to tell me before?" So I told him, and he said, "You know where you can shove that."

He went back to his girlfriend's home, and begged her for a second chance. She turned him down. He tried the tavernkeepers. They turned him down. So he walked back, and asked, "What was that you tried to tell me?" I said, "Pete, I've stuffed it. Now the only thing I can offer you is an old mattress. You can sleep on that. If you need a blanket during the night, I can furnish that. If it rains, you can pull the mattress under the eaves. But I don't think it is going to rain. And there's an outdoor faucet. In the mornings, you can rap at the kitchen door, and my wife will give you a can of pork and beans. You are good to the gate. And if you want me to confiscate your boots, you will have to beg me."

He came into the back yard, sat down on the yard furniture, and started thinking. That afternoon, my daughter and 15 year old granddaughter arrived from Michigan. They saw this man, big man nude to the waist, looking extremely sick, sitting in the back yard, and they saw a great big scar over his chest. Of course, my daughter immediately said, "Who is that in the back yard?" I told her, "A patient of mine, an alcoholic who walked 18 miles today, in that heat, trying to sober up."

She asked if she could talk to him. I told her, yes, he was an ex-convict, and told her the things he had said to me. My granddaughter's eyes bugged out and she wanted to know if she could sit in on that talk.

Now Pete welcomed company. He was lonesome. He spent the afternoon talking to the two girls, and my daughter said, very kindly, "What would you like for dinner?"

Pete said, "A pint. But I know I won't get that." She said, "No you won't get it. Now tell me what you would like in the way of food." He said, "Just anything."

She was a gourmet cook, and prepared a wonderful dinner for him. She felt she owed him something for all the information he had given her. And that horrible scar in his chest. He had been shot in the heart by a policeman during a burglary, rushed to emergency room and operated on in open-heart surgery. The next day the two girls went and talked to him again, and prepared a gourmet meal. Now Pete stayed there four days and four nights. He talked freely to the girls, giving his entire history very frankly, and when the girls weren't talking to him, he watched the basset hound, short-legged, slow movement. You know bassets, do you not? (Yes.) She climbed up the trunk of that Palo Verde tree in the back yard, to get an elevated view of life. (Chuckles) And Pete watched her with a great deal of admira- tion, a short-legged dog, so laboriously climbing that trunk. And he petted her, and Sarah Lee liked petting. After four days, he asked permission to go to his girlfriend's house, where he had an old car parked. He said he thought he could repair it sufficiently so he could sell it for twenty-five dollars, and get sufficient cash to start life anew. He fixed the car, sold it for twenty-five dollars, returned and spent the night, and asked permission to go out and find a job the next day. He located two jobs. One for a horse wrangler, which had low pay, and a factory job, which had good pay. He slept overnight to decide which job he would take. And in the morning, he announced he was going to take the factory job. So I gave him permission to go to work. He had twenty-five dollars to rent a room and pay for food, until his first paycheck came in.

The first Thursday, he called on his girlfriend, and said, "You are coming with me to Alcoholics Anonymous." At Alcoholics Anonymous, when he made his maiden speech to AA, he said, "Any old drunk, no matter how absolutely worthless he is, can get sober and stay sober. All he needs is a back yard launching pad."

Now the only therapeutic thing I did for him was to say, "You are good to the gate. And if you want me to confiscate your boots, you'll have to beg me." I know convicts. I worked my way through medical school examining convicts. I put him on his convict's honor not to run away. He didn't realize it. He just sensed in some way he couldn't run away. He had some complaints about my daughter and granddaughter. "Those girls don't belong in this world. They are the kind of creatures I have never seen before."

He has been sober and industrious for four years now. So has his girlfriend. Just knowing the right the thing to say, and only doing the right amount, placed him on his convict's honor.

In handling alcoholics, you have to know their personality fairly well. In 1942, an unkempt, unshaven dirty man staggered into my office, and said, "I am a norsky and you are a norsky, and norskies are not afraid to talk straight from the shoulder. I am a drunk. I have just come off a three-month binge. This is the third day I have been sobering up."

"And what did you do before you went on this last three-month binge?"

He said, "I sobered up from the previous three-month binge. I am norsky; you can talk turkey to me. I brought a scrapbook with me to prove I am worth saving." He was one of the early aviators. He established transcontinental records. He had been a fellow student pilot with General Hap Young of the Air Force. He was the 22nd member of the caterpillar club. People don't know the names of those people anymore. You have to let your engineer bail out first, and then at the last possible moment you bail out of your plane and hopefully you land safely. If you land safely and live, you become a member of the caterpillar club. And he was the 22nd member to survive a forced jump.

He described his scrapbook, and when he finished showing me, he allowed me to start on him. I turned to him and said, "Yes, I am of Norwegian descent, just as you are. I will talk turkey to you. In the first place, you're a liar. That is not your scrapbook. That belongs to a decent man. Now I will tell you what a low-down kind of a cuss you are." I let him have all the invective I could think of for about an hour. I learned he started drinking on his drunken spells by walking in to a bar, ordering two beers, and he'd lift them up to his face, and drain them, and follow them with a whiskey chaser. He always put his car keys on the bar, for the bartender to take care of. After about an hour, he became so infuriated at the invective I threw at him, he said, "God damn you, I don't need any of your name calling." He rushed down to the parking lot, got in his car, raced down Michigan Avenue, turned into the Middle Belt Tavern, ordered his two schooners of beer and a whiskey chaser. As he was lifting the schooners to drink, he said, "That's what that God damn bastard said you would do." He put them down, paid for them and went home, and came in the next Saturday, and told me.

I said, "Yes, and you are making a big deal about having put down the schooners and not drinking them for a week. But you have been living on goof balls for a whole week, eating your mother's cooking, and being supported by your parents. And you want me to give you credit? Let me tell you what kind of a no-good scoundrel you are." He listened meekly, and I told him if he wanted any further help from me, he would have to promise me certain things. One, when he wanted to get drunk, he would pick me up, and we would both go to town and see who could drink the other under the table first. Or, if he had a bottle of rum, and felt he couldn't handle it, bring it over, and we could drink it, the two of us. So for the next few weeks he went down to the gym and put in a ten-hour day, working to get himself in shape. This was in September. In November, he applied for admission to the Air Corps, was accepted as a captain, on ground status. He called me from the airport, and said, "I've got a bottle of rum here, and a powerful desire to drink it."

And I said, "Bring it over to me. I'll have the glasses and the ice ready." He came over, with his bottle of rum. I put the ice in the glasses, filled them up, picked mine up, and said, "Here's mud in your eye." And I drank it.

"God damn your soul, you would do that. Keep that damn bottle, I don't need it." He went back to the air base.

Some time later he came back to the office, said, "Get in the car. We're going down to Detroit and get drunk." That was about twenty miles.

I talked about the weather, every innocent subject I could think of. He kept looking at me angrily, we got about halfway there, and he stopped the car and cursed me fluently, saying, "God damn son of a bitch, you *are* going to go with me and keep your word, to see who can drink the other one under the table."

I said, "That's what I promised."

"Damn your lousy soul, you are not going to do that." He turned the car around and went back to the air base. Shortly thereafter he was given flying status and made a major, and in time served in the Pentagon, where he served as official chauffeur* for all the big shots, for members of the arms committee, personally chauffeured General Hap Arnold when Hap Arnold came stateside. He was eventually made a lieutenant colonel. Now and then he would call me from Washington and say, "I need to hear your voice." And so we had a casual conversation.

In 1963, he and his wife showed up in Phoenix. He took us out to dinner. Betty and I had a Daiquiri, so did his wife; he had a glass of milk. He had often taken us out to dinner when he was at the air base in Detroit.

LDJ: I understand part of that. He wanted you to rescue him. You refused to do that. You put the responsibility back on him.

MHE: *All* the responsibility back on him. . . . [Regarding the alcoholic] he is trying to shift the responsibility to you, and you have to put it back, where it belongs. I was of Norwegian descent, as he was. It gives him a sense of identification with me.

LDJ: You cursed him. I can think of one reason for that, to show him you knew everything he said to himself.

MHE: I said everything I thought he could have said to himself, although I may have had a better vocabulary. I've done that with fat people. "You are the fattest bucket of lard I've ever seen."

LDJ: You told her she couldn't tolerate the things you needed to tell her until she went into trance.

MHE: You talk to patients and see to it they take their responsibility.

JAY WILIMEK (JW): I would think many people who are like that would have many people speak to them like that, tell them they are fat. Is the difference that you don't take responsibility for them at the same time?

MHE: You say the things they have been telling themselves and not believing it, and they hear you saying their ideas. They also know you are not afraid to tell the truth. They can rely on you to tell the truth. They are compelled to face themselves.

LDJ: I don't know that fat people are told that. They may be told, "You are a little overweight; maybe you should lose some weight." But people treat them gently.

MHE: Gently and politely.

LDJ: You are unusual in that you are willing to do that. Even most psychiatrists and psychologists are unwilling to tell them directly things like that.

MHE: How can you do therapy unless you deal with a patient where he is at?

A man came in and said, "I am a retired policeman, medically retired. I have emphysema, high blood pressure. As you can see, I am obese. I smoke three packs of cigarettes a day, drink a fifth a day, and I want to jog. My physician says with my emphysema, high blood pressure, it isn't safe to jog. He says I should walk, and I'd really like you to help me. I'd really like to jog."

---

*Author's note: Perhaps Erickson means the official pilot.

I said, "I will take you at your word. You want to jog. And before you jog you will have to do some walking. Now your treatment is rather simple and easy. Are you married?" He said he was a bachelor.

"Who prepares your food for you?"

He said, "I prepare most of it. There is a handy little restaurant around the corner from where I live I like to eat at frequently. And there is a handy little grocery around the corner by that restaurant."

I said, "All right, all you need to do is walk to that handy little grocery, and buy just enough food for breakfast, and just enough for breakfast so there will be none left over. So you won't overeat. And take another walk to buy enough food for lunch, no leftovers. And a third walk for your dinner.

"Now where do you buy your cigarettes?" At that same handy little grocery store. "All right, where do you buy your liquor?"

"There's a handy little liquor store next to the restaurant."

"How do you buy your cigarettes?" He bought them two cartons at a time. I said, "You don't buy your cigarettes for the present, you buy them for the future."

"Ah, yes."

"All right, your problem is already solved. You buy your cigarettes one pack at a time from a store that is one mile away. I will get you walking, it will be healthy for you too. You want to dine out? There's a good restaurant at least a mile away. You can enjoy eating at a good restaurant. And for your liquor, take all you want. Take your first drink at a bar a mile away. Enjoy. Go to another bar a mile away for your second drink. Enjoy. Go to another bar a mile away for your third drink."

He left the office cursing me. He told me what kind of a fraud I was, and so on. A month later a new patient came in. He said, "My friend, the retired policeman, says you are the only psychiatrist in town that knows what he is talking about."

LDJ: You gave him very straightforward instructions.

MHE: He was a retired policeman. He knew what discipline was.

LDJ: You understood that about him and you knew he would do it.

MHE: I understood what convict honor is, too. He really had self-discipline. And he cursed me because I made him see that. And there is no way he could ever delude himself again.

A woman came to me recently for cigarette smoking, and she lived in a rather lonesome area. She stressed to me how modest she was and how obedient she would be to anything I said. I said, "All right. Buy your cigarettes one pack at a time. It is only a half mile to the nearest store. Go there in the nude."

She said, "You know I wouldn't do a thing like that."

"You know, you can go there in the nude for every cigarette you wish." She quit smoking.

A woman 53 years old called me up and said she wanted an appointment with me to quit smoking cigarettes. She said she was a psychotherapist. "A psychotherapist? Fifty-three years old? Who wants to quit smoking? That does not seem to be sincere. You will have to prove it, by climbing Squaw Peak, at sunrise, every morning for a week." Squaw Peak is that mountain over there. She climbed it every morning at sunrise, for a week, and then she called for an appointment.

So I asked her, "How many cigarettes do you have in your handbag?"

"I have two packs. Shall I throw them away?"

"I don't know that you want to throw them away. You can put them on my desk, and I will let them stay there for three weeks, and you can come anytime to get them."

She put them on my desk, and said, "Do you want my matches too?"

"Certainly. I will keep them for you."

After she put her matches down, she said, "Shall I go home and get the rest of my cigarettes?"

I said, "Since you've phrased that question, I think that would be a good idea." So she immediately left, and came back with over a pack of cigarettes, put them on my desk. "I'll keep them there for three weeks. Now what is your real reason for coming to see me?"

"I have a boy 19 years old, and a girl, 21, and my husband is a professor at the University of Arizona, and when we got married, he promised me that he would help with the housework and the cooking. He likes gourmet food, but he has me do all the cooking. I bring home as much money as he does. And he never lifts his hand to do anything around the house. He is a scholar. He published a book. The house has been his. The kids, if they wanted to be noisy, had to go out and play at the neighbors' homes. And when he was studying at home, everybody had to be very quiet, because he was a student, a scholar.*

I said, "Well, if you have a 21-year old daughter, and you haven't collected any of his promises yet, what hope is there for you?"

"But he ought to keep his promises."

"Well, you can come in same time, next week, and tell me what's going on."

She came in a week later and said, "I asked my husband to type a letter for me. He didn't want to, said he was tired and wanted to go to sleep. I said I needed that letter and he would type it, and he just closed his eyes and started to go to sleep. I got mad. I yanked the covers off him, and I hauled him out of bed, onto the floor, and told him, 'I want that letter written.'

"He went in to the study, he typed that letter, slammed the door behind him, typed that letter, brought it out and handed it to me. . . . It's impossible to make that many mistakes in one letter. That really made me mad. I went in the bedroom, and hauled him out, and told him, 'Get in that study and type it correctly,' and I slammed the door behind him. He typed it perfectly."

I said, "You now know you can enforce your wishes, and he promised you he would do his share of the cooking, and you would like to have him do his share. How badly do you want that? He said one week he would do it. One week you would do it. Well, why don't you tell him?

"When his week comes, he can fry hamburgers and boil potatoes, that's all."

---

*Author's note: It is impossible to communicate in print the subtle disdain and sarcasm Erickson conveys in his voice as he says, "a student, a scholar."

"That's all right. Let him fry the hamburgers and boil potatoes. And when you sit down at the table, you and your daughter and your son take out from your lap boxes of take-home food you bought from a restaurant. He can eat the hamburgers and the boiled potatoes."

She did that, and came in and said, "It is my turn this week to do the cooking."

I said, "Be respectful in doing that. As he has cooked hamburgers and boiled potatoes, you do the same for him, as he cooked for you. And bring your own take-home food for the children and yourself."

LDJ: Be respectful.

MHE: Respectful of his cooking. Cook the same thing he did.

Some of my students saw her at the top of Squaw Peak. She continued to climb Squaw Peak every morning. They saw her up there, and she recognized them. She picked up a cigarette butt and turned to the students and said, "Isn't it disgusting that people will make a nice trip like this and smoke a filthy thing like this and litter up the scenery?"

Reviewing the conversation, I realize that, like many of Erickson's comments, it had a greater impact on me much later than at the time. While his comments were confusing and multifaceted (as usual), they contained hope that there was help for the substance abuser through a variety of ways, from hypnosis to paradox. I felt empowered in my supervision. Some time later, I encountered William Miller and Reid Hester's (1986) review of outcome studies of alcoholism treatment. It appeared from their comprehensive review of the literature that there was no advantage to be had from inpatient treatment of alcohol abuse. It seems that most of our treatment models, such as the disease model, the 12-step models, and group and individual counseling, cannot be validated and have unknown therapeutic power. Even such shibboleths as group treatment must be run by recovering counselors could not be said to be differentially effective. It appeared that psychologists who had never been alcoholics could be rehabilitated into being effective therapists for alcoholics.

The treatment models which did show scientific validity were not in general use, since they typically used some combination of behavior therapy, family therapy, self-control training, and so on. These programs with good results were mainly located in research settings. It appeared that brief treatment was as good as or better than long-term treatment, and outpatient as good as or better than inpatient.

There is general consensus that chemical abuse problems must be addressed before efforts to change other areas of life are attempted (Budman & Gurman, 1988). Certainly, therefore, a brief therapist must investigate the use of mood-altering chemicals by patients. However, the notion that the use of drugs is a disease (as opposed to a bad habit) or that untreated alcoholism/drug use must always lead to death appears to be more in the nature of religious conviction than scientific fact (Holder, Longabaugh, Miller, & Rubonis, 1991; Peele, 1989). The Holder et al. review found that brief interventions appeared to be as helpful as (or more so) and far less expensive than intensive programs, such as chemical aversion treatment, inpatient, residential treatment, intensive outpatient, and so on. In fact, Holder suggested that there was an *inverse* relationship between expense and effectiveness of treatment in chemical dependency, with the least expensive programs often having the most robust effects, when compared with intensive and comprehensive ones.

Recent literature tends to support the use of fairly brief, behaviorally oriented treatments (Miller & Hester, 1986). It seems that the focus on attainable behavioral goals is superior to a total lifestyle change, if only in terms of cost. In other words, while AA seems to be quite helpful to some addicts (and is certainly cost-effective), it does not appear to have any unique or necessary components, and for those who do not like the group format or the emphasis on spirituality, alternatives should be made available. For example, William Miller has emphasized a motivational interview style of intervention that has more impact than confrontational interviewing, and is again less resource-intensive (Miller & Rollnick, 1991).

Based on my experience consulting with Scott Miller and reviewing the literature, I began to seek opportunities to attempt brief treatment with alcoholics. The model two colleagues and I adopted included:

1. a strong emphasis on the responsibility for change being placed squarely on the patient
2. a primary orientation toward strengths, and especially toward exceptions in abuse patterns
3. utilization of patient attitudes, interests, and patterns of behavior
4. focus on patient goals in lieu of imposing the goal of complete abstinence
5. avoidance of confrontation as a means of creating change

Although Erickson had emphasized the usefulness of confrontation (e.g., the story of the Norse aviator), we were not sure we had the interpersonal skill to carry it off, and evidence seemed to indicate that confrontation did more harm than good (Miller & Rollnick, 1991). Instead, eliciting cooperation and understanding was to be emphasized.

Our approach was to be behavioral and solution-focused in nature. We borrowed heavily from de Shazer and the BFTC group, and Insoo Berg and Scott Miller's (1992) techniques were followed closely. We utilized the strategic therapy techniques of the MRI group at times (Fisch, Weakland, & Segal, 1982; Watzlawick, Weakland, & Fisch, 1974). We decided to utilize individual and family or couples psychotherapy and not offer any group treatment. We considered the AA model to be a useful approach for some patients, and certainly supported patients' attending AA meetings, but we did not require it.

We attempted to reframe patient complaints in ways we felt would surprise and make memorable our interventions. We did not demand that patients quit drinking, and we tried to support any and all efforts they made to improve their lives. Relapses were reframed by asking patients whether they were still drinking or using drugs there in the session. When they responded they were not (and in each case, the relapse had already been confronted by the patient, who felt upset and disappointed about the lapse), we specifically inquired about how they had made the decision to stop the relapse. These helpful techniques, as well as many others, are in Berg and Miller (1992).

The results of our small investigation were quite positive. Generally, relapse (used as a measure of failure in most studies) seemed to be less than the 50–90% generally reported. Of 15 patients treated over a one-year period, nine were satisfied with their level of control over drinking at follow-up. Four appeared no better; two could not be located. While some were abstinent, others (per their own goals) were "controlled drinkers." Sessions ranged from 3 to 36 (in the case of a woman with multiple problems, including panic disorder, family dysfunction, and some personality disorder characteristics). We found we were effective with patients for whom AA was not helpful, those who had been told they would never be free of alcoholism until they accepted and worked the AA program. One woman, at follow-up, said she had gone to an AA meeting and said she was now sober and she had not admitted she was powerless. In fact, she felt quite powerful. This announcement was met with less than complete support.

Another group of successes we found were those who did not consider themselves alcoholics, but did feel their drinking was a problem to them. In these cases, family therapy was very helpful, as well as de Shazer's ideas about customer status. We looked for the "hidden customer" (Berg & Miller, 1992), but limited our efforts to those areas that the patient wanted to change. Thus we avoided the confrontive style of treatment, which we now speculate causes more drinking than a more respectful and collaborative style (W. Miller et al., 1993). Following are illustrative cases from the work of my colleagues and myself. These are presented to encourage therapists who are not specialists in treating chemical abuse to experiment with strategic and solution-focused approaches. This is not to discount the well-researched role of behavioral and family approaches, only to suggest there are many techniques which can be helpful.

Case Example: I Am Here Against My Will

A 31-year-old man presented for treatment, saying he would lose his wife if he didn't come to see me. She came with him and complained bitterly about his weekend drinking. He was sober during the week, but starting on Friday night he would drink beer heavily until he was quite intoxicated. During the day on Saturday he would gradually sober up, and then start drinking again with his friends, returning home in the early hours of the morning. He would again sober up Sunday, lying around feeling very sick. Then he went to work on Monday morning. He took pride in not missing work.

For the wife the final straw came when he went into their nine-year-old son's room at 3 a.m. one Saturday and began to explain how much he loved the son. The next day the son, quite worried, came to talk to his mother about how dad came into his room drunk.

The man told me he bitterly resented his wife's trying to force him to quit his drinking, but he felt he had no choice but to do so, so as not to lose his family. He did not see his drinking as a problem.

Part of this treatment model is to accept and meet the patient in his view of the world. I agreed it was quite unfair for his wife to demand he quit drinking, and told her that if she succeeded he would only relapse after the current crisis had passed. He agreed with my analysis. I also said it was possible that he had a great deal of fun in the weekend drinking. He asserted that he did in fact enjoy it very much, and that he would be severely harmed if he could not get drunk with his friends on weekends. I agreed that was possible, although I couldn't be sure. I wondered whether his drinking was as much fun as the drinking wanted to seem to him. I thought it was possible that it was very much a fun experience; it was also possible the drinking was not living up to its promises, but he was too drunk to know, so the drinking was able to get away with this confidence game. It was very hard to tell.

I suggested any man who quit drinking just because his wife told him to do so was a fool, and wouldn't deserve my respect or his own. But at the same time, a man who believes everything others tell him is a fool, and certainly he was foolish if he believed everything the beer companies told him about how drinking beer makes you fun, sexy, and intelligent. I proposed a simple scientific experiment. I suggested he flip a coin, and if the coin came up "heads" he would not drink that weekend, but would go out with his friends as usual. If the coin came up tails, he had to drink that weekend.

Whatever the coin came up, he would do the opposite the next weekend. Therefore, if he didn't drink this weekend, he would keep careful note of how much fun he actually had without drinking. The following week he was obligated to drink, and he should keep careful note of how much fun he had by drinking. Then he would compare the two weekends. He returned in four weeks and to his amazement reported that he had actually enjoyed the weekends more when he did not drink. He had a totally sober weekend one time, drank and found it was not as fun as he expected, and the next weekend drank only very lightly and enjoyed himself, as did his wife who accompanied him. The fourth weekend he was likewise sober and enjoyed that. He was thinking the family rule that one could only have fun by drinking heavily may be in error. He was seen a total of four times. At follow-up eight months later his wife was satisfied with his sobriety and involvement with the family on weekends.

Case Example: I Can Never Tell When I'll Drink

A 37-year-old man presented saying his drinking was ruining his business. He would be seized by impulses to drink and felt he had to drink. This happened two to three days per week. When he started drinking, he would continue to drink throughout the day and his small business would be thrown into chaos. He felt desperate. If he tried very hard he could postpone the drinking for 24 hours, but then the next day his resolve would crumble and he would begin to drink.

He was unable to describe any helpful difference between the days he drank and the days he did not drink. He could not predict when he would drink and when he would not drink. He consistently described himself as helpless before the impulses. He reiterated when asked that he would do whatever he had to do to get control of this problem. Because of this helplessness I asked him to take a special coin that had been blessed by a holy man. He smiled a bit and took the coin. I asked him to flip the coin the next morning. If the coin came up heads, he had to be sober all day, whether he felt like it or not. If the coin came up tails, he had to drink that day, whether he felt like it or not. If he really didn't like the result of the coin flip, he could go for two out of three.

My patient was angry. He said that was not what he wanted to do and that he didn't see how it could help. He wanted me to create a way for him to quit, not for him to drink more. I insisted that he would learn and this assignment would be of help to him. He agreed grudgingly to do the homework.

He returned in two weeks, and reported. He had flipped the coin three days, feeling all the time a good deal of anger toward me. The first two days, to his relief, he did not have to drink. On the third day, the coin demanded he drink. He rebelled, saying "To hell with that thera-pist," and from that day on, felt no compulsion to drink.

Case Example: The Three-Day Miracle

A woman in her thirties presented with a complaint of alcoholism. She complained that she had never been sober for more than three days except for the times when she was inpatient in the 28-day programs she had tried twice. After discharge she relapsed immediately. After taking her history the counselor asked her how long it had been since her last drink. She reported that it was three days. The counselor was impressed and asked her how she had managed to say sober for that long. She seemed surprised by this question but replied that there were a few things she could to keep herself sober for a few days at a time. As she listed what she had done to stay sober, the therapist was fascinated and wondered how she had discovered those things (which mostly consisted of distracting herself and staying busy). He wondered whether she was likely to keep doing those after the session, and how it would help if she did continue doing those things.

She said she thought she could do them a bit more, although she seemed surprised that he did not emphasize the standard information she had already received about admitting she was powerless over alcohol and attending AA. She was told that attendance at AA was fine, but she could decide what was best for her and do that.

At her second visit, she had been sober for ten days, the longest time she could remember. She was pleased. They spent the session reviewing how she had done that. The counselor congratulated her on her success and wondered whether she would like to continue that lifestyle. She said she would and made an appointment for a week later.

When she returned for her third visit, she had a lapse to report. She had drunk for three days that week. The counselor asked her how long it had been since her last drink, and she said, "Two days." He asked her how she had decided when it was time to stop drinking. What made her decide drinking wasn't the solution she had been led to think it was? She looked amazed and began to talk about how she stopped. The lapse was normalized as something which happens, but emphasis was placed on the importance of her stopping, how much insight and determination that must have taken, and so on. She ended the session saying how relieved she felt about how her lapse had been handled, and how she had expected to be confronted.

The fourth session was two weeks later; she was still sober. The therapist continued to see her until she had 42 days of consecutive sobriety. She then announced that she was determined to go to an AA meeting and tell the people there that helplessness is not necessary to achieve sobriety, that she was not helpless and had not turned her life over to anyone but herself, and she was feeling great.

Case Example: Coke Keeps Me Company

A woman was referred to me by her clergyman. She had exhausted the family savings snorting cocaine over the past six months. She and her husband had both been alcoholics when they married; they had gotten active in AA and become sober. He became very involved and active in his church; she joined him in that but lacked conviction and dedication. She reported that he would criticize her for not being spiritually support- ive and not being a good example to their children. She felt he did not love her and would buy coke whenever she felt that way.

Her exceptions to the problem of coke use involved times when she felt cared about and supported by others. She wanted that feeling from her husband, but had some friends in the neighborhood who were caring and supportive and from whom she could receive good feelings. She was instructed to continue to do what helped her stay sober. She was espe- cially congratulated on telling her neighbors she needed some company, and encouraged to continue that.

Her husband attended the next session, and we discussed times when he was able to provide the kind of attention and support she felt she needed. We identified several times, and he agreed he could continue and even increase those. She was free of cocaine use for over three weeks at this point.

In the third session, with her husband absent, she identified clearly the feeling of needing attention and company which preceded her search for cocaine. She had experienced those feelings but had not given in to them during the past week. She identified ways she had accomplished that, and was congratulated for discovering those, most of which dealt with reaching out to others when she felt the need. Based on the MRI views of the problem being the attempted solution, we tried create a second-order change. She was asked to try and experience the trouble- some feeling during the session. After some encouragement, she was able to do that. Then she was asked to intensify the feeling and give it a rating. On a 1-10 scale she rated it 6, with 9 or 10 meaning she would be compelled to search for cocaine. With some effort she raised it to a 7. She was then instructed to lower it to a 6 again, using only her mind and her imagination in whatever way seemed helpful and useful to her. Again with some effort she managed to remember a pleasant scene, and the feeling lowered to a 5. She then raised it to 7 or 8, and lowered it to 4. This pattern continued, with the therapist giving almost no actual training, except encouraging her to use her own imagination and ability. By the end of the session, she rated the feeling of loneliness as "2 or less" and was quite pleased. Her homework was to induce the bad feeling and use her own resources to lower it, without help from anyone else.

By the fourth session, she felt strong and capable. She had begun spontaneously to attend some AA and NA groups, and had carried out her homework. After six more sessions, she felt ready to break from treatment.

Six months later she returned, having relapsed into cocaine again. Her husband was much less supportive this time, and was threatening divorce. With similar approaches, she was able to again remain free of cocaine, and even submitted to urinanalysis on a random basis, so as to prove to her husband she was still sober.

The marriage eventually ended in divorce. A follow-up six months from the last contact found the patient was intermittently sober and living with a son by a previous marriage. The patient was seen for 19 visits. She was not viewed as a success or as a failure, since she was continuing to drink occasionally, although she did claim she was not using cocaine. She does not see her level of drinking as causing a problem for her, and she has not sought any other help.

We received a morale boost in our efforts from a program on National Public Radio which ran during the week of October 4, 1993. Morning Edition featured five segments on treatment of alcohol abuse. The programs suggested alternatives to traditional treatment, including a report of a British treatment approach that accepts moderate drinking instead of abstinence as a goal. Paradoxically, this program in Britain seems to achieve higher levels of abstinence than do programs emphasizing total abstinence as the only legitimate goal. The research from England demonstrates that brief counseling emphasizing controlled drinking is easily as helpful and effective as expensive inpatient treatment (Chapman & Huygens, 1988; Chick, Ritson, Connaughton, Stewart, & Chick, 1988).

Of course, social psychologists have long warned us that when we make something unavailable we make it more desirable (Cialdini, 1984). And if abstinence is the only legitimate goal, then a patient who lapses *even temporarily* into drinking is considered a treatment failure, not only by researchers but also by him or herself. However, alcohol often fails to live up to its promises of relief from problems, and if the patient is looking only at quality-of-life issues (and is not feeling forced to abstain because of a strict doctrine), that patient often freely chooses to forego alcohol simply because it is a disturbing force and delivers little actual relief.

The NPR series referred to a report by the Institute of Medicine which challenged the uniform approach to alcohol treatment. Instead of a procrustean bed of 28-day inpatient treatment followed by daily attendance at AA, the report recommended a community-based, flexible approach to treatment, emphasizing brief, less intensive treatment with a majority of patients. Since cost-effectiveness should be considered by clinicians treating substance abusers, and accountability are the watchwords of the present environment, such an approach seems ideally suited for today's treatment strategies.

RECOMMENDATIONS

How can psychotherapists best address the needs and problems of the chemically dependent? Traditionally, treatment of the chemically dependant has not been accountable, but has instead relied on emotion and rigid commitment to treatment models that are not scientifically validated. The treatment philosophy of AA, while showing excellent results in many cases in voluntary, no-cost peer led groups, has been adapted and forced into inpatient and intensive outpatient programs. These programs are notorious for their rigid and uncompromising approach, forcing all patients to fit the same model. The alternative — emphasis on individual assessment and tailoring treatment to fit the patient — requires a strong background and understanding of behavior change techniques and skills. Many of the counselors in recovery programs are recovering addicts themselves, are emotionally committed to the 12-step programs, and will not consider alternatives for selected patients.

This is not to say that there is anything wrong with AA. It is an inspiring program and has been a miracle in the lives of many alcoholics. It should not be discouraged; attacks on it because of its spiritual roots are foolish at best and possibly malicious. But it cannot be the only choice; rather, a variety of choices must be made available. Controlled drinking may well be a valid goal for many people. A broader view of what constitutes successful treatment must be fostered in the profession. Erickson's statement about AA being better than most psychiatrists and psychologists would no longer appear to be true, considering recent developments in theory and technique (cf. Berg & S. Miller, 1992; Peele, Brodsky & Arnold, 1991; W. Miller & Rollnick, 1991). The British experience suggests the opposite may be the case.

But the fact remains that the addictions treatment field is controlled by recovering persons who believe deeply that they owe their lives to following the 12-step model, and therefore every other addict must follow the same procedure. No amount of scientific data can possibly influence such powerful and personally useful beliefs, so we can expect treatment to continue to be characterized by a great deal of rigidity.

Funding sources, both public and private, can facilitate change by not funding expensive treatment programs. This option of mandated change, while desirable, does not seem likely, since the population of recovering patients is a considerable constituency. Efforts to move toward more efficient treatments will likely be stymied by the sincere and well-meaning efforts of this group.

Thus, we are very pessimistic about the possibilities for change in this field. It is quite unlikely that the present treatment industry will voluntarily change, even in light of the considerable scientific support for more effective treatment strategies. Instead, the present program directors will gradually grow old and retire from the field. In the meantime, it seems likely that therapists who have never had addictions personally may make considerable contributions by treating as many chemically addicted persons as possible, using the behavioral, motivational, and solution-focused tools that are now available and well validated in the scientific literature.

In other words, what needs to happen is that mental health counselors should have better training and supervision in effective CD treatment. They should seek to be primary treatment resources for alcohol and drug problems. As they then successfully treat a new generation of patients, many of these patients will get graduate degrees and enter the mental health profession themselves. They field will gradually change by attrition and by main-line therapists co-opting the chemical abuse field.

Of course, there is another possibility, which should be considered. Perhaps patients treated in this way will not see how hard it is to overcome chemical dependency. They may not understand what a powerful role the therapist has played in their recovery. And therefore they may not be interested in a career in mental health, but instead consider that they solved the problem themselves and continue in other fields of work. Thus, it may be a danger for therapists to make treatment too easy, since we will fail to create true believers to carry on the message.

I do not consider myself an expert in the field, but my own experience is instructive: Treating addiction is not a difficult process. Perhaps I have not seen the most difficult cases, but I have seen some cases of serious drug and alcohol abuse. Severity of the case did not seem to be a controlling factor. If the counselor is reasonably well trained in brief treatment ideas, has adequate supervision or consultation, and is willing to apply a broad range of treatment strategies in place of the "one size fits all" approach of the past, then a good deal of effective therapy can be done.

TREATMENT PROTOCOLS

While we had excellent response with Berg and Miller's (1992) model, there are a variety of models available. The research evidence clearly indicates that 12-step programs should never be the center of a treatment philosophy. Instead, a behavioral approach or perhaps a solution-focused approach (which still needs validation in better studies than mine) is preferred.

The "illness" model should not be taught to patients. This model suggests that chemical dependency is a progressive illness inevitably resulting in deterioration and eventually death. Instead, the British model should be taught — that abusing chemicals has certain disadvantages which might lead a person to live a less robust and enjoyable life than one might otherwise. The emphasis should always be on how the client might structure his or her life to live more fully.

Twelve-step programs should clearly be an option to patients, and they should be made aware of the good that many patients have found there. Places and times of AA and other meetings should be communicated, as a likely route toward a healthy lifestyle. But the tradition in AA is to not charge for such attendance, and that should be carried over when AA is made a part of professional treatment programs. The AA model is basically a religious model, something I personally approve of, being a religious person myself. At the same time, no one should ever be charged for attending church; all financial support must be given completely freely and voluntarily. I would never ask people to pay admission to religious services, and treatment centers requiring people to pay for religious instruction are similarly inappropriate.

Some kind of "readiness" assessment (either de Shazer's evaluation of customer status or Prochaska's stages of readiness) should be used, and the emphasis should be on giving the patient what he wants at each stage of treatment readiness. In saying this, I am quite aware that some gifted therapists have the ability to create customers in every session; however, this should not be expected of the rest of us, who find the readiness models quite helpful.

I personally am quite uncomfortable with treatment programs being staffed preferentially by former addicts and substance abusers (in their own vocabulary, "recovering persons"). There seems to be no actual evidence from outcome studies that going through the addiction process makes for a better counselor, and it does seem likely it could impair, at least in some instances. Some (not all, by any means) "recovering" counselors are addicted to 12-step programs, find life has become unmanageable without 12 steps, and need to turn over their 12-step dependency to a higher power.

In other words, addiction counselors are either unaware or willfully ignorant of the evidence that therapists can do a good deal of harm as well as good, and that the therapist with the strongest and most rigid agenda going into the therapy relationship is most likely to do that harm. Conversely, the therapist who can maneuver, stays flexible, and adapts to what the patient presents and works for what the patient wants is less likely to do harm. Forcing people into a mold, no matter how helpful it may be for some members of a population, is not helpful and should be avoided.

When former substance abusers recover from their own recovery process, they can and should be welcomed into any branch of mental health for which their training and intelligence equips them. But no special status should be accorded because of their struggle, and the possibility of that struggle blinding them to alternative routes others may find helpful should be clearly pointed out. Unless and until addiction counselors can demonstrate that their techniques are more helpful than behavioral methods, or more powerful than the family-based treatments described in the next chapter (which focuses on conduct disorders as well as substance abuse), claims to special insight cannot be allowed.

CHAPTER 11

Effective Treatment of the Adolescent Client

There's nothing wrong with teenagers that telling them won't aggravate.

— Lawrence J. Peter, 1977

Teens can be difficult, even in the best of circumstances. Adolescent problems may be exacerbated when parents or caretakers apply ineffective strategies for encouraging good behavior. This is especially true if the caretakers then persist in those strategies, applying more of what hasn't worked. In such cases, family-oriented interventions become the most logical approach. This view, the systems approach, can be seen at work in the most powerful and successful programs for behaviorally disordered children and adolescents. Therapists working with children and teens may not utilize family-based approaches, but they should understand the professional literature and be able to justify choosing approaches that either are less effective or have not been validated, in light of the existence of approaches that have received robust validation and support.

Some family therapists disdain research, but it is not at all clear that there is any alternative. Postmodern rhetoric notwithstanding, accountability means testing our ideas in a consistent and relevant way. Keeney and Ray (1992) may call for aesthetics taking precedence over pragmatics, but even that assertion is capable of being empirically investigated (Shadish, Montgomery, Wilson, Wilson, Bright, & Okwumabua, 1993). The Shadish review demonstrates that pragmatic, outcome-oriented treatment is clearly superior to approaches emphasizing "aesthetics" of family therapy. Certainly, a therapist working with teens and their problems has an obligation to be aware of what the literature says about the more effective treatment approaches.

While some therapists take exception to the family-focused view of teen disturbance, preferring an individual approach, what cannot be challenged is that teens are consuming a good deal of our mental health financial resources. Much of the savings that managed care programs have demonstrated has come from reducing hospitalization of teens. These patients are typically aggressive and behaviorally disordered, with the most typical diagnosis being "major depression," the depression diagnosed on the basis of the aggressive behavior. Often these teens do not meet traditional criteria for major depression; instead of the passive set of symptoms seen in adults, a more agitated and troublemaking style prevails.*

Traditionally, hospitalization was reserved for adolescents who showed clear delusional behavior or who were very extreme in their actions, such as persistent suicidal or homicidal behavior. And certainly, if there is no other way to assure the safety of a very suicidal person (e.g., a patient with a strong desire to suicide, with a specific plan and the means to carry it out), the inpatient setting is appropriate. However, with the rise of for-profit psychiatric hospitals came the discovery that difficult teens had insurance that would cover 30, 60, 90, or more days of inpatient hospitalization. Some hospitals seemed to develop inpatient treatment packages tailored to the benefit package, so that the adolescent who had 60 days of inpatient coverage would need just that many days of treatment. The difficulty lies in demonstrating what type of therapy is most effective for teens. Can institutionalization be avoided? Must teens be "sent away" for extended residential treatment, or can the treatment be done in the natural environment?

The practice of institutionalizing teens, even "crazy" ones, is actually not well supported. Kiesler (1982) has pointed out many disadvantages of inpatient treatment, suggesting that as a rule the harm from inpatient treatment may well exceed the benefit. For one thing, Kiesler points out how inpatient treatment can actually often foster regression and loss of social and job capabilities, especially when the teen looks at him or herself. A loss of self-esteem is only natural; after all, the authorities seem to see one as incompetent and worthy of being locked up, so one's self-concept may well follow that lead.

In addition, being in a hospital fosters a loss of contact with parents, family, and other significant persons. In the teen years, one is especially needy of such contact and to proscribe or interfere with it seems unreasonable. In its place, the teen is placed around other deviant teens, certainly an excellent training ground for more deviancy. Instead of being encour-

---

*In reviewing these cases, I have always been suspicious that providers were fearful that a diagnosis of conduct disorder, which seems to fit the symptoms much better, would not be reimbursed by the insurance company.

aged to get work, show up, get a paycheck, and spend it on interesting and educational adventures, the teen is unable to work or spend the fruits of her or his labors. And while those objectives are easily addressed and even achieved within family therapy, no such emphasis is realistic when the teen is hospitalized.

In addition, Eamon (1994) points out that the best use of inpatient facilities is not to treat the teen but rather to change the fit between the teen and her or his environment, namely the family caring for that child. Unfortunately, Eamon points out, hospitals often fail in this most central mission. The facility may be a distance from the parents. The parents may not want to participate, since their own anxieties are lowered by having the teen out of the home, and they are not particularly motivated to take the adolescent back. Furthermore, Eamon reviewed evidence that only one-third of inpatient teens actually meet generally accepted diagnostic criteria, such as psychosis or severe depression or organic disorder; most were reacting to troubled or inadequate family environments. The implication of her argument is that the family is the proper focus for intervention. It makes little sense to remove the teen, treat, and then place the patient into a dysfunctional system that is likely to cause a relapse of the problem behavior.

In reality, the problems of many institutionalized teens (perhaps even those who appear to be appropriate for inpatient care) may be the result not of internal conflicts or early learning problems, but rather of ineffective helping strategies being applied over and over (Morrissette & Bodard, 1989). In other words, the impact of current family, school, and peer influence is greater than the impact of presumably vital early learning experiences and object relations. Typically, the misbehavior of the teen is correctly seen by parents and therapists as having potentially disastrous consequences unless interdicted. That is a justification for strong coercive efforts to control the teen. These efforts are nearly always of the same nature as previous efforts to interdict less extreme behavior. They include:

1. Confronting the teen
2. Labeling and blaming
3. Removing rewards and increasing punishments; however:
   (a) The removal of rewards by one parent may be undermined by a person (often another parent) who feels sorry for or sympathetic toward the teen.
   (b) Alternatively, the parent may soften or repent of the harsh penalties and relent regardless of the teen's behavior.

4. Ejecting the teen from the family, or creating the "throwaway" child (as Morrissette & McIntyre, 1989, point out, homeless young people are more often "throwaway" than "runaway")

It can be argued that even the teen placed in a residential setting is a type of "throwaway" because of the reality of the teen being removed from the home. Obviously, this harsh characterization should be tempered by the observation that such a situation implies a return to the family when the teen is "fixed." However, it remains that such a removal suggests the teen is the cause of the problems and the family has no responsibility to change.

It is not uncommon for methods of change for teens to center around coercion, a natural but ironic fact, when the therapist reflects on the social psychological theory of reactance (Brehm, 1966). This theory postulates that a subjective feeling that one is free to act is helpful in terms of survival value, and that when one perceives that freedom is being limited or removed, a feeling of reactance, resentment, or a desire to do the opposite is produced. Obviously, there are many more ineffective influence strategies. The point is that persisting in what doesn't work will only produce more of what is not wanted. Yet, when one is enmeshed in an ineffective strategy, there must be some way of changing the viewing so that the doing can also change.

TREATMENT OF TEENS: WHAT WORKS?

It may well be that families' natural strategies for dealing with teens often work quite well, since a very small portion of people who have problems ever seek professional help. Of the 90% of people who admit to having faced (and feel they successfully handled) serious problems, including problems with health, emotions, addictions, or lifestyle, only 3% seek professional assistance (Gurin, 1990). Even coercion-based interventions may work well in some cases. Or it may be that the families who handle these problems effectively employ distinct strategies. Alexander's research comparing delinquent families (families with a delinquent adolescent) with functional families suggests just that (Alexander & Parsons, 1982). And certainly, Brehm's (1966) analysis provides sufficient scientific rationale to assume that the successful families seem to handle their problems without causing extreme levels of reactance.

In any case, for adolescents who end up seeing therapists, the coercion-based approaches have not worked. It would be a grave error, then, for therapists to mirror those approaches. Unfortunately, in my experience reviewing cases for managed care, this is precisely what is often attempted.

The teen has been subjected to coercive methods at the hands of caretakers and parents. These methods have failed or exacerbated the problem. The parents then turn the problem over to professionals, who try to confront the teen into behaving better and finally support ejecting the teen from the family and placing him or her in an inpatient program or a residential treatment facility. Unfortunately, the record for residential treatment appears to be unsatisfactory, to say the least (Morrissette & McIntyre, 1989). It is common for teens to go from one placement to another with recurring problems. Yet therapists tend to overlook the fact that they have become part of the social equation and may be maintaining bad behavior through applying ineffective interventions similar to those already tried. It is necessary for therapists to do something different (Morrissette & McIntyre, 1989).

If we focus on treatment programs that empirically have shown a strong ability to help difficult children and teens, there are three main sources: James Alexander at the University of Utah, Jose Szapocznik at the University of Miami School of Medicine, and (focusing on preadolescents) Gerald Patterson at the Oregon Social Learning Center. While there are many fine therapists of teens and many high quality training programs in family therapy, these three are unusual in their *research*-based program development. All three programs have focused on a difficult problem area, and all three have used research to help refine and empower their work. Alexander has focused on teens who are referred to Juvenile Court, Szapocznik has focused on the problems of Cuban-American families, especially those where a teenage member is abusing drugs, and Patterson has developed treatment approaches with oppositional and defiant children.

These programs have in common an emphasis on treating the here-and-now problem, rather than examining early learning or object relations. They emphasize treatment within the family rather than individual, and they all assume the current family interactions are vital target areas for intervention. Both Alexander and Szapocznik have roots in structural and strategic family therapy approaches (Haley, 1963, 1976; Minuchin, 1974; Minuchin & Fishman, 1981); Patterson shares a systems orientation and is informed by social learning theory.

Along with the research-based treatments, Fisch, Weakland, and Segal (1982), Haley (1976), Madanes (1981), Selekman (1993), and many others offer clinical approaches to treating adolescents. These excellent approaches share one failing: There is no systematic research base underlying the techniques, so there is no way of knowing what power they bring to treatment. After all, the only thing separating therapists from shamans is our belief that systematic application of the scientific method is an effective way of improving our skills and understanding. While those pragmatically based treatment programs offer useful and powerful intervention strategies, this review will emphasize the treatment programs with robust research foundations.

Reframing Skills with Adolescents

It appears essential the "bad" behavior of the adolescent be reframed for himself and for the significant others. As Bergman (1985) has noted,

> Reframing in itself has enormous therapeutic power. Patients react to an effective reframing with responses such as surprise, startle, and sometimes, excitement. When a reframing is accepted, not only the perception but also the affect associated with the perception change. Patients seem to become unstuck from their old position in their lives or in their families. And often, one finds that changes in behavior follow this change in perception. (p. 41)

Furthermore, studies into therapeutic relationships with teens suggest that therapist warmth is not generally related to a positive bond between therapist and patient. Instead, effective reframing is a powerful factor in creating a therapeutic alliance (Alexander & Parsons, 1982; Robbins, Alexander, Newell, & Turner 1994). In other words, the typical adolescent has to see the therapist do something of value before valuing what the therapist can do. Changing the way the family characterizes the teen may be something of immediate of value.

In order to engage adolescents at a public mental health center, where the therapist rarely has contact with the family before the first session, Richard Ebling has found it useful to start each session by first explaining that he will "collect" opinions from everyone there, in turn. He then asks, "First, I need to know, what are some things that you are good at?" The adolescent's responses are carefully explored, adding positive labels or benign connotations to client statements, and sometimes extracting (from client or parent descriptions of delinquent behavior) some skill or talent that can be deemed praiseworthy. Further inquiry is made regarding the teen's talents, interests, favorite music, artistic/writing endeavors, work experience, etc. When a teen balks at this request, it is simple to ask, "What do your friends think you're good at? What do other people think you have talents in? If I asked someone who knows you well, what might he say?" Ordinarily, after this sort of discussion, an adolescent is ready for the question, "What would you like to accomplish by coming here today?" and is often willing to give a description of needed changes — *before* the parents get a chance to tell about the teen's misdeeds.

This approach to treatment follows the principle of complimenting visitors, complainants, and customers, and helps connect with the adolescent by using surprise (emphasizing positive qualities, in a context where the adolescent expects further criticism), helping the client save face, and expressing interest in him as a person. The approach is reminiscent of Erickson's report that he would ask an obsessive washer what kind of soap she used, and when she washed, would she start at her feet and work up or would she start at her head and work down? When Jay Haley asked why he would do that, he replied, "So that she would know that I was *really interested*."

Usually, the parents, who have brought the teen to the clinic, can tolerate the wait. If they begin their turn by criticizing the teen, Ebling will start asking them *what things the teen does right*.

A useful reframing for parents is to invite them to think of teens as being genetically programmed to oppose what adults say (giving parents a developmental rationale for this is sometimes useful), but as possessing a core of good judgment and willingness to "do good." However, their judgment and good nature are eclipsed by the importance of opposing adults — *as long as* the nearby adults are giving them something to oppose. A former client — senior in high school, athlete — suggested that drug prevention efforts would be most effective with the following strategy: Tell teens of the possible results of chronic drug use — not in terms of physiology, but in observable terms (fighting with parents, gradually lower grades, gradual decline in motivation, almost imperceptible diminution of cognitive skills) — and suggest that they observe people they know who have been using for one or two years, then notice what happens in the lives of those persons, and decide if that's what they want in life. Brehm (1966) has pointed out that this oppositional tendency is not just limited to adolescents, although it may be easier to see in them. Rather, it is a general tendency in most people to oppose any force that seems to limit or take away freedoms or options. This *reactivity* causes persons to act in ways that may seem obstructionistic or even irrational, but that are understandable when analyzed in the light of the reactivity effect Brehm describes. In consultation, John Weakland suggests mentioning the possible ill-effects of (undesirable) behaviors, then saying, "But that *might not* happen, so (doing those behaviors) *might* be worth it."

A related framework suggests that teens seem incapable of fear if they are being told they should be afraid. Helping them save face and refraining from direct criticism, while offering kinder explanations for their behavior, seem to give them the opportunity to examine and criticize their own behavior. Parents often desire to punish bad behavior. If they insist on this, certain kinds of punishment seem much more useful than others. Specifically, punishments that are predominantly *inconvenient* (as opposed to painful or humiliating) are more effective.

Selekman (1993) proposes that one of the best ways to achieve a useful reframing with the teen patient is to attempt to achieve the teen's goals. As an example, he describes "Julie," who has been deteriorating in school, shoplifting, and smoking marijuana. Her goal is not to change any of those behaviors but rather to get her parents to quit complaining. Selekman accepts that goal and begins to create a well-formed outcome focus (e.g., If the parents don't complain, then what will they do instead? Have there been times they did that? What was Julie doing when they did the other things?), which Julie is willing to work toward.

In contrast, if the therapist were to attempt to offer Julie a relationship based on insight, Julie would be likely to perceive this as "more of the same" that she had been offered. In her perception, she might hear the therapist saying, "Let me help you (*a one-up relationship*) understand (*you are ignorant and I am expert*) what is wrong with you (*you are defective*)." In fact, her perception might not be far from the truth. If her diagnosis were "oppositional/defiant disorder" (ODD), the therapist would see or judge her as defective. By accepting the patient's goals and actually trying to help her achieve them, the therapist conveys respect.

Morrissette (1992) offers five reframing techniques that he finds helpful in working with homeless youth.

1. Spend a good deal of time letting the youth learn about the setting and in small talk. Enthusiasm is dangerous at this juncture, since a teen may be "treatment wise" and have experience with therapists promising more than they can deliver. Instead, the therapist should emphasize "pacing" or nonverbal synchronicity with the patient, as well as small talk and finding common interests.
2. Instead of assessing the teen, encourage the teen to assess the therapist. This phase of *assessment reversal* empowers and conveys respect to the client. Morrissette points out that the phrase "I would like to help you" immediately places the young person in an inferior position to the helper, creating a feeling in the patient of being undermined. Instead, the assessment reversal supports the teen's need to feel in control.
3. Caution the young person against prematurely trusting the helper. Morrissette claims that the notion that the teen has been exploited in the past supports this caution; after all, if the therapist understands that the teen has suffered at the hands of well-intentioned adults, such "go slow" advice is not paradoxical at all, but profoundly sensible.
4. Find personal strengths to compliment in the young person. Morrissette suggests the therapist share (instead of hiding) moments of surprise or even confusion if the teen is ready to trust the therapist, in view of what the youth has presumably already experienced. Such willingness to trust shows a good deal of courage.

5. Emphasize that the teen should continue to nurture his or her current social network, and encourage significant others and friends to attend the planning meetings or conferences (terms Morrissette uses instead of "therapy"). This is a reversal of the typical stance that the teen may have experienced, in which he is encouraged to give up the current friends because of their "bad influence."

Morrissette gives as an example "Kelly," who sought help at the shelter for homeless youth. He suggested she should go slowly and ask as many questions as needed in order to decide whether his shelter was helpful for her. He emphasized that she was there by her own choice, and should leave if she was not satisfied. He says, "Kelly appeared surprised and somewhat humored with this suggestion. She immediately noted that in the past she felt like she was always being cross-examined or under a microscope" (p. 450).

Both Selekman and Morrissette describe interventions that surprise the teen. The expectations are shifted or even upended, and a state of beneficial uncertainty is created. Similarly, Ebling's emphasis on the positive aspects of the teen, early in the therapy, may be a vital component of his success with difficult families.

Szapocznik, Kurtines and contributors (1989) suggest a meta-analysis of positive reframing, which they call the *acceptance paradox*. By this they mean that the patient is accepted and validated so that he or she may change. They refer to the process of conveying that acceptance as *joining*, which includes nonverbal acceptance as well as tacit initial agreement with family rules. Acceptance of positive features or intentions behind "bad" behavior is vital, and often the patient will respond with actual shock when the therapist sincerely congratulates him for the behavior.

Reframing with Significant Others

The MRI group (Fisch, Weakland, & Segal, 1982) uses reframing extensively in preparing patients to change. Since they view the essential question as "What maintains the problem?" and since they usually find the patient's or the significant others' efforts to solve the problem are precisely what maintains it, they strive to shift the understanding of the problem. For example, if the family sees the teen as "bad," the reframing might emphasize the "sick" explanation; if they see the teen as "sick," then a helpful emphasis might be toward "bad." In other words, shifting understanding prepares the ground for a shift of behavior.

This systems view is essential in understanding many of the effective approaches to changing the adolescent. The notion is that the change of behavior by significant others may have a more powerful impact on the adolescent than any attempts at giving insight or understanding.

Fisch, Weakland, and Segal give an example in which the parents complain of an unreasonable daughter who gives arbitrary and confusing answers. Since the parents try hard to be reasonable and rational, and since they resent the daughter, the therapist reframes their efforts as being controlled by unreasonableness, and suggests that they give her some of her own medicine. They are assigned to be more unreasonable than she is. In the next session, with the parents present, the therapist then recommends that the daughter continue to ask "Why not?" when the parents say "no" as a way of maintaining her power in the family. The therapist then points out that, while this may land her in Juvenile Hall and perhaps result in her being in a chronic state of rage, it is a small price to pay to maintain her high level of power in the family. After all, the therapist confides, she would be a fool to give up the power she has in the family. This paradoxical reframing has the desired effect of empowering the parents to reverse their particular strategy for dealing with their daughter. In this case, the paradoxical injunction to the daughter pointed out to the parents the power inherent in acting in an arbitrary manner. When they increased their own use of arbitrary behavior, the daughter improved in her behavior.

In a comparative study, Szykula et al. (1987) found that strategic therapy of the MRI variety was equal in therapeutic impact to family-based behavioral treatment. The notion that parents need to be taught to be better teachers and managers (an underlying principle of much child and adolescent behavior modification) is not well supported, since such an idea would contradict the strategic approach. Rather, the key seems to be a shift of meanings and attributions, which then changes the way the whole system relates. Thus, the act of reframing, the shifting of meanings from one framework (usually "bad" or "crazy") to another (i.e., "well meaning but flawed," "needing to find ways to be independent," or "wanting more closeness but approaching it ineffectively," among many others) exerts a freeing effect on the system, allowing many of the participants (not just the identified patient and the parents) to behave more freely and unpredictably. Since both behavior modification and strategic therapy appeared to work equally well, it seems likely the common factors account for the improvement.

COMPARING TREATMENT STRATEGIES
WITH ADOLESCENTS

While there are many opinions about how to treat teens effectively, there are relatively few actual comparative studies. In a large study of status offenders referred to the juvenile court in Salt Lake City, Alexander and Parsons (1973; Parsons & Alexander, 1973) treated and tracked treatment effects. Status offenders are adolescents whose behavior has caused them to be referred to the justice system, even though the behavior in question would not be an offense in an adult. In other words, a teen would be referred for smoking, drinking, or being ungovernable; many adults engage in similar behaviors but are not brought to court because they are "old enough" to do them without legal repercussions.

Alexander and Parsons demonstrated that these "status offenders" did tend to progress into criminal offenses if not treated. If no treatment were offered, approximately 50% would be back in court for similar or more serious offenses within 6–18 months.

Three active treatment conditions were compared with a "no treatment" condition. A family therapy program developed by Alexander, emphasizing a combination of strategic and behavioral principles, was offered (functional family therapy, FFT), along with client-centered and dynamic individual psychotherapy conditions. Since at the time it was common to refer juveniles to individual treatment, these conditions were ideal for creating the comparison. FFT was partly developed from Alexander's studies of normal families, in which he found a variety of differences between their problem-solving techniques and those of delinquent family systems. He then advocated a "matching to sample" philosophy, in which the therapist would attempt to influence the delinquent family to behave more like the symptom-free families. Alexander was also strongly influenced by strategic therapy (emphasizing positive reframing and emphasis on presenting problems) and by behavioral approaches (emphasizing exchange theory and behaviorally specific contracting).

Systems theory would suggest that there is a tendency for siblings from the same family to engage in similar behavior. In this case, when follow-up by examining court records was accomplished, it was found that within three and a half years, 66% of teens who had been through the court system would have a sibling referred to the court. There were then two questions: first, would family therapy be more effective than individual therapy for treating these status offenders, and second, would family therapy (with its emphasis on changing the system or the structure of the family) reduce sibling delinquency? Several subsequent studies addressed these questions, and those results were reported in Alexander and Barton (1976). Those results are summarized in Table 11.1. The family therapy condition had significantly more impact on both the identified patient and on siblings than did the individual therapy conditions.

Replications of Alexander and Parsons

Later research demonstrated a similar powerful effect on teens who were about to be ejected from their families. Barton, Alexander, Waldron, Turner, and Warburton (1985) trained state protective service caseworkers

Table 11.1 Effect of Functional Family Therapy and Comparison Treatment on Delinquent Family Process and Outcome*

	Group Recidivism 6–18 months	Sibling delinquency 2½–3½ years
no treatment (control group)	50%	66%
client-centered (individual)	47%	59%
dynamic (individual)	73%	63%
FFT	26%	20%

*Adapted from Alexander & Barton, 1976.

in Alexander's functional family therapy model. The trained caseworkers integrated the FFT skills into their interventions with families who requested help because a teen was ungovernable at home. After they had used FFT with 109 cases, they compared the results of their interventions to the results of caseworkers who had not taken the family therapy training.

The caseworkers performing this study focused on rates of utilization of foster family placement. While the idea behind foster family placement was to provide a cooling off period for the adolescent, it had actually become very difficult to return the teen to the family. Both the identified patient and the family resisted returning to the stressful situation of the teen at home.

The target was to promote family change that would allow the teen to remain at home, thereby avoiding the "throwaway" phenomenon. The results were quite impressive. Before the training, the trained caseworkers referred 48% of their cases to foster care; a matched group of caseworkers who did not receive the training referred 43%. After the training, the caseworkers referred only 11% of their cases to foster care, while the matched group continued to refer a high proportion (49%) out of the family.

Barton et al. (1985) also reported on intervention with hard-core incarcerated delinquent adolescents. Following release, a comparison group (achieved by examining court records and matching post hoc to the experimental group) had a recidivism rate of 93% in one year; in other words, nearly all of these teens would be in legal trouble one or more times within a year of release. Prior to their release from the training school where they were incarcerated, the experimental group began to receive family therapy designed to shift the family structure and promote functional family interaction. As the teens were released, family therapy continued. After FFT treatment, the recidivism rate was 60%, and as a group those who received treatment committed less than half the offenses they had previously. A comparison group was offered residential treatment, job training, remedial education, and school placement. The comparison group continued to commit serious offenses at the same rate as before, so the traditional package of treatment, organized around residential treatment, appeared to have no effect.

Family-based interventions are a robust and viable alternative to the "get rid of" strategies of residential and inpatient care. Those working in residential settings would naturally object to being characterized as enabling a "throwaway" mentality in parents, and rightfully so. These therapists are sincere and deeply caring people who want to help. The question is not who cares the most, but what is the most helpful and least disruptive. In this regard, a replication of the Alexander FFT approach is quite enlightening. Gordon, Arbuthnot, Gustafson, and McGreen (1988) compared a residential placement with Alexander's family therapy approach in adolescent delinquents. At follow-up (over two years later), the family therapy treatment group showed an 11% recidivism rate while the control (residential) group showed a 57% rate. From the original studies up to the present, FFT has been shown to have powerful advantages over individual and residential treatment for very difficult teens. Since it is common for teens with disorders of conduct and behavior to be labeled "depressed," these findings speak directly to the treatment of a wide spectrum of teen problems.

Reexamining the Results

I was taking a family therapy practicum from Bruce Parsons when he and Alexander were finishing the original studies, and later worked at the same juvenile court where the studies had been done. I was so influenced by those results that for some time after that I foolishly resisted seeing adolescents individually, out of the fear that I would somehow contaminate them. I misunderstood these results to suggest that no treatment except family therapy was useful to the adolescent.

What I should have learned from these data is something quite different. Functional family therapy was developed out of a kind of marriage of systems-strategic thinking and behavior therapy, so the teen is seen as part of a system, and the behavior of that teen makes sense within that social context. Thus, individual treatment informed by the principles we have already discussed—namely, focusing on the goals of the patient, creating a working alliance, working for limited goals, and emphasizing homework that changes the context and the relationship patterns—can help, as can family therapy (Szapocznik et al., 1986). Perhaps the problem was with the particular therapists offering the individual treatment; they may have violated some of the ground rules, such as trying to make the patient change in ways foreign to his or her interests and values. Instead, they needed to emphasize the influence the teen client has on his family, and the influence the family has on the client. In other words, the teen is likely to be interested not in insight into himself but into strategies of influencing others and resisting unwanted influence from others.

What was lacking in my understanding at the time was the customer status distinction. Were the teens I saw from the juvenile court customers to change themselves, or were they complainants or visitors? Perhaps the family therapy had more impact simply because there was a better chance of finding a customer for change in the family. Obviously, with the whole family present, it is likely that someone in the family will be willing to work hard, even if the identified patient is not. And if individual therapy is necessary, it must offer changes the teen is likely to be a customer for. Better yet, we should carefully discover what the teen is interested in, and help him achieve some change or sense of mastery in that area.

Family Therapy and Children

Although it appears that family therapy or therapy informed by family and systems thinking is the treatment of choice for adolescents, can we say the same for children? Szapocznik, Kurtines and contributors (1989) compared structural family therapy, psychodynamic child play therapy, and a recreational control condition in treating 69 six-to-twelve-year-old Hispanic boys presenting with behavioral and emotional problems. While this group is a distinct population from the adolescents we are discussing, the study is an important one. The three conditions were designed to provide the most common elements of treatment, including "play therapy" as a condition that arouses placebo factors, provides hope-promoting experiences, and fosters warm and supportive interactions. The emphasis was on play and recreation, and there were no attempts to discuss emotional or behavioral problems or give advice.

So the study is well-suited to comparison of active treatment conditions: What effect does it have on the patient and on the family to be treated with a systems-oriented family treatment, as opposed to an individually-oriented insight treatment? How much growth comes from general conditions of warmth and attention, as compared with interventions which are presumed to create psychological health?

Several important conclusions can be derived from the Szapocznik study. First, specific treatment approaches are much more likely to retain patients than the recreational approach. Forty-three percent of the subjects in the recreational condition dropped out, mostly the older patients. While the younger children continued to attend, the older ones appeared to require active treatment. In contrast, family therapy and individual therapy had lower dropout rates of 16% and 4% respectively.

Second, all three conditions (both active treatment conditions and the control condition) were equivalently helpful to the children, whether this improvement was measured on psychodynamic or behavioral assessments. In this study, family therapy was not superior to individual therapy in terms of helpfulness to the patients. However, there was a significant and marked difference between the two treatment conditions when assessed at a one-year follow-up. The experimenters were shocked to find that family functioning had dramatically improved for those in the family therapy condition, while family functioning in the psychodynamic group had deteriorated! It may be that as the "identified patient" improves, the family deteriorates because of not being able to scapegoat and blame someone for the problems. Oddly enough, the families of patients in the control play condition did not deteriorate, even though those children also improved.

Interestingly, Szapocznik and his colleagues do not comment on the fact that the placebo "play" condition produced improvement in the children who stayed in therapy. While having a clear focus seems to help the children stay in therapy, those who do stay in spite of no focus (the "play" condition) did improve. On measures of symptom relief, the nonspecific play condition was more effective than psychodynamic play therapy, although not significantly. Even on psychodynamic measures of improvement, family therapy produced greater (but not statistically significantly greater) improvements than did the individual psychodynamic therapy.

Szapocznik's results suggest that structural family therapy is the treatment of choice for behavioral and emotional problems in preadolescent boys, since it improves family structure and function, and therefore improves the family's ability to help its members. For many children, simple positive attention is enough to mobilize their natural tendencies to improve and adapt in a positive way. For example, in his 1985 review, Phillips concluded there was very little evidence that play therapy was more effective than simple placebo in producing positive adaptation in children. It may be that time itself is the operant factor in the improvement seen in the children. This implies that children are more robust and strive more vigorously toward health than is usually assumed by psychotherapists. After all, it is in our own self-interest to see children and teens as needing our special expertise and ministrations. That the opposite may be true is not a fact we would welcome.

THE QUESTION OF RESISTANCE

It is common in solution-focused discussions to assert that resistance to psychotherapy is an artifact of the way in which therapists approach the family or, more radically, that resistance itself is merely a construction of the therapist and doesn't "really exist." This view derives from constructivism, a philosophical approach postulating that all of our knowledge is really our own construction, and doesn't represent anything "real"—in other words, reality cannot be independently known.

Such ideas have wide currency in strategic and solution-focused therapy, and many have misunderstood them to indicate that research itself is futile and that any and all constructions of reality have equal validity. De Shazer (1982, 1985) has argued that the concept of resistance is not a useful nor helpful one, a position echoed by Selekman (1993). The position suggests that the therapist is an integral part of the system he or she is treating, so (in the spirit of constructivism) if we look for resistance, we create the very phenomenon we purport to observe. Instead, the therapist should assume that the system and all persons in it are always cooperating to the best of their ability; the job of the therapist is to discover in what ways the client will cooperate with the therapist. Therapists agreeing with the solution-focused view of therapy often sound like religious fanatics in their rejection of any such "thing" as resistance.

A different view is advanced by the Miami group, Szapocznik and his colleagues (Szapocznik, Kurtines and contributors, 1989). They utilized a systemic-strategic view of resistance, presupposing that the therapist is, to some extent, separate from the system and can reduce the tendency of some families to resist treatment.

Adolescent drug abusers are difficult to treat. There appears to be a high failure rate associated with proposing 12-step programs to individual adolescent drug abusers (Berg & Miller, 1992), but unfortunately this is typically the only program available. Szapocznik and his colleagues have demonstrated that while strategic family therapy appears to be quite effective with this population, keeping the families in treatment is a substantial obstacle. Regardless of how clinicians may wish to suggest everyone is cooperating in unique ways, the fact is that, in the Miami experience, very few families actually follow through with needed treatment. Of 650 initial contacts who investigated possible treatment, only 250 came in for a screening interview, only 145 completed the intake procedure, and only 72 completed treatment.

The Miami group analyzed types of resistance and were able to identify four general family resistance patterns (in their population, Cuban-American families in the Miami area). First, the identified patient (IP) was very powerful in the family and resisted therapy. Second, the mother was ambivalent about therapy, and tended to protect the IP. In this case, the father tended to be in a peripheral role. Third, in some families there was little or no cohesiveness or alliance between the parents. Often the father was not only disengaged but also refusing to attend therapy. And finally, in some families, the investigators were able to identify a family secret which the members feared exposing. The first pattern, the powerful IP, was the most common.

Then they developed interventions designed to implement family structural changes that would neutralize the resistance (see Szapocznik, Kurtines and contributors, 1989, for a detailed description of the interventions). These interventions formed the experimental condition, while engagement as usual was the control. When the results were analyzed, it was apparent that deliberately dealing with resistance had been enormously successful. At the beginning of the study, families contacting the center were assigned to "engagement as usual" or "strategic structural systems approach." While 58% of the families in the control condition failed to come to the mental health center for intake, only four families (7.1%) failed to attend in the experimental condition. Furthermore, of the patients completing treatment, 80% were drug-free, and the experimental group was no less successful than the control group. That is, once engaged in therapy, both groups received the same type of structural family therapy.

In other words, we cannot assume that (as is often said) the patient must be strongly motivated and get to treatment on her or his own, if treatment is to be successful. That requirement may itself be a symptom of an ineffective approach. It is obvious from this study that if the family will come to treatment, the strategic family therapy approach stands an excellent chance of being very helpful. Active efforts on the part of the therapist to engage the patient in therapy (i.e., overcome whatever resistance to therapy happens to be present in the family) are remarkably successful.

Since in my own training the concept of a motivated patient had been strongly modeled as a necessity for successful treatment, these results came as a personal shock. As I recovered from that shock, I began to make more effort to engage patients into treatment from the very first telephone call. Once again, a cherished old belief has fallen by the wayside, as I have found consistently that there is no difference between patients who are eager to engage in therapy and those who are quite reluctant. On the contrary, some of the most reluctant have become some of the most successful.

Another useful analysis of family resistance comes from the social learning view of Patterson and Chamberlain (1992). Patterson and his group at the Oregon Social Learning Center have documented what is certainly the most well-investigated approach to treating preadolescent antisocial children. Using a behavioral or social learning approach, Patterson has achieved some remarkable results with this difficult population (cf. Patterson, Reid, & Dishion, in press). Patterson and Chamberlain collapsed their analysis of resistance into two general categories: *I can't* and *I won't*. They found the "I can't" responses related both to "I won't" statements and to failure to complete homework assignments. Their analysis suggested that parental resistance was the result of three determinants: (a) parental traits such as depression and antisocial personality traits; (b) external factors such as stress and social problems; and (c) skill of the therapist in confronting and teaching the parents. In regard to the last, they noted that more experienced therapists experienced less resistance from families, which supports the interactional view rather than the social or intrapsychic formulation. They now intend to investigate the therapist's role in producing the resistance, something de Shazer has been alluding to for some time now.

So the assertion that "resistance is not a helpful concept" may not be itself very helpful. A careful examination of what is meant by resistance yields some very useful interventions. Now in reality the disciples of de Shazer do deal with resistance when they follow customer status treatment protocols, and they deal with it very effectively. It is more useful to concentrate on the commonalities between strategic, systemic, social learning, and solution-focused approaches. In any case, an awareness of the interactional determinants of resistance seems to be more profitable than looking at it as something "inside" of the patient.

TREATMENT PROTOCOLS FOR ADOLESCENTS

Our review of the literature indicates that family therapy, utilizing either systems or behavioral techniques, is the treatment of choice for children and adolescents (Szykula et al., 1987); strategic or systems-oriented approaches in individual therapy also appear effective. Depressed adolescents have shown a positive response to cognitive-behavioral treatment, although according to a recent review of the literature, they do not show any response to antidepressant medication, when compared with placebo (Peterson, Compas, Brooks-Gunn, Stemmler, Ey, & Grant, 1993). Insight-oriented individual approaches seem to have a number of drawbacks and should not be recommended.

Engagement and Resistance

Agencies and therapists should develop assertive engagement strategies to involve the teenage patient in therapy when the first inquiry is made.

The strategies should acknowledge the inherent ambivalence about therapy and aim at restructuring the family relationship so as to remove restraining forces. Acceptance and reframing appear to be essential elements in this process.

This means that the initial telephone call should be handled by a skilled clinician or a very well-trained paraprofessional. The call is viewed as a therapeutic contact and potentially an important event in helping the family. Outreach, including home visits by a therapist, should be a component of restructuring efforts. For example, to engage a powerful and resistant teen, it is often necessary to make the home visit, to meet the adolescent on his own turf (Szapocznik, Kurtines & contributors, 1989). Then the therapist can engage the teen by learning what would motivate him to enter treatment and providing a way he can achieve that.

The Miami group reaches out assertively to "no show" clients, trying to track them down, diagnose what type of resistance is present in the family, and enable the family to deal with that resistance. Adolescent treatment programs should include such outreach to broaden their impact. Compensation schemes must be modified to allow for fair and reasonable coverage for such activities as outreach, home visits, and collateral contacts or visits with stepparents, school or probation personnel, and other network members.

Initial intakes should be valued and rewarded by the agency. Therapists who have a good track record of attracting new patients (low no-show rate, reflecting an effective outreach strategy) and a good retention record (patients remaining in treatment for a mutually agreed-upon time) are therapy superstars and should be rewarded accordingly. Thus, it is necessary to track those attributes in the management information system.

The customer status protocol appears to be a useful tool for predicting the types of interactions to which an identified patient (or any other family member) will response positively. While further refinement of this tool is likely, the present understanding is a useful starting point. It should be kept in mind that customer status can rapidly change, depending on how effective the therapist is at identifying the needs of the family members. This system, or the Prochaska approach (e.g., Prochaska, DiClemente & Norcross, 1992), should be utilized routinely to inform therapists of interventions that will not make things worse (e.g., forcing therapy on a noncustomer, or ignoring the customer in the family and working only with the identified patient), and which have a good chance of making things better (e.g., giving assignments to collect data to complainants or patients in the contemplation stage, but giving homework for behavior changes to customers and action-level patients).

The Role of Diagnosis

Alexander and Parsons (1982) recommend a phased approach to treatment, with an assessment phase determining how the therapist would engage the family. Family therapists tend to use interactional tools rather than individually oriented approaches, such as asking the family to plan an activity together and observing the interactional patterns. For example, consider the processes of merging versus separating. In family therapy, some families will show a good deal of merging between some members, and much separating between others. Symptoms may occur when one person wants more closeness and the other wants more distance. Family therapy can modify the ways these desires are carried out.

The diagnosis we are discussing here is not a *DSM-IV* diagnosis. Such categorization is helpful only for insurance and government entities who insist on it; the diagnosis is seldom helpful for treatment. Instead, the diagnosis should address interactional aspects, such as Alexander's (see Alexander & Parsons, 1982) three-part individuation scheme: *separating/ distancing* (characterized by withdrawal, cold sarcasm, many outside activities or runaway); *midpointing* (characterized by passive contact, depression, hysteria, and alcoholism/drug abuse); and *merging* (characterized by phobias and insecurities, overcompensation, hypomania, and caretaking). Each of these is seen as a possible strategy for the adolescent to accommodate to the stresses of the teen years (as contrasted with the *DSM-IV* assumption that depression, hysteria, and so on are *conditions inside the person*), and each can be directed toward one or more family members. For example, a child could be merging with a mother and distancing/separating from a father. The mother could then be distancing from the father, leading him to feel isolated and ineffectual. Alternatively, a child could be midpointing toward the parents when they are striving toward merging, creating conflict over the level of involvement defined as appropriate in the family.

Alexander and Parsons also focus on the family presentation as a diagnostic variable. Some families attend to behavior, some to feelings or cognitions, and some to relationship variables. Each type of family must be recognized and responded to appropriately by the therapist.

Szapocznik's (Szapocznik, Kurtines and contributors, 1989) sophisticated diagnostic scheme is somewhat more complex and yet complementary to Alexander's. He and his colleagues consider six structural dimensions: (1) *structure*, including aspects of leadership, behavioral control, and guidance; (2) *flexibility*, which refers to shifts in communication, alliance, and subsystem formation; (3) *resonance*, referring to enmeshment, disengagement, and differentiation; (4) *developmental stage*, assessing whether ages, roles, and tasks are appropriate in the family; (5) *identified patienthood*, measuring the extent to which the family members agree all family problems are due to a single person, the identified patient; and (6) *conflict resolution* stages, from denial to resolution.

Since the treatment programs with the best research and outcome data do use interpersonal diagnostic schemes, the accountable family therapist is advised to use them or at least to understand them well. It is possible Selekman's contention that diagnosis is not an important activity will turn out to be the case, but so far it is far from well established. Solution-focused family therapy, as portrayed by Selekman, has great advantages in that the interventions are quite transparent and obvious, arising from the powerful and concise decision tree explicated by de Shazer (1988). Both de Shazer (1988) and Selekman (1993) suggest decision trees which suggest interventions. These decision trees could greatly simplify family psychotherapy and would be a significant advance for the field. But without a fair and comprehensive set of trials, comparing them with well-documented approaches, they remain hypotheses.

Both Szapocznik and Alexander have identified specific populations, made efforts to design effective treatment programs, and conducted sophisticated and energetic follow-up to determine the result of interventions. As a result, it can be argued that their approaches constitute treatments of choice for teens. Solution-focused treatment, in comparison, has been developed from strong and focused efforts to improve treatment strategies in a general outpatient population, consisting of people who make appointments and follow through with them. There are no data available on the power or effect size of the approach. Those who use the solution-focused ideas and techniques find them powerful and useful and a significant advance over systems such as those of Haley and Minuchin. This is because of the basic simplicity of the model. In contrast, the Alexander and Szapocznik approaches are more demanding of the therapist, requiring more intense training and supervision.

At the Brief Therapy Center in Salt Lake City, our assessment centers on:

1. *What is the family structure?* Is/are parent(s) in an authoritative position or a helpless or powerless position? Do they actively try to influence the teen or take a passive or uninvolved position? Does each family member behave consistently with his age? Who colludes with whom in the family? Each position may help to maintain the problem and may be a target for intervention through reframing and homework assignments to shift or modify family structure.
2. *What does each person say he or she wants to accomplish by coming in?* To what extent can the therapist reframe the situation and find common ground

on which to base interventions? How can the therapist work to simultaneously help each person achieve something of value? What is the customer status of each person in the system? Can it be modified or simply
accepted?

3. *What is the style of language and response?* Is the language direct and concrete or symbolic? Is it vague or specific? When cooperation is requested, is there: (a) direct cooperation, (b) direct defiance, (c) changing or altering the assignment, e.g., a collaborative style, or (d) ignoring
   of requests?

4. *Does the family communicate in a particular style?* Do family members interrupt and mind-read (suggesting an attempt to merge), or contradict/
   bicker (midpoint), or withdraw, refuse to respond (separate)? Can they
   utilize each other's comments? Do they interrupt with new information
   or with derailing and bickering?

Interventions

The most common intervention is to focus on changing the family interaction patterns, using reframing as a basis for changes in behavior. There
is an implicit or explicit diagnostic scheme behind interventions. For example, Alexander and Parsons suggest a change of sequence with a child who
starts fires. Instead of the sequence of fire-setting, mother's subsequent
upset feelings which she expresses to father, and father's punishment, a
new sequence is begun. Based on the frame that the boy needs to understand about fires, the family is given the assignment of getting the boy to
set fires and put them out under the close supervision of the (previously
isolated) father.

Alexander and Parsons strongly emphasize the value of communication-
training exercises, in this way differing from their strategic roots. The
functional family therapy view is that therapy does not teach patients new
skills; it merely enables them to become receptive to learning them. Many
of these specific skills were defined by observing how functional, healthy
families communicate about challenging issues. Individuals in the effective
families tended to make shorter statements, were direct and responsible
when making a request, distinguished between rules (consequences follow
violation) and requests (no consequence for refusal), and were skilled at
generating alternatives.

One characteristic that distinguishes delinquent from functional families
is their flexibility in response to feedback. In adaptive families, members
may interrupt to provide feedback or new information or to ask for clarifi-
cation. In dysfunctional families, the interruptions do not contain new
information. In functional family therapy the therapist actively shapes fam-

ily communication by noting positive examples as well as suggesting better ways to discuss heated family issues.

Behavioral techniques in FFT include contingency contracting (agreeing to exchange valued behaviors through the use of a contractual agreement), token economies (exchanging valued tokens for specific desired behaviors), charting behavior, and a variety of interpersonal tasks, such as conflict-management training.

Selekman's approach is again simpler; he relies primarily on reframing through the use of de Shazer's questions, with thoughtful augmentations from other sources. However, the basic theme, of shifting meanings and behaviors in the family, remains constant. We can derive then a general model of intervention, namely, promoting change primarily at the level of interpersonal and interactional behavior and avoiding a focus on internal change. In examining the confluence of themes, we see the development of a view of human change radically different from the traditional approach, one which emphasizes the essential group nature of our consciousness. We are creatures of the group, and to ignore this is to ignore some of the most powerful determinants of our behavior.

Herein lies the essential paradox: The effective therapist for adolescents sees the teen as acting on and being acted on by the many groups of which he or she is a member. At the same time, the essential quality of psychotherapy is that, by changing one's mind, one can change the world. So we act as if the teen is a creature of the family and an independent being capable of free exercise of will. And both are simultaneously correct.

It appears that effective treatment will primarily emphasize the social nature of adolescents, through informed efforts to restructuring networks, especially the family. While individual approaches can also yield helpful results (Kazdin, 1993), more convincing evidence supports the efforts to modify the family.

At the Brief Therapy Center, our treatment protocol emphasizes the importance of each family member's having some kind of new experience, either in the session or later, through homework. Clearly, the treatment of adolescents relies to a greater extent on the use of novel or surprising elements than would the treatment of the trauma survivor or the substance abuser. Novelty, surprise, and entrancement appear essential in working with difficult adolescents. But of course, when we remember our own sense of immortality and omniscience as adolescents, the central role of surprise is not surprising.

Yet surprise for its own sake is insufficient — any good movie produces that. Rather, the surprise must be about the teen, not about the world generally. The skilled therapist must convey the idea that "I noticed this about *you*. Perhaps I shouldn't even mention it." And the quality that is noticed should be positive. So when homeless teens come to Morrissette's treatment program (Morrissette, 1992), he asks them for advice about how to survive on the streets, no mean feat in the Canadian winters. Seeing the teen as an expert on survival is a therapeutic surprise (since the teen is likely to be accustomed to people treating him or her as a victim or a troublemaker).

By the same token, when parents behave in a new or surprising way in response to the teen's usual challenges or symptoms, they are so valued and central to the teen's world that the message is clearly, "This is about you." The message is even more powerful when the parents overtly deny the change of behavior is about the teen, as the MRI group recommends, e.g., "I don't know why I am acting this way; I don't seem to be myself these days." Then the message "This is about me" is heard by the teen, though it is not overtly given (indeed, denied) by the parent. As Brehm (1966) would predict, an apparently hidden message is more powerful and unlikely to result in reactance or resistance than a direct one ("This is about you"). If the teen overhears something, it has more impact than if he is told directly.

So positive messages (which support more freedom to act) can be directly given, while consequences to problem behavior might be better given in some indirect way.

Protocol for families

Specifically, our intervention protocol emphasizes:

1. At the initial contact and to some extent throughout therapy, a strong attempt is made to help the identified patient save face through a discussion of strengths and abilities, i.e., positive attributes. Strong efforts are made to attend to those strengths.
2. The therapist attempts to cooperate with the teen's goals, even if only partially.
3. Behavioral change on one person's part is defined as a shift in direction (e.g., "It seems you have really turned a corner,") and the idea of reciprocity is raised ("I wonder how the members of your family are going to keep up with that change?").
4. In the session the distinction is made between rules (that have consequences if not obeyed) and requests (which don't have consequences for noncompliance). When a parent makes a rule that is not followed by a consequence, this is reframed as a request (this is more respectful and connotes an adult-to-adult type of relationship).
5. Formal contracts for behavior change are often created as an example of

how to create changes in behavior through the positive use of rules, i.e., a good behavior results in a good consequence.

6. When possible, the attempted coping strategies are reversed, especially when there is a confusion between rules and requests. If the parent does not have the power or ability to follow through with a rule, a strong attempt is made to help the parent take a one-down position, making only requests.

7. Termination is achieved by spacing out sessions whenever possible and discussing the possibility that a monthly "booster" session should accomplish what is needed, as well as suggesting a "break" from therapy when progress seems to be reasonably stable. Relapse factors are openly discussed and often humorously recommended by suggesting advantages of the old problem-laden behavioral patterns.

Case Example: The Single Mother's Revenge

A single mother presented to me asking for help with her 14-year-old son. She complained of his skipping school, being disobedient and argumentative at home, failing to do chores, running around with a group of drug abusers, acting at times like he was on drugs, and no longer being affectionate and caring toward her or his 16-year-old sister. The son was clothed in gang-like attire, with an unusual haircut that involved shaving part of his head and growing his hair long on other parts, and wore a jacket with swastikas and death's heads. He was quite unresponsive in the interview, except to offer his opinion that his mother was stupid or crazy to bring him there and that there was nothing wrong with him. A search for the "hidden customer" was futile, and his current relationship with the therapist was judged as "visitor."

After a half-hour of this, the young man was told that his life did seem to be going just about how he would like it to, so I would be foolish to tell him to change his behavior just to make his mother happy. He was excused to sit in the waiting room, and I turned to the mother. I suggested that, while the young man needed therapy, he was not yet ready, and might not be ready for some time to come. I asked the mother if she were willing to work hard to help her boy become ready for therapy. She replied that she was used to working hard and had done so ever since the boy's father had left the family many years ago. She agreed to do whatever it would take.

I offered a tentative diagnosis of the son who was, I thought, suffering from a very dangerous condition, namely an excess of certainty. The boy seemed to be pathologically certain that nothing bad would ever happen to him and that he had no need of cooperating or compromising with anyone. There was some possibility that the mother had contributed to a small degree to that, by being predictable, leading the boy to think he had her completely figured out. The first homework assignment to her was to quietly discover ways to surprise him.

On the second visit, the daughter attended. She believed there was a problem in the family, but felt it was not her place to be involved with it. In any case, she was busy in school trying to be on the honor roll and active in clubs so that she might have a chance to attend college. Therefore she would not be willing to work hard to help her brother. I congratulated her on her good sense and agreed that the problem had little to do with her. I asked if she could collect some information for me, and she agreed to collect data. Her assignment was to watch for times when the brother's behavior seemed less bad or even somewhat good. She was to try to see what seemed to make those times happen and whether she could predict when he would be good again. The mother, in the meantime, had made some efforts to surprise her boy, and was encouraged to continue.

The mother attended alone the third visit. She said her daughter thought I was the best counselor they had been to, and couldn't understand why her brother didn't want to attend the sessions. When the mother then asked more about how to surprise her son, I introduced the concept of being one-down or incompetent. She had worked very hard to be one-up and competent, but perhaps this had unwittingly supported his pathological certainty. She had overperformed. I asked if she would make a painful but necessary sacrifice for her son, which she was willing to do. I asked whether she could try to imply to her son that she was having a nervous breakdown, or that she was functioning at a lower and lower level. She agreed to think of ways she could do that.

On the fourth visit, she reported that her son was in the habit of calling her after school, at her work. She typically encouraged him to do his chores, and he angrily refused, said he was going with his friends and wouldn't be home until late. This week when he had called, she mumbled that he should run around some and have fun, before it was too late, and then stifled a sob. He asked in a worried tone, "Mom, what's wrong?" She replied it was nothing, it had nothing to do with him, and he should try to forget about her problems. When she arrived home, all the chores were done and he was studying his classwork assignments.

On the fifth visit, she reported that she had found a stash of pornography in his room and had dealt with it by cutting out tiny parts of the pictures that were offensive to her with a razor and then replacing the magazines. She seemed to have enjoyed this. She also reported that the son's best friend had been placed in a drug rehabilitation program for the next 28 days, and this had upset her son. We brainstormed more signs of incompetence she could try.

On the sixth visit, she had washed her son's jacket and somehow a great deal of bleach had gotten in the water and much of the artwork which adorned the jacket had been destroyed. When he angrily confronted her, she was perplexed and frightened that she didn't seem to know what she was doing anymore. She wondered what other stupid things she might have done. She went to her room to think about it, forgetting to fix supper.

Another serendipitous event occurred when the boy discovered a peeping tom spying on his sister and chased him down the street with a baseball bat. He seemed to feel proud of his role as a protector of his sister, and the women agreed they did feel safer with him around the house.

After eight visits over three months, the mother and I agreed that there was no longer a pressing need for her to come in. The boy was cooperating at home, helping out and doing chores. He spent more time at home and on his schoolwork. He was looking forward to the summer vacation.

I next heard from the family several months later when the mother called in August asking if the therapist could write a letter of recommendation. She said her son had asked her if he could transfer to another school, since when he went to the old school he fell in with the wrong crowd (his first admission that he had ever had a problem), and was afraid that if he went back there he would get into trouble again. She learned that a doctor's note was useful in getting the district to agree to the transfer. I gladly provided that note.

This is an example of utilizing the powerlessness of the mother, who had been acting as if she had the authority to enforce her rules but who in reality did not. When she adopted a one-down position, even in a playful way, the son responded with increased responsibility. In my experience this is a common occurrence. Such experiences lead me to have a strong faith that teens want to behave in helpful and responsible ways, but are often caught in reactive and resistant positions, maintained by the parents' well-meaning attempts to improve things or at least keep them from deteriorating.

Case Example: Drying Up

A 14-year-old client with a history of psychotic symptoms and a diagnosis of schizophrenia was brought to a mental health center by his mother.

She complained that he read the Bible loudly all the time, quoted Bible verses to her, which annoyed her, prayed for hours on end, bathed only weekly, and argued with teachers at school (as well as arguing with her at home, complaining about her procession of boyfriends). He had been admitted to the inpatient unit of the local children's hospital on at least two occasions and was, according to his mother, near another hospitalization.

The therapist wondered about his strengths and goals. He stated that he wanted to be left alone by his mother, get off medications, stop wetting the bed, and get a job. His mother seemed quite unhappy about his goal of getting off his medications, expressing a variety of fears of what would happen if he did that.

His mother was reputed to be a chronic recreational user of street and prescription drugs; she became agitated and stormed out of the office when the therapist asked how *she* was doing. She refused to attend the next two sessions, but consented to return once she was assured that the focus would be on the boy. Meanwhile, the boy did attend, and explained to the therapist his grandiose theories of saving the world, encouraging international cooperation, and reducing crime (mainly through prayer). He also reported that his mother wanted him to keep getting prescriptions for his medications (one of which was a benzodiazepine) so that she could sell them or take them herself; he stated that he had taken his medications only intermittently for the past month. He expressed his concern for his mother's well-being and offered the opinion that she suffered a great deal from stress. He hoped that he could convince her to enter treatment for her substance abuse and probable mental illness.

The therapist told him that it did indeed appear that his mother had a lot of stress, and that possibly she would be willing to allow him to help reduce that stress. Of course, she had a hard time accepting help from others, so the discussion would have to *appear* to be focused on helping him remain stable. He readily agreed to this way of approaching it, saying, "Yeah, she'd get really mad if she got the idea that you think there's something wrong with her."

The therapist called the mother and assured her the emphasis would only be on her son. She agreed to return. At the family session, the mother had to be frequently redirected in order to develop a well-formed goal statement (as previously, she would only describe her complaints about the client, and her fears that he would need immediate rehospitalization if he went off medication). The therapist asked, "If, somehow, your son were cured of his problem, how would you know? What would he do that would tell you that he was over the problem and didn't need medication anymore?" Her negatively framed answers were gradually negotiated into the well-formed goal statement that he would (1) bathe nightly, "even if he didn't think he needed it," (2) attend school daily and do his homework, (3) share no more than one or two short scriptural verses with her per day, and (4) read the Bible for no more than 30 minutes a day, silently, in his room with the door closed. She then agreed that, if he did those things for three weeks in a row, she would accept a reduction in his medications, as long as he remained functioning.

The therapist had a silent agreement with the teen to improve so that there would be some chance his mother could get counseling. The identified patient used the goals negotiated with his mother as his homework tasks. His superordinate goal was to get a reduction in his medication approved by the medical doctor.

Telephone contacts with mother and schoolteacher revealed sustained improvement by client, who stated in later sessions, "You know, I was getting kinda carried away with all that Bible-reading I was doing . . . a person can take that too far." He obtained a part-time job at a local fast-food restaurant and continued to attend school. Currently, he returns to the clinic "just to check in" every three to four months, or more often when his mother is abusing drugs consistently or kicks him out of the home for a few days (most likely due more to her mental condition than to his behavior). He has currently been off medications for approximately eight months and is learning to manage his own responses to stress.

From his psychiatric history and case notes: His first contact with mental health services was in 1984. He was five years old. His mother's complaint was that "he is cranky when he comes home from school, he has a smart mouth and doesn't stick up for himself." The therapist at the time said, "Client is very compliant to the point where he is nonassertive. He is fearful of disagreeing with other children. He is disciplined by threats from his father and spanking. His parents complain he is disrespectful. He appears to need improved social skills, as his parents lack ability to model appropriate social behaviors. Parents report that child is helpful and kind to other children. He is able to dress and care for himself. He interacts minimally with peers . . . client has had no previous counseling. Father carries diagnosis of bipolar affective disorder; has had two hospitalizations in the past year. Mother carries diagnosis of schizophrenia." Client was seen once with father and twice in group; then "parents decided he did not need to come in."

Next contact with that center was in 1993, when client was referred after discharge from inpatient treatment. He had been hospitalized in another state twice (one of those was in a state psychiatric hospital). His complaint at that time was that he had started hearing voices one year previously, was also having much suicidal ideation, and wanted to die. Voices and depressive symptoms were eliminated with medications within two months; the client only came to clinic for medical appointments until seven months after intake.

First session with Richard Ebling, at which time he presented alone and stated his goals: "I want to stop wetting the bed, and to get off medication. . . . My mom said to ask if you'd talk to the doctor about getting me off pills for the bedwetting." He agreed to work on non-medication methods for the enuresis, reported one "dry spell" lasting several months a year ago; now wets bed 20–22 days/months. Reports history of using creative writing; history of "resisting the opportunity to argue"; accepts personal responsibility orientation regarding changing behavior.

Second session: "You know what started my mental illness? I wasn't sleeping, thought I was talking to God, couldn't sleep, was seeing things. I don't think it was really God, because he was not understanding at all, said you have to be perfect, do all these things." Client was preoccupied with religious themes, didn't see this as unusual, but didn't expect others to agree with him on all points; reported believing that "Dreams are messages sent by God, telling you how you are doing." Stated, "My father's mentally ill, thought he was Jesus." Reported having all "dry days" since last session, "except for three days" (14 of 17 days were dry). Stated, "If I know I'm asleep in the dream, I'll know to wake up and go to the bathroom" (at end of previous session, had stated that wetting pattern was that he would wet the bed when he thought, in a dream, that he was awake and using the toilet; he was asked to pay attention to exceptions).

Third session, 18 days later: "I only wet the bed one or two times, I've been sleeping out on the porch because it makes it easier to wake up." No reference to religious themes, stated that he hadn't been taking medications for several weeks, and felt OK (looked slightly hypomanic). However, he had gotten refill on medication (including a benzodiazapine) on mother's insistence, stated that she wanted him to keep taking medication.

In this case, we see a common pattern in mental health centers, where a drug-abusing and/or mentally ill parent brings in a child for treatment. Careful attention must be paid to all members of the family, so that the parent will stay involved in treatment. While it is important to attend to the child's reasons for being in treatment, it is just as important to convey to the parent that his or her needs are also being met through the treatment process.

It appears that many oppositional children improve rapidly when a parent is treated for depression, leading us to suspect that the oppositional behavior is actually an attempt on the child's part to help the parent, perhaps by distracting the parent from internal pain by causing external trouble. In other words, perhaps the child unconsciously senses that it is easier on the parent to attend to the child's misbehavior than to the internal sense of despondency and hopelessness. While we would not offer that reframing to the parents, it is very useful to us in seeing the child as helpful. Certainly, this attitude "leaks out" the therapist's respect toward the child.

While we think family therapy is the treatment of choice for most children, a systemic view of individuals, focusing on their relationships instead of intrapsychic problems, often leads to simple and effective individual interventions.

Case Example: The Torment of Peers

A seven-year-old girl was brought to treatment by her parents, who said she was refusing to attend second grade because she was afraid the other children would tease her. The parents said she was convinced this was absolutely a fact. Her parents had attempted to talk her out of that belief and to take her to school anyway, without effect. She remained paralyzed with fear.

Since this child was interested in ways to overcome the teasing she thought she would face (and not a customer to overcome her fears), the therapeutic strategy used was to tell her about how to play tricks on those kids. She was instructed to say a "silly thing" (non sequitur) whenever they came up and said something rude or teasing to her. It was pointed out how confused and distracted the children would be when she did this. She practiced in the office and started a list of silly things to memorize and work on at home. It was suggested rather repetitively that "it would be a terrible shame, if, after all that work of developing silly things to say (to the teasing peers), they forgot to tease you." It was noted that her parents seemed to become visibly relieved as they saw the girl become less anxious; all three of them seemed glad to have a plan.

On follow-up both she and the parents reported no more problems with teasing; the girl was resuming normal social interactions (but wished that she'd had a chance to say those "silly things" to confuse her tormentors).

This case illustrates both joining the patient in her goal (to handle or cope with teasing) as opposed to convincing the patient she needed something for which she was not a customer, such as exploration of her fears, as well as the principle of therapeutic surprise. She was startled by the idea of a non sequitur as a valid response, but rapidly accepted it and practiced with some gusto. While this case does not involve a teenager, it does illustrate some of the principles of good family-based work, being parsimonious and respectful of both the family and the client.

WHERE DO WE GO NEXT?

At the University of Miami they are beginning a program of home-based interventions with very delinquent teens. While it is too early to assess, the initial results appear very good. In this program, there is a very intense outreach to the families of teens involved in violence, drugs, and gangs. The therapist works in the community, going to the homes of the families, and does not ask them to come into the office. All therapy is done in a naturalistic setting. Strenuous efforts are made to involve the teen. Dr. Angel Perez-Vidal, at age 72, has pioneered this energetic outreach, going once to a disco to locate an uninvolved adolescent (he supposed his grandfatherly demeanor made him stand out in that setting), and another time tracking down a teen on his preferred street corner at 11 p.m. With dedication and effort, he has been able to involve teens who would have never appeared appropriate or motivated for family therapy, with excellent results.

Therapists in this pilot program may carry no more than six clients, since especially in the early phases the counselor may spend several hours each week working with a family. As the family structure is changed and the teen finds home a healthier place to be, the therapist begins to withdraw, until after three months he spends only an hour per week. Project director Sergio Aisenberg points out that while carrying only six cases would be inadequate in an outpatient practice, the true comparison for these teens is with residential treatment or with other intensive programs; as such, the economics should be obvious (cf. Lima, 1995, for a discussion of psychiatric nurse home visits and the economic benefits of in-home care). A case manager/therapist approach emphasizing the home-based structural/strategic treatment model can be much less costly and may prove far more effective.

References

Alexander, J.F., & Barton, C. (1976). Behavioral systems therapy with families. In D.H. Olsen (Ed.), *Treating relationships*. Lake Mills, Iowa: Graphic Publishing Company.

Alexander, J.F., & Parsons, B.V. (1973). Short term behavioral intervention with delinquent families: Impact on family process and recidivism. *Journal of Abnormal Psychology, 81*, 219-225.

Alexander, J.F., & Parsons, B.V. (1982). *Functional family therapy*. Carmel, CA.: Brooks/Cole.

Alexander, F., & French T.M. (1946). *Psychoanalytic psychotherapy: Principles and applications*. New York: Ronald Press.

Andreas, C., & Andreas T. (1994). *Core transformations: Reaching the wellspring within*. Moab, UT: Real People Press.

Autism and writing to close the gulf (1992, Nov. 11). *USA Today*, pp. 1D, 2D.

Barlow, D.H. (1988) *Anxiety and its disorders: The natural and treatment of anxiety and panic*. New York: Guilford.

Barlow, D.H., & Craske, M. (1990) *Mastery of your panic and anxiety*. Albany, NY: Center for Stress & Anxiety Disorders.

Barlow, D.H. (Ed.) (1993). *Clinical handbook of psychological disorders* (2nd ed.). New York: Guilford.

Barry, D. (1985). *Dave Barry's Bad Habits*. New York: Holt.

Barter, J.T. (1988). Accreditation surveys: Nit-picking or quality seeking? *Hospital and Community Psychiatry, 39*, 707.

Barton, C., Alexander, J.F., Waldron, H., Turner, C.W., & Warburton, J. (1985). Generalizing treatment effects of functional family therapy: Three replications. *American Journal of Family Therapy, 13* (3), 16-26.

Beahrs, J.O., & Torem, M. (1990). MPD, traumatic dissociation and self-deception: A dialogue with John Beahrs, M.D. *Trauma and Recovery, 3* (2), 3-11.

Beahrs, J.O., Butler, J.L., Sturges, S.G., Drummond, D.J., & Beahrs, C.H. (1992). Strategic self-therapy for personality disorders. *Journal of Strategic and Systemic Therapies, 11*, 33–52.

Beahrs, J.O. (1982). *Unity and multiplicity: Multilevel consciousness of self in hypnosis, psychiatric disorder and mental health.* New York: Brunner/Mazel.

Beck, A.T., Rush, A.J., Shaw, B.F., & Emery, G. (1979). *Cognitive therapy of depression.* New York: Guilford.

Beck, J.T., & Strong S.R. (1982). Stimulating therapeutic change with interpretations: A comparison of positive and negative connotation. *Journal of Counseling Psychology, 29*, 551–559.

Beckham, E.E. (1992). Predicting patient dropout in psychotherapy. *Psychotherapy, 29*, 177–182.

Beier, E.G. (1966). *The silent language of psychotherapy.* Chicago: Aldine.

Beier, E.G., & Young, D. (1984). *The silent language of psychotherapy* (2nd ed.). Chicago: Aldine.

Berg, I.K., & Miller, S.D. (1992). *Working with the problem drinker.* New York: Norton.

Bergin, A.E., & Lambert, M.J. (1978). The evaluation of therapeutic outcomes. In S.L. Garfield & A.E. Bergin (Eds.), *Handbook of psychotherapy and behavior change: An empirical analysis* (2nd ed., pp. 139–189). New York: Wiley.

Bergman, J. (1985). *Fishing for barracuda: Pragmatics of brief systemic therapy.* New York: Norton.

Berne, E. (1964). *Games people play.* New York: Ballantine.

Bordin, E.S. (1979). The generalizability of the psychoanalytic concept of the working alliance. *Psychotherapy: Theory, Research, and Practice, 16*, 252–260.

Brehm, J.W. (1966). *A theory of psychological reactance.* New York: Academic press.

Budman, S.H., & Gurman, A.S. (1988). *Theory and practice of brief therapy.* New York: Guilford Press.

Burns, D., & Nolen-Hoeksema, S. (1992). Therapeutic empathy and recovery from depression in cognitive-behavioral therapy: A structural equation model. *Journal of Consulting and Clinical Psychology, 60*, 441–449.

Calhoun, K.S., & Resick, P.A. (1993) Post-traumatic stress disorder. In D.H. Barlow (Ed.), *Clinical handbook of psychological disorders.* New York: Guilford.

Chapman, P.L.H., & Huygens, I. (1988). An evaluation of three treatment programmes for alcoholism. *British Journal of Addiction, 83*, 67–81.

Chick, J., Ritson, B., Connaughton, J., Stewart, A., & Chick, J. (1988) Advice versus extended treatment for alcoholism. *British Journal of Addiction, 83*, 159–170.

Cialdini, R.B. (1984). *Influence: How and why people agree to things.* New York: Morrow.

Conner-Greene, P.A. (1993). The therapeutic context: Preconditions for change in psychotherapy. *Psychotherapy, 30*, 375–382.

Cordova, J.V., & Jacobson, N.S. (1993). Couple distress. In D.H. Barlow (Ed.) *Clinical handbook of psychological disorders.* New York: Guilford.

Cummings, N.A. (1991). Intermittent therapy throughout the life cycle. In C.S.

Austad & W. H. Berman (Eds.), *Psychotherapy in managed health care: The optimal use of resources*. Washington, DC: American Psychological Association.

Da Verona, M., & Omer, H. (1992). Understanding and countering chronic processes with mental patients: An interpersonal model. *Psychotherapy, 29*, 355–365.

de Shazer, S. (1982). *Patterns of brief family therapy*. New York: Guilford.

de Shazer, S. (1985). *Keys to solution in brief therapy*. New York: Norton.

de Shazer, S. (1988). *Clues: Investigating solutions in brief therapy*. New York: Norton.

de Shazer, S. (1991). *Putting difference to work*. New York: Norton.

Derogatis, L.P., & Melisaratos, N. (1983). The Brief Symptom Inventory: An introductory report. *Psychological Medicine, 13*, 595–605.

Derogatis, L.R. (1977). *SCL 90-R manual*. Baltimore, MD: Johns Hopkins University Press.

Dolan, Y. (1991). *Resolving sexual abuse*. New York: Norton.

Durrant, M., & Kowalski, K. (1993) Enhancing views of competence. In S. Freeman (Ed.), *The new language of change: Constructive collaboration in psychotherapy*. New York: Guilford.

Eamon, M.K. (1994). Institutionalizing children and adolescents in private psychiatric hospitals. *Social Work, 39*, 588–594.

Elkin, I, Shea, M.T., Watkins, J.T., Imber, S.D., Sotsky, S.M., Collins, J.F., Glass, D.R., Pilkonis, P.A., Leber, W.R., Docherty, J.P., Fiester, S.J., & Parloff, M.B. (1989). National Institute of Mental Health treatment of depression collaborative research program: General effectiveness of treatments. *Archives of General Psychiatry, 46*, 971–982.

Elliott, R., Stiles, W.B., & Shapiro, D.A. (1993). Are some psychotherapies more equivalent than others? In T. Giles (Ed.), *Handbook of effective psychotherapy*. New York: Plenum.

Evans, M.D., Hollon, S.D., DeRubeis, R.J., Piasecki, J.M., Grove, W.M., Garvey, M.J., & Tuasor, V.B. (1992). Differential relapse following cognitive therapy and pharmacotherapy for depression. *Archives of General Psychiatry, 49*, 802–808.

Eysenck, H.J. (1993). Forty years on: The outcome problem in psychotherapy revisited. In T. Giles (Ed.), *Handbook of effective psychotherapy*. New York: Plenum.

Fisch, R.J., J.H. Weakland, & L. Segal. (1982). *Tactics of change*. San Francisco: Jossey-Bass.

Fischer, J., & Corcoran, K. (1994a). *Measures for clinical practice, Vol. 1: Couples, families and children*. New York: The Free Press.

Fischer, J., & Corcoran, K. (1994b). *Measures for clinical practice, Vol. 2: Adults*. New York: The Free Press.

Flexner, J.T. (1984). *Washington: The indispensable man*. New York: Signet.

Foa, E.B., Riggs, D.S., Dancu, C.V., & Rothbaum, B.O. (1993). Reliability and validity of a brief instrument for assessing post-traumatic stress disorder. *Journal of Traumatic Stress, 6* (4), 459–474.

Foa, E.B., Rothbaum, B.O., Riggs, D.S., & Murdock, T.B. (1991). Treatment of posttraumatic stress disorder in rape victims: A comparison between cognitive-behavioral procedures and counseling. *Journal of Consulting and Clinical Psychology,* *59,* 715–723.

Frank, E. (1991). Interpersonal psychotherapy as a maintenance treatment for patients with recurrent depression. *Psychotherapy, 28,* 259–266.

Frank, J. (1974). *Persuasion and healing.* New York: Schocken.

Fuhriman, A., Paul, S.C., & Burlingame, G.M. (1988). Eclectic time-limited therapy. In J.C. Norcross (Ed.), *Handbook of eclectic psychotherapy* (pp. 226–228). New York: Brunner/Mazel.

Gaston, L. (1990). The concept of the alliance and its role in psychotherapy: Theoretical and empirical considerations. *Psychotherapy, 27,* 143–153.

Gelso, C.J., & Johnson, D.H. (1983). *Explorations in time-limited counseling and psycho-therapy.* New York: Teachers College Press.

Gelso, C.J., & Carter J.A. (1985). The relationship in counseling and psychother-apy. *Counseling Psychologist, 13,* 155–243.

Giles, T. (Ed.) (1993). *Handbook of effective therapy.* New York: Plenum.

Gordon, D.A., Arbuthnot, J., Gustafson, K.E., & McGreen, P. (1988). Home-based behavioral-systems family therapy with disadvantages juvenile delin-quents. *American Journal of Family Therapy, 16,* 243–255.

Greenberg, R.P., Bornstein, R.F., Greenberg, M.D., & Fisher, S. (1992). A meta-analysis of antidepressant outcome under "blinder" conditions. *Journal of Consulting and Clinical Psychology, 60,* 664–669.

Gurin, J. (1990). Remaking our lives. *American Health,* March, 50–52.

Gustafson, J.P. (1986). *The complex secret of brief psychotherapy.* New York: Norton.

Hadley, T.R., & McGurrin, M.C. (1988). Accreditation, certification, and the quality of care in state hospitals. *Hospital and Community Psychiatry, 39,* 739–741.

Haley, J. (1963). *Strategies of psychotherapy.* New York: Grune & Stratton.

Haley, J. (1973). Uncommon therapy: *The psychiatric techniques of Milton H. Erickson, M.D.* New York: Norton.

Haley, J. (1976). *Problem solving therapy.* San Francisco: Jossey-Bass.

Herman, J. (1992). *Trauma and Recovery.* New York: Basic Books.

Hill, C.E. (1989). *Therapist techniques and client outcomes: Eight cases of brief psychother-apy.* Newbury Park, CA: Sage.

Holder, H., Longabaugh, R., Miller, W.R., & Rubonis, A.V. (1991). The cost effectiveness of treatment for alcoholism: A first approximation. *Journal of Studies of Alcohol, 52,* 517–540.

Horowitz, M. (1986). *Stress response syndromes.* Northvale, NJ: Jason Aronson.

Horowitz, M., Marmer, C., Krupnick, J., Wilner, N., Kaltreider, N., & Waller-stein, R. (1984). *Personality styles and brief psychotherapy.* New York: Basic Books.

Horowitz, M., Wilner, N., & Alvarez, W. (1979). Impact of Event Scale: A measure of subjective stress. *Psychological Medicine, 4,* 209–218.

Horvath, A., & Greenberg, L.S. (1986). Development of the Working Alliance Inventory. In L.S. Greenberg & W.M. Pinsof (Eds.), *The psychotherapeutic process: A research handbook* (pp. 529–556). New York: Guilford.

Howard, K.I., Kopta, S.M., Krause, M.J., & Orlinsky, D.E. (1986). The dose-effect relationship in psychotherapy. *American Psychologist, 41,* 159–164.

Hoyt, M.F. (1990). On time in brief therapy. In R. A. Wells & V. J. Gianetti (Eds.), *Handbook of the brief psychotherapies* (pp. 115–143). New York: Plenum.

Hoyt, M.J. (1995). On time in brief therapy. In M.J. Hoyt (Ed.), *Brief therapy and managed care* (pp. 64–104). San Francisco: Jossey-Bass.

Hoyt, M.F., Rosenbaum, R., & Talmon, M. (1992). Planned single-session therapy. In S.H. Budman, M.F. Hoyt, & S. Friedman (Eds.), *The first session in brief therapy*. New York: Guilford.

Jacobson, N.S. (1992). Behavioral couple therapy: A new beginning. *Behavior Therapy, 23,* 493–506.

Johnson, L.D. (1988). Naturalistic techniques with the "difficult" patient. In J.K. Zeig & S.R. Lankton (Eds.), *Developing Ericksonian therapy: State of the art* (pp. 397–413). New York: Brunner/Mazel.

Johnson, L.D., & Miller, S.D. (1994). Modification of depression risk factors: A solution-focused approach. *Psychotherapy, 31,* 244–253.

Johnson, L.D., & Morrissette, P.J. (1995). Treatment focus in brief psychotherapies. Manuscript submitted for publication.

Karon, B.P., & VandenBos, G.R. (1975). Treatment costs of psychotherapy as compared to medication for schizophrenia. *Professional Psychology, 6,* 293–298.

Karon, B.P., & VandenBos, G.R. (1976). Cost-benefit analysis: Psychologist versus psychiatrist for schizophrenics. *Professional Psychology, 7,* 107–111.

Karon, B.P., & VandenBos, G.R. (1981). *Psychotherapy of schizophrenia: The treatment of choice.* New York: Aronson.

Kazdin, A.E. (1993). Adolescent mental health: Prevention and treatment programs. *American Psychologist, 48,* 127–141

Keeney, B.P., & Ray, W.A. (1992, Spring). Kicking research in the ass: Provocations for reform. *AFTA Newsletter, 47,* 67–68.

Kiesler, C.A. (1982). Noninstitutionalization as potential public policy for mental patients. *American Psychologist, 37,* 349–360.

Kernberg, O. (1975). *Borderline conditions and pathological narcissism.* New York: Jason Aronson.

Kilpatrick, D.G., Veronen, L.J., & Resick, P.A. (1982). Psychological sequelae to rape. In D.M. Doleys, R.L. Meredith, & A.R. Ciminero (Eds.), *Behavioral medicine: Assessment and treatment strategies.* New York: Plenum.

Kilpatrick, D.G., & Amick, A.E. (1985). Rape trauma. In M. Hersen & C. Last (Eds.), *Behavior therapy casebook.* New York: Springer.

Klein, D.F., Zitrin, C.M., Woerner, M.G., & Ross, D.C. (1983). Treatment of phobias: Behavior therapy and supportive psychotherapy: Are there any specific ingredients? *Archives of General Psychiatry, 40,* 139–145.

Klerman, G.L., Weissman, M.M., & Rousaville, B.J. (1984). *Interpersonal psychotherapy of depression.* New York: Basic Books.

Kluft, R.P. (1982). Varieties of hypnotic interventions in the treatment of multiple personality. *American Journal of Clinical Hypnosis, 24,* 230–240.

Kohut, H. (1971). *The analysis of the self.* New York: International Universities Press.

Koss, M.P., & Butcher, J.N. (1986). Research on brief therapy. In S.L. Garfield

& A.E. Bergin (Eds.), *Handbook of psychotherapy and behavior change* (4th ed., pp. 627–670). New York: Wiley.

Kraft, R.G., Clairborn, C.D., & Dowd, E.T. (1985). Effects of positive reframing and paradoxical directives in counseling for negative emotions. *Journal of Counseling Psychology, 32,* 617–621.

Kurtines, W.M., Hervis, O., & Szapocznik, J. (1989). Brief strategic family therapy. In J. Szapocznik, W.M. Kurtines, and contributors, *Breakthroughs in family therapy with drug abusing and problem youth* (pp. 59–76). New York: Springer.

Lambert, M.J. (1992). Psychotherapy outcome research: Implications for integrative and eclectic therapists. In J.C. Norcross & M.R. Goldfried (Eds.), *Handbook of psychotherapy integration.* New York: Basic Books.

Lambert, M.J., DeJulio, S.S., & Stein, D.M. (1978). Therapist interpersonal skills: Process, outcome, methodological considerations, and recommendations for future research. *Psychological Bulletin, 85,* 467–489.

Lambert, M.J., Shapiro, D.A., & Bergin, A.E. (1986). The effectiveness of psychotherapy. In S.L. Garfield and A.E. Bergin (Eds.), *Handbook of psychotherapy and behavior change* (3rd ed., pp. 157–211). New York: Wiley.

Lankton, S.R., & Lankton, C.H. (1986). *Enchantment and intervention in family therapy.* New York: Brunner/Mazel.

Lima, B. (1995). In-home behavioral care: The missing link. *Behavioral Health Management, 15* (2), 17–19.

Linehan, M.M. (1987). Dialectical behavior therapy for borderline personality disorder: Theory and method. *Bulletin of the Menninger Clinic, 51,* 261–276.

Linehan, M.M. (1981). A social-behavioral analysis of suicide and parasuicide: Implications for clinical assessment and treatment. In H.G. Glazer & J.F. Clarkin (Eds.), *Depression: Behavioral and directive intervention strategies.* New York: Garland Press.

Lipke, H.J., & Botkin, A.L. (1992). Case studies of eye movement desensitization and reprocessing (EMDR) with chronic post-traumatic stress disorder. *Psychotherapy, 29,* 591–595.

Luborsky, L., Crits-Christoph, P., Mintz, J., & Auerbach, A. (1988). *Who will benefit from psychotherapy? Predicting therapeutic outcomes.* New York: Basic Books.

Luborsky, L., McClellan, A.T., Woody, G.E., O'Brian, C.P., & Auerbach, A. (1985). Therapist success and its determinants. *Archives of General Psychiatry, 42,* 602–611.

Luborsky, L., Singer, B., & Luborsky, L. (1975). Comparative studies of psychotherapies: Is it true that "Everyone has won and all must have prizes"? *Archives of General Psychiatry, 32,* 995–1008.

Luborsky, L. (1984). *Principles of psychoanalytic psychotherapy: A manual for supportive-expressive treatment.* New York: Basic Books.

Lytle, R. (1993). An investigation of the efficacy of eye movement desensitization in the treatment of cognitive intrusions related to memories of a past stress event. Unpublished doctoral dissertation, University Park, PA: The Pennsylvania State University.

Madanes, C. (1981). *Strategic family therapy.* San Francisco: Jossey-Bass.

Malan, D.H. (1976). *The frontiers of brief psychotherapy: An example of the convergence of research and clinical practice.* New York: Plenum.

Malan, D.H., Heath, E.S., Bacal, H.A., & Balfour, F.H.G. (1975). Psychodynamic changes in untreated neurotic patients: II: Apparently genuine improvements. *Archives of General Psychiatry, 32,* 110–126.

Mann, J. (1973). *Time-limited psychotherapy.* Cambridge, MA: Harvard University Press.

Mann, J., & Goldman, R. (1982). *A casebook in time-limited psychotherapy.* New York: McGraw-Hill.

Masterson, J.F. (1981). *The narcissistic and borderline disorders.* New York: Brunner/Mazel.

McConnaughy, E.A., DiClemente, C.C., Prochaska, J.O., & Velicer, W.F. (1989). Stages of change in psychotherapy: A follow-up report. *Psychotherapy, 26,* 494–503.

Meichenbaum, D., & Turk, D.C. (1987). *Facilitating treatment adherence: A practitioner's guidebook.* New York: Plenum.

Meltzoff, J., & Kornreich, M. (1970). *Research in psychotherapy.* New York: Atherton Press.

Milgram, S., & Sabini, J. (1975) *On maintaining norms: A field experiment in the subway.* Unpublished manuscript, City University of New York.

Miller, S., Hubble, M., & Duncan, B. (1995). No more bells and whistles. *The Family Therapy Networker, 19* (2), 52–63.

Miller, W.R., Benefield, R.G., & Tonigan, J.S. (1993) Enhancing motivation for change in problem drinking: A controlled comparison of two therapist styles. *Journal of Consulting and Clinical Psychology, 61,* 455–461.

Miller, W.R., & Hester, R.K. (1986). Inpatient alcoholism treatment: Who benefits? *American Psychologist, 41,* 794–805.

Miller, W.R., & Rollnick, S. (1991). *Motivational interviewing: Preparing people to change addictive behavior.* New York: Guilford.

Minuchin, S. (1974). *Families and family therapy.* Cambridge, MA: Harvard University Press.

Minuchin, S., & Fishman, H.C. (1981). *Family therapy techniques.* Cambridge, MA: Harvard University Press.

Molnar, A., & Lindquist, B. (1989). *Changing problem behavior in the schools.* San Francisco: Jossey-Bass.

Morrissette, P.J. (1989). Benevolent restraining: A strategy for interrupting vicious cycles in residential care. *Journal of Strategic and Systemic Therapies, 8,* 31–35.

Morrissette, P.J. (1992). Engagement strategies with reluctant homeless young people. *Psychotherapy, 29,* 447–451.

Morrissette, P.J., & Bodard, K. (1989). Troubled youth and their troubling ways: A conceptual framework for youth care workers. *Child and Youth Care Forum, 20,* 5, 365–373.

Morrissette, P.J., & McIntyre, S. (1989). Homeless young people in residential care. *Social Casework, 70,* December, 603–610.

Muerer, K.T., & Glynn, S.M. (1993). Effective psychotherapy for schizophrenia. In T. Giles (Ed.) *Handbook of effective psychotherapy.* New York: Plenum.

Norman, G. (1990). *Bouncing back*. Boston: Houghton Mifflin.

Nylund, D., & Corsiglia, V. (1994). Becoming solution focused/forced in brief therapy: Remembering something important we already knew. *Journal of Systemic Therapies, 13*, 5-12.

Ogles, B.M., Lambert, M.J., & Sawyer, J.D. (1995) Clinical significance of the National Institutue of Mental Health Treatment of Depression Collaborative Research Program data. *Journal of Consulting and Clinical Psychology, 63*, 321-326.

O'Hanlon, B., & Beadle, S. (1994). *A field guide to possibility land: Possibility therapy methods*. Omaha, NE: The Center Press.

O'Hanlon, W.H. (1987). *Taproots: Underlying principles of Milton Erickson's therapy and hypnosis*. New York: Norton.

O'Hanlon, W. H., & Weiner-Davis, M. (1989). *In search of solutions*. New York: Norton.

O'Hanlon, W., & Wilk, J. (1987) *Shifting contexts*. New York: Guilford.

Omer, H. (1991). Dialectical interventions and the structure of strategy. *Psychotherapy, 28*, 563-571.

Omer, H., & London, P. (1988). Metamorphosis in psychotherapy: End of the systems era. *Psychotherapy, 25*, 171-179.

Orvis, B.R., Kelley, H.H., & Butler, D. (1976). Attributional conflicts in young couples. In J.H. Harvey, W.J. Ickes, & R.F. Kidd (Eds.), *New directions in attribution research* (Vol. 1). Hillsdale, NJ: Erlbaum.

Parsons, B.V., & Alexander, J.F. (1973). Short term family intervention: A therapy outcome study. *Journal of Consulting and Clinical Psychology, 41*, 195-201.

Patterson, G.R., Reid, J.B., & Dishion, T.J. (in press). *A social learning approach: IV. Antisocial boys*. Eugene, OR: Castalia Press.

Patterson, G.R., & Chamberlain, P. (1992). A functional analysis of resistance (A neobehavioral perspective). In H. Arkowitz (Ed.), *Why don't people change: New perspectives on resistance and noncompliance*. New York: Guilford.

Paul, G.L., & Lentz, R.J. (1977). *Psychosocial treatment of chronic mental patients: Milieu vs. social learning programs*. Cambridge, MA: Harvard University Press.

Peele, S., Brodsky, A., & Arnold, M. (1991). *The truth about addiction and recovery: The life process program for outgrowing destructive habits*. New York: Simon & Schuster.

Peele, S. (1989). *Diseasing of America: Addiction treatment out of control*. Lexington, MA: Lexington Books.

Pekarik, G. (1985). The effects of employing different termination classification criteria in dropout research. *Psychotherapy, 22*, 1, 86-91.

Pekarik, G., & Wierzbicki, M. (1986). The relationship between clients' expected and actual treatment duration. *Psychotherapy, 23*, 532-534.

Peter, L.J. (1977). *Peter's quotations: Ideas for our time*. New York: Bantam Books.

Peterson, A.C., Compas, B.E., Brooks-Gunn, J., Stemmler, M., Ey, S., & Grant, K.E. (1993). Depression in adolescence. *American Psychologist, 48*, 155-168.

Phillips, R.D. (1985). Whistling in the dark? A review of play therapy research. *Psychotherapy, 22*, 752-760.

Prochaska, J.O., & DiClemente, C.C. (1986). The transtheoretical approach. In

J.C. Norcross (Ed.), *Handbook of eclectic psychotherapy* (pp. 163–200). New York: Brunner/Mazel.

Prochaska, J.O., DiClemente, C.C., & Norcross, J.C. (1992). In search of how people change: Applications to addictive behaviors. *American Psychologist, 47,* 1102–1104.

Resick, P.A., & Schnicke, M.K. (1992). Cognitive processing therapy for sexual assault victims. *Journal of Consulting and Clinical Psychology, 60,* 748–756.

Robbins, M.S., Alexander, J.F., Newell, R.M., & Turner, C.W. (1994, February). The immediate effects of positive reframing on client attitudes in the initial session of functional family therapy. Paper presented at the North American Society for Psychotherapy Research, Second Regional Chapter Conference. Santa Fe, New Mexico.

Segal, L., & Watzlawick, P. (1985). On window shopping or being a non-customer. In S. Coleman (Ed.), *Failures in family therapy* (pp. 73–90). New York: Guilford.

Selekman, M.D. (1993). *Pathways to change: Brief therapy solutions with difficult adolescents.* New York: Guilford.

Seligman, M. (1990). *Learned optimism.* New York: Knopf.

Shadish, W.R., Montgomery, L.M., Wilson, P., Wilson, M.R., Bright, I., & Okwumabua, R. (1993) The effects of family and marital psychotherapies: A meta-analysis. *Journal of Consulting and Clinical Psychology, 61,* 992–1002.

Shapiro, F. (1989a). Efficacy of the eye movement desensitization procedure in the treatment of traumatic memories. *Journal of Traumatic Stress, 2,* 199–223.

Shapiro, F. (1989b). Eye movement desensitization: A new treatment for post-traumatic stress disorder. *Journal of Behavior Therapy and Experimental Psychiatry, 20,* 211–217.

Shapiro, F. (1991a). Eye movement desensitization and reprocessing procedure: From EMD to EMDR-A new treatment model for anxiety and related traumata. *Behavior Therapist, 14,* 133–135.

Shapiro, R. (1991b). Eye movement desensitization and reprocessing: A cautionary note. *Behavior Therapist, 11,* 188.

Shapiro, F. (in press). *Eye movement desensitization and reprocessing: Principles, protocols, and procedures.* New York: Guilford.

Shapiro, D.A., & Shapiro, D. (1982). Meta-analysis of comparative therapy outcome studies: A replication and refinement. *Psychological Bulletin, 92,* 581–604.

Shearin, E.N., & Linehan, M.M. (1989). Dialectics and behavior therapy: A metaparadoxical approach to the treatment of borderline personality disorder. In L.M. Ascher (Ed.), *Therapeutic paradox* (pp. 255–288). New York: Guilford.

Sifneos, P. (1979). *Short-term psychotherapy and the emotional crisis.* Cambridge, MA: Harvard University Press.

Silberschatz, G., Curtis, J.T., Sampson, H. & Weiss, J. (1991). Mount Zion Hospital and Medical Center: Research on the process of change in psychotherapy. In L.E. Beutler & M. Crago (Eds.), *Psychotherapy research: An international review of programmatic studies* pp 48–55. Washington, DC: American Psychological Association.

Sledge, W.H., Moras, K., Hartley, D., & Levine, M. (1990). Effects of time-limited psychotherapy on patient dropout rates. *American Journal of Psychiatry, 147,* 1341–1347.

Sloane, R.B., Staples, F.R., Cristol, A.H., Yorkston, N.J., & Whipple, K. (1975). *Psychotherapy versus behavior therapy.* Cambridge, MA: Harvard University Press.

Smith, M.L., Glass, G.V., & Miller, T.I. (1980). *The benefits of psychotherapy.* Baltimore, MD: Johns Hopkins University Press.

Smith, M.L., & Glass, G.V. (1977). Meta-analysis of psychotherapy outcome studies. *American Psychologist, 32,* 752–760.

Steenbarger, B.N. (1994). Duration and outcome in psychotherapy: An integrative review. *Professional Psychology, 25,* 111–119.

Stein, D.M., & Lambert, M.J. (1995). Graduate training in psychotherapy: Are therapy outcomes enhanced? *Journal of Consulting and Clinical Psychology, 63,* 182–196.

Stiles, W.B., Shapiro, D.A., & Elliot, R. (1986). "Are all psychotherapies equivalent?" *American Psychologist, 41,* 165–180.

Stiles, W.B., & Snow, J.S. (1984). Counseling session impact as viewed by novice counselors and their clients. *Journal of Counseling Psychology, 31,* 3–12.

Strupp, H.H., & Binder, J.L. (1984). *Psychotherapy in a new key: A guide to time-limited dynamic psychotherapy.* New York: Basic Books.

Szapocznik, J., Foote, F.H., Perez-Vidal, A., Hervis, O.E., & Kurtines, W. (1985). *One person family therapy.* Miami, FL: Miami World Health Organization Collaborating Center for Research and Training in Mental Health, Alcohol and Drug Dependence, Department of Psychiatry, University of Miami School of Medicine.

Szapocznik, J., Rio, A., Murray, E., Cohen, R., Scopetta, M., Rivas-Vazquez, A., Hervis, O., Posada, V., & Kurtines Rio, A, Murray, E., Cohen, R., Scopetta, M., Rivas-Vazquez, A., Hervis, O., Posada, V., & Kurtines, W. (1989). Structural family versus psychodynamic child therapy for problematic Hispanic boys. *Journal of Consulting and Clinical Psychology, 57,* 571–578.

Szapocznik, J., Kurtines, W.M., Foote, F., Perez-Vidal, A., & Hervis, O. (1986). Conjoint versus one-person family therapy: Further evidence for the effectiveness of conducting family therapy through one person with drug-abusing adolescents. *Journal of Consulting and Clinical Psychology, 54,* 395–397.

Szapocznik, J., Kurtines, W. M., and contributors (1989). *Breakthroughs in family therapy with drug abusing and problem youth.* New York: Springer.

Szykula, S.A., Morris, S.B., Sudweeks, C., & Sayger, T.V. (1987). Child-focused behavior and strategic therapy outcome comparisons. *Psychotherapy, 24,* 546–551.

Talmon, M. (1990). *Single-session therapy: Maximizing the effect of the first (and often only) therapeutic encounter.* San Francisco: Jossey-Bass.

Taube, C.A., Burns, B.J., & Kessler, L. (1984). Patients of psychiatrists and psychologists in office-based practice: 1980. *American Psychologist, 39,* 1435–1447.

van der Kolk, B. (1987). *The therapeutic self: Developing resonance in interpersonal relationships.* New York: Human Sciences Press.

"Vicki" (1994). Vicki: A blind woman's two near-death experiences. *IANDS Vital*

Signs, 13, 1–8. East Windsor Hill, CT: International Association for Near-Death Studies, Inc.

Watzlawick, P., Weakland, J.H., & Fisch, R. (1974). *Change: Principles of problem formation and problem resolution*. New York: Norton.

Weakland, J.H., Johnson, L.D., & Morrissette, P.J. (in press). Brief therapy supervision: The Mental Research Inbstitute Model. *Journal of Systemic Therapies*.

Weiner-Davis, M., de Shazer, S., & Gingerich, W.J. (1987). Building on pre-treatment changes to construct the therapeutic solution: An exploratory study. *Journal of Marital and Family Therapy, 13*, 359–363.

Wells, R. (1982). *Planned short-term treatment*. New York: Free Press.

White, M. (1986). Negative explanation, restraint and double descriptions: A template for family therapy. *Family Process, 25* (2), 169–186.

White, M. (1987, spring). Family therapy and schizophrenia: Addressing the 'In the corner lifestyle.' *Dulwich Centre Newsletter*.

White, M. (1984). Pseudo-encopresis: From avalanche to victory, from vicious to virtuous cycles. *Family Systems Medicine, 2* (2), 150–160.

White, M., & Epston, D. (1990). *Narrative means to therapeutic ends*. New York: Norton.

Williams, D. (1992). *Nobody nowhere*. New York: Times Books.

Williams, M.H. (1985). The bait-and-switch tactic in psychotherapy. *Psychotherapy, 22*, 1, 110–113.

Yapko, M.D. (1988). *When living hurts: Directives for treating depression*. New York: Brunner/Mazel.

Yeomans, F. (1993). When a therapist overindulges a demanding borderline patient. *Hospital and Community Psychiatry, 44*, 334–336.

Index